Language and disadvantage

MW01114710

EDWARDS

LANGUAGE AND DISADVANTAGE

STUDIES IN DISORDERS OF COMMUNICATION

SECOND EDITION

W

WHURR PUBLISHERS
LONDON   JERSEY CITY

© Whurr Publishers Ltd 1989

First published 1979 by
Edward Arnold (Publishers) Ltd
Second edition 1989 published by
Cole and Whurr Limited
Reprinted 1990 and 1991 by Whurr Publishers Ltd
19b Compton Terrace, London N1 2UN

British Library Cataloguing in Publication Data

Edwards, John
    Language and disadvantage. – 2nd ed.
    (Studies in disorders of communication).
    1. Socially disadvantaged persons. Language skills. –
    Sociological perspectives
    I. Title   II. Series
    306′.4

ISBN 1 870332 95 4

All rights reserved. No part of this publication may be reproduced, stored in a retrieval system, or transmitted in any form or by any means, electronic, mechanical, photocopying, recording or otherwise, without the prior permission of Whurr Publishers Ltd.

This publication is sold subject to the condition that it shall not, by way of trade or otherwise, be lent, resold, hired out, or otherwise circulated without the publisher's prior consent in any form of binding or cover other than that in which it is published and without a similar condition including this condition being imposed upon any subsequent purchaser.

Printed and bound in Great Britain by Athenaeum Press Ltd, Newcastle upon Tyne

Contents

To my mother and father

General preface

This series is the first to approach the problem of language disability as a single field. It attempts to bring together areas of study which have traditionally been treated under separate headings, and to focus on the common problems of analysis, assessment and treatment which characterize them. Its scope therefore includes the specifically linguistic aspects of the work of such areas as speech therapy, remedial teaching, teaching of the deaf and educational psychology, as well as those aspects of mother-tongue and foreign-language teaching which pose similar problems. The research findings and practical techniques from each of these fields can inform the others, and we hope one of the main functions of this series will be to put people from one profession into contact with the analogous situations found in others.

It is therefore not a series about specific syndromes or educationally narrow problems. While the orientation of a volume is naturally towards a single main area, and reflects an author's background, it is editorial policy to ask authors to consider the implications of what they say for the fields with which they have not been primarily concerned. Nor is this a series about disability in general. The medical, social, educational and other factors which enter into a comprehensive evaluation of any problems will not be studied as ends in themselves, but only in so far as they bear directly on the understanding of the nature of the language behaviour involved. The aim is to provide a much needed emphasis on the description and analysis of language as such, and on the provision of specific techniques of therapy or remediation. In this way, we hope to bridge the gap between the theoretical discussion of 'causes' and the practical tasks of treatment—two sides of language disability which it is uncommon to see systematically related.

Despite restricting the area of disability to specifically linguistic matters—and in particular emphasizing problems of the production and comprehension of spoken language—it should be clear that the series' scope goes considerably beyond this. For the first books, we have selected topics which have been particularly neglected in recent years, and which seem most able to benefit from contemporary research in linguistics and its related disciplines, English studies, psychology, sociology and education. Each volume will put its subject matter in perspective, and will provide an introductory slant to its presentation. In this way, we hope to provide specialized studies which can be used as texts for components of teaching courses, as well as material that is directly applicable to the needs of professional workers. It is also hoped that this orientation will place the series within the reach of the interested layman—in particular, the parents or family of the linguistically disabled.

David Crystal
Jean Cooper

Preface

This book treats the problems of disadvantaged speakers as essentially a socio-linguistic issue and, in the course of the text, I hope to demonstrate that this is the most appropriate view to take. This is not to say that difficulties faced by such speakers are any the less real or important if they derive from social attitudes to speech rather than from linguistic deficiency itself. Indeed, problems whose existence depends upon prevailing social norms are among the most intractable.

To do justice to the topic, many areas of research have had to be considered and thus a rather large amount of ground has been covered here. This has resulted in fairly brief treatment of many subjects which, although having a definite relation to the main theme, are also full topics in their own right. I have attempted, where appropriate, to indicate to the reader, therefore, sources which treat these topics more comprehensively. In addition, I have tried to combine here the findings of the most relevant investigations from both sides of the Atlantic. Since some areas of concern have received more attention in some places than in others, an awareness of work carried out elsewhere is likely to be useful to workers in any given context.

The initial approach to the book was governed by my belief that, before dealing with language *per se*, it is necessary to provide some background information about the broader area of disadvantage itself. Since the issue under discussion is one which depends largely upon social forces, it would have been rather unwise to skip too lightly over the milieu in which disadvantage is seen to arise, and which gives it definition. Thus, the first chapter considers some of the theoretical approaches to the causes of disadvantage. Does disadvantage have a genetic basis, can it be attributed to environmental deprivation, or is it simply a manifestation of sociocultural difference? Is disadvantage merely the latest euphemism for poverty? These are some of the questions to be tackled at the outset.

In the second and third chapters, the language of disadvantaged speakers is examined. Here the argument really centres upon the so-called 'difference-deficit' controversy—is disadvantaged language merely a variant, neither better nor worse than other language varieties, or does it represent an inaccurate and illogical mode of expression? I give some attention here to the work of Bernstein who has often been taken to support the 'deficit' view, and to the investigations of Labov, which are firmly within the 'difference' camp. To this framework is appended the work of others, as well as some comment upon the implications and applications of the two broad theoretical approaches.

In chapters 4 and 5, the working assumption is that the difference viewpoint is the most reasonable and, therefore, that the problems associated with disadvantaged speech are ones of sociolinguistic convention and attitude. Thus in chapter 4 general reactions towards, and evaluations of, various forms of nonstandard language are examined. In chapter 5, this line is continued with specific reference to the issue of nonstandard speech in the educational context. The brief sixth chapter draws attention to the special case of disadvantage among immigrant populations and ethnic minority groups.

Throughout the book the work of therapists, teachers and others directly concerned with the problems of the disadvantaged speaker is considered. I make few specific recommendations, however, nor do I suggest a 'cure' for disadvantaged speech. This is because the explanation of the problem can also provide its solution. That is, the difficulties of disadvantaged speakers do not reside in themselves so much as in the attitudes of those around them. Consequently, any 'solution' to the problem must lie, in the long term at least, in the moderation or eventual elimination of prejudicial attitudes towards certain speech styles. Therefore, the purpose of this book is simply to examine the relevant issues and to bring them to the attention of the reader. In so doing, it is hoped that a picture of disadvantaged language will emerge which reflects reasonably well the current state of research and theory. My own views on the matter will become obvious.

I must acknowledge here the assistance received from David Crystal, who has been a source of encouragement from the start; Bernadette MacLellan, who assisted with the preparation of the manuscript; and my wife Suzanne for her forbearance during the writing of the book.

JRE
August, 1978

Preface to the Second Edition

There are two main reasons why a second and somewhat enlarged edition of this book makes sense a decade after its original publication. The first is simply to make the point that, unfortunately, disadvantage is still very much with us. Basic issues like group intelligence differences and the aetiology of disadvantage are still being debated, and the notion of environmental deficit still has widespread appeal (indeed, the very term "disadvantage" connotes only a deficit view for many; see Edwards 1981a). Thus the language of the disadvantaged continues in many quarters — including academic ones — to be seen as substandard. It is important, then, to review some of the recent writings to demonstrate once again the popular hold on the imagination possessed by a deficit philosophy.

At the same time, I shall try to re-emphasize the original insight of this book — namely, that linguistic disadvantage remains a socially-determined pheno-menon. In the original preface I noted that problems whose existence depends upon social norms are among the most difficult to resolve, and in chapter 4 I observed that linguistic disadvantage reflects political, social and economic power and its uneven distribution across society. Not made sufficiently clear, perhaps, was the corollary that issues intertwined with socioeconomic realities are liable to recur even in contexts in which one might have thought, naively, that the force of evidence would have won the day. The price of accuracy in such matters is enduring watchfulness and continuing dissemination of psychological, educa-tional and linguistic information. For, in the last ten years, we can still find writers who talk about the "lunatic notion" of black children being taught "in the gibberish of the streets" (Reed 1981, 29), who claim that linguistic insights supporting the validity of all varieties of language are without basis (Honey 1983), who wish to reinforce a linguistic deficit theory associated, perhaps inaccurately, with Bernstein (Mason 1986).

Thus, this second edition will allow an updating of relevant material, while sustaining the force of the original argument — which can remain unchanged in the main since the analysis first presented has stood time's test quite well. New supplementary information will be presented here, dealing with intervention programmes, black English, language attitudes, standard/nonstandard varieties, bilingual education, and so on.

The second major reason for a new edition is that it permits the introduction of one or two strands which were not formerly present at all. For example, Ogbu's (1978) discussion of the "castelike" status of some minority groups has led to some interesting and relevant debate. Also, the emerging emphasis upon ethno-methodological and ethnographic approaches to an understanding of behaviour embedded in its real-life context is worthy of some attention here (see Garfinkel 1967), as is the more specific trend to study language in its community setting (e.g. Milroy 1980) and to undertake conversational and discourse analysis — particularly in the classroom (see Edwards and Mercer 1986).

I also wish here to briefly explore the relationship among education, language, identity and pluralism. I mentioned in chapter 6 the special difficulties presented by ethnic minority group members whose language is not that of the larger society surrounding them. Immigrant groups (including the *gastarbeiter*) and indigenous minorities may be seen as being at risk of sociocultural assimilation and, in that sense, doubly disadvantaged — for they are also very often socioeconomically disadvantaged, occupy subordinate positions in society and, in learning the majority language, may often acquire a nonstandard variety of it. Thus it has been argued that the school, in particular, has a double role to play — to help overcome (or at least not exacerbate) this disadvantage which is shared with other socially disadvantaged groups, and also to attempt, usually through language pro-grammes, to maintain and possibly enhance mother-tongue competence. Chapter 6 mentioned the possibility of American bilingual education functioning in this way, rather than merely as a form of compensatory education, but the issue is much broader and more important than was indicated there. The central matters include: (a) the nature of the relationship between language and identity; (b) a consideration of assimilation, cultural pluralism, and their interplay; (c) the role of schools in effecting social change. Further to (c) are four other points: (i) can schools support group identities at risk of change, and contribute to enduring pluralism and diversity?; (ii) can they do this by attending principally to language?; (iii) what is the place of multicultural education?; (iv) can schools promote diversity *and* provide a strong core curriculum? These are matters discussed at length elsewhere (Edwards 1985), but the issue of language and identity, and particularly its educational ramifications, is clearly relevant to a discussion of disadvantage, and so should be mentioned here.

Overall, I hope that this new edition will prove useful by re-presenting a large amount of data and discussion still highly relevant, and by adding to this some cursory indication of developments over the last ten years. My feeling is that linguistic disadvantage is still all too prevalent, that teachers and others continue to need guidance in dealing with disadvantaged children and, most generally, that language variation continues to be one of the most important and problematic areas of human social interaction.

The addendum to the first edition is presented here as chapter 8. I have written this as a single undivided essay and, while it *can* be read alone as an overview of recent developments and interests, it really presupposes an awareness of themes discussed in the preceding chapters. Certainly, my intention when writing it was to provide an updating of original material.

JRE
August, 1988

1

Disadvantage

'Poverty is a great enemy to human happiness; it certainly destroys liberty,
and it makes some virtues impracticable and others extremely
difficult.'   Samuel Johnson

'The greatest of evils and the worst of crimes is poverty.'   G B Shaw

To be at a disadvantage is to suffer unfavourable conditions or circumstances and,
in this ordinary sense of the word, virtually everyone can claim to have been at
a disadvantage at some time, in some situation. In the psychological and educational literature, however, disadvantage most often signifies a relatively enduring
condition descriptive of the lifestyles of certain social groups—the working class,
immigrant populations and ethnic minorities among them—which contributes to
poor academic achievement for children at school, and generally lowered chances
of success in the larger society.

Passow (1970, 16), for example, defines the disadvantaged child as one who

> because of social or cultural characteristics (e.g. social class, race, ethnic origin, poverty,
> sex, geographical location, etc.) ... comes into the school system with knowledge, skills
> and attitudes which impede learning.

This broad and general definition simply implies that membership in a social group
which differs in important ways from society at large may create difficulties at
points of interaction with that larger society. Of primary interest here is the relationship between home and school. The definition implies that, from the time of
first entry into school (which generally reflects the attitudes and values of middle-
class society), a child may be at a disadvantage relative to other children if his
early home life is somehow discontinuous with life at school. There are several
important factors to be considered here.

First, disadvantage is seen as sociocultural in nature. That is, there is no need
to invoke any genetic intellectual disability to account for disadvantage (although
the definition does not explicitly rule out the possibility of cognitive deficits arising
from home environment). Rather, disadvantage can be viewed as the result of class
and/or cultural differences in patterns of early socialization. An obvious example
is the immigrant child who comes to school with little or no understanding of the
national language. It is not difficult to see that such a child is at a considerable
disadvantage regardless of his cognitive and intellectual skills. In general,

adherents of Passow's view of disadvantage would argue that, for ethnic and racial minorities, and for lower-class social groups, there are many aspects of lifestyle, child-rearing practice, etc. (most of them much more subtle than the example just given) which diverge considerably from those of the middle class, and which are sufficient to place group members at a disadvantage.

A second, related factor is that disadvantage receives its definition at points of contact between groups which are at once distinguishable and yet part of the same larger society. This, as mentioned above, is most noticeable in the school situation, since school is the single most important of such contact points. It is only in such a context that the values, attitudes and behaviour of one group, or of one group member, can be seen to be less than ideal within some larger framework. If there were no contact between certain social groups and the surrounding society, disadvantage, as viewed here, would not exist. It is precisely because groups can differ from one another and yet still share many features in common that disadvantage, a relative term, can be reasonably applied. To continue with the example mentioned above, we would not expect the language difficulty of the new immigrant to have existed in his home country. Disadvantage always involves a comparison, most often from a particular value position. Thus, as we shall see, many of the things considered disadvantageous are only so when judged against a middle-class standard.

A third factor of importance in Passow's definition is that it does not simply equate disadvantage with poverty. Certainly, within areas of high unemployment, poor housing and low income, one expects to find a concentration of social or educational disadvantage. It is also true that ethnic and racial minorities are very often poor. But, since such external and visible cues may mask a great deal of heterogeneity, it would be incorrect to assume that all those who can be classed within such gross categories are *ipso facto* disadvantaged. On the other hand, it is equally incorrect to equate more comfortable physical surroundings with absence of social disadvantage. It was Wiseman (1968) who noted that there are many 'good' homes in working-class neighbourhoods and many 'bad' ones in middle-class suburbia.

Kellaghan (1977) has considered Passow's definition of disadvantage, commenting in particular upon the latter's emphasis on the 'knowledge, skills and attitudes which impede learning'. These arise in the home situation in the first instance, become characteristic ways of dealing with the world, and yet may be inappropriate in a school system which stresses different values and approaches to life. This, in general, is the crux of the matter. More particular is the question of whether or not disadvantage, which clearly involves *difference*, also implies *deficit*. Is it the case that home-school discontinuity arises because of different, but equally valid, lifestyles, patterns of socialization, etc.? Can one, on the other hand, say that some 'knowledge, skills and attitudes' are inherently better than others? Does a simple dichotomy between difference and deficit oversimplify the issue? Such questions force us to consider more closely the aetiology and definition of disadvantage in general, and anticipate, very directly, the later discussion of language in particular.

1.1 Disadvantage and poverty

While one should not simply equate disadvantage with poverty, there is no doubt that the two often coexist. Since the poor constitute a social group of long standing,[1] it is not surprising that *disadvantage* is but one in a rather long list of terms—many simply euphemisms—used to characterize the poor. Before discussing some of the viewpoints associated with these terms, however, I should like briefly to consider a more general treatment of poverty.

Rainwater (1970) outlines five major perspectives on poverty. These are seen to result from the combination of two polarized dimensions. First, the poor may be seen as either weak or potent; second, they may be considered as either virtuous or bad. The interaction of these two dimensions gives rise to four conceptions of the poor.

In the *moralizing* perspective, the poor are seen as having considerable strength, or at least as having the same potential grasp on the environment as anyone else; at the same time, however, they are somehow lacking in virtue or goodness. The picture, then, is essentially that of a group morally different from the rest of society. Rainwater considers this view to be, historically, the oldest approach to poverty. The immorality and sinfulness of the poor set them apart—they are 'meant to suffer ... they live in a deserved hell on earth' (16).

A moralizing perspective leads to a basic desire to contain the poor and to prevent the spread of immorality, while at the same time making heroic and altruistic efforts to save them. One suspects that this view would find fewer overt supporters now than, for example, in Victorian times, yet elements of it doubtless colour many modern and apparently more sophisticated approaches to poverty.

The *medicalizing* perspective stems from seeing the poor as bad, but weak. Rainwater suggests that this view is a natural successor to a moralistic stance, inasmuch as what was once considered sin can now be seen as sickness. Since many types of social behaviour are, in contemporary times, seen to derive from mental illness rather than from sin, moral flaw or demonic possession, it is not surprising that a medical model of poverty should arise. Viewed from this angle, poverty represents a type of social pathology; thus remediation is possible. Compensatory intervention, for example, would seem to follow from an adherence to this view of the poor. In addition, more large-scale programmes aimed at reorganizing entire social communities may be attempted.

If poverty is seen to result from a combination of virtue and weakness, then Rainwater feels that a *normalizing* perspective is in operation. Bluntly stated, the poor are like everyone else, but have less money and are hence unable effectively to handle the exigencies of life. Just as the medicalizing perspective suggests intervention to cure the sickness of poverty, so this normalizing viewpoint sees a need to provide the poor with greater opportunity. There is here a strong element of helping people to help themselves, and of providing initial aid and guidance to set them on their feet, as it were. This view appears to be most prevalent, for

---

[1] From biblical times, at least; see the well-known quotation in *St John* XII:8.

example, among agencies concerned with helping the poor in the so-called 'under-developed' countries.

A fourth view of the poor is one which holds that they are both strong and good; Rainwater terms this the 'apotheosizing' perspective. One thinks inevitably of Rousseau, the noble savage, and of man born free only to be kept in social shackles. Viewed in this way, the poor can be seen as defiantly disdaining to enter the mainstream of a society which has alienated and denaturalized middle-class man. The Nietzschean superman will more likely be found among the ranks of the poor than in a bourgeois society which is soft, corrupt and dull. In Rainwater's words, 'there is no more *lumpenproletariat*, for among the disinherited lie the real proletariat who have not been co-opted and bought off by materialistic society' (22).

An implication of this view is that the poor are more to be seen as a pool of radical creativity, with the potential for reorganizing the whole society, than as a group standing in need of assistance. This of course has serious corollaries for those who feel that there may be at least some poor people in need of at least some outside help. It is one thing to consider that there exist strengths and virtues in the poor community, but quite another to romanticize over the position of the poor—a point of view which has historically proved seductive to disaffected members of the middle class.

These four perspectives on poverty are all essentially descriptive insofar as they represent views of the lives of the poor rather than explanations of how the poor came to be so. Rainwater provides, however, a fifth approach to the subject, which he describes as an effort to go beyond value judgements. In this *naturalizing* perspective, attempts are made to provide explanations for poverty, and to do so in a scientific (i.e. objective and impersonal) way. It is clear that since science itself, however, is not a value-free exercise, the naturalizing perspective cannot be as objective and disinterested as it sometimes presents itself as being. It is, nevertheless, the view which most directly animates current reactions to poverty. It comprises two quite dissimilar themes.

First is what Rainwater refers to as 'biological determinism' in which inferior intelligence, a function of heredity, is seen to characterize certain racial and social class groups. For rather obvious reasons, a strong adherence to this view is less respectable now than it once was, although recently there has been some considerable interest in the issue (see Section 1.1.1 below). The perceived utility of eugenics and, more generally, a concern to look after people who are considered unable to judge what is best for themselves are characteristics of what Rainwater sees as the 'benign totalitarianism' associated with this view.

The other broad theme emerging from the naturalizing perspective on poverty is one which stresses cultural difference. The lifestyle of any group is seen as adequate for its immediate environment, and has in fact developed in ways most appropriate for that environment. A strong adherence to this 'cultural difference' view may imply that no intervention at all in the lives of the poor is called for. The fact, however, that subgroups within society may come into contact with the middle-class mainstream suggests that certain aspects of lifestyle may be disadvantageous outside a fairly strictly confined geographical and/or psychological space. Proponents of cultural difference often, therefore, support intervention which attempts to broaden the range of opportunities open to the poor, without condemning what they already possess, or do.

Overall, Rainwater's discussion of poverty and its descriptions is a useful and informative starting-point for further discussion. Although his presentation may not be exhaustive, and although the perspectives may not exist in 'pure' form, it seems hard to deny that there are *at least* this many ways of looking at the poor. The value of Rainwater's approach is that it provides some sort of reference-point for what follows; the reader may wish to bear Rainwater's categories in mind when considering the contents of the rest of this chapter.

Of most direct relevance to what follows are the two themes constituting the naturalizing perspective, since they roughly correspond to what are often referred to as the (genetic) deficit and difference views of poverty and, by extension, of disadvantage. It is as well to point out before proceeding further, however, that these labels, at first apparently representing opposite positions, may not be as dichotomous as they seem. On the one hand, it is not difficult to understand that a deficit view of poverty also implies difference. But, equally, a difference viewpoint may encompass deficit. Rainwater notes, for example, that those espousing this latter view show a lack of interest in biological determinism. This may be taken to imply that, from a difference view, proven biological inferiority would only be of practical importance insofar as it reflected itself in differences. These differences, then, might or might not be important, depending solely upon the degree and type of interaction of one group with another.

In attempting to make more specific some recent views of disadvantage, I think it useful to consider three approaches, none of which are 'pure' in the sense that a proponent of one inevitably rejects the others. In fact, throughout the relevant literature, there is a great deal of ground-shifting. This means not only that individual theorists and researchers are capable of changing their minds, but also that the whole topic itself is less than clearcut. It is important, however, to attempt to introduce some minimal clarity at this point. It is futile to consider the relationship of language and disadvantage without first attempting to come to grips with disadvantage itself.

1.1.1   Genetic deficiency: the work of Jensen

The view described by Rainwater (above) as 'biological determinism' has received its most recent and forceful exposition in the work of Jensen. In his well-known article in the *Harvard Educational Review* (1969a), Jensen proposed that compensatory education for disadvantaged children had failed, largely because its proponents ignored genetic, social class and racial differences. Because of the large overlap between disadvantage and race in the United States, Jensen's comments were generally presumed to apply essentially to black-white differences in intelligence and, indeed, this forms the major impact of his work.

Thus, the first, most vociferous and most predictable response to Jensen's paper was that it espoused a racist view of society. Cronbach (1975), in a valuable commentary on 'Jensenism' notes, for example, that 'Jensen scorned the Zeitgeist and became a target of scorn himself' (12). This is because, at the simplest level, Jensen argued against what was then (and still is) the prevailing assumption concerning group differences in achievement and intelligence test performance: that they result from environmental difference or deficit. Cronbach points out that earlier views that genetic and environmental contributions to group differences cannot be separated had, from about 1940, altered to become an assumption that no major genetic differences exist. Further, this assumption of the 1940s 'had crystallized into a combative assertion in the 1960s' (2). Thus, when Jensen's article appeared it was clearly bucking a strong environmentalist tide which meant that, regardless of the rights or wrongs of the case, Jensen's views would be considered inflammatory in many quarters.[2] To quote Cronbach once again: 'In the America of 1969, to make a statement about race differences even at the level of hypothesis was to offend blacks and threaten their political interests' (6).

It is, therefore, of some importance to bear in mind the social and temporal context of Jensen's remarks, for science—and especially social science—does not operate in a vacuum. Statements with social implications bring about social reactions, however 'scientifically' they may be couched. The researcher who fails to realize this is naive indeed. The scientist whose work is seen as more or less directly related to social policy must, therefore, be concerned not only with the usual demands of good scientific practice but also with what might roughly be called the politics of his work. This is clearly important in Jensen's case and, indeed, for the larger topic with which this book deals.

It would be wrong, I believe, to dismiss Jensen solely on the basis of general charges of racism. As general background to his more famous pronouncements on race, class and educability we can see that his viewpoint has not been static, but rather has changed considerably before emerging under the spotlight of public notoriety.[3]

In 1967, Jensen noted that the over-representation of blacks and Mexican-Americans in the lower socioeconomic ranks of society

> cannot be interpreted as evidence of poor genetic potential.... It seems a reasonable hypothesis that their low-average IQ is due to environmental rather than genetic factors. (10)

In 1968, he stated that

> I find little information about the extent to which Negro-white differences have a genetic basis. (22)

In the *Harvard Educational Review* paper, however, Jensen claims that

> the preponderance of the evidence [i.e. concerning black–white academic performance differences] is, in my opinion, less consistent with a strictly environmental hypothesis

[2] Cronbach supplies several examples of the oversimplified and emotional responses to Jensen which appeared in the popular media (but see also Daniels 1973). More scholarly references to Jensen and racism were also evident (e.g. Baratz and Baratz 1970, Deutsch 1969).

[3] For much of the next two paragraphs, Cronbach (1975) has again proved a useful guide (see also Dworkin 1974, Jensen 1974a).

than with a genetic hypothesis, which, of course, does not exclude the influence of environment or its interaction with genetic factors.   (1969a, 82)

Later still, in 1973, Jensen's review of the situation leads him to entertain 'serious doubts on the currently popular explanations in terms of environment' (1) and, further, that the

failures of an enormous variety of compensatory education programs ... would seem to constitute impressive evidence against the theory that environmental influences are paramount as a cause of differences in IQ and achievement.   (23).

I reproduce these quotations here because they rather imply that it is not reasonable to call Jensen a racist. He has apparently altered his views from an environmental position, to one of uncertainty, and then to one emphasizing genetic factors. This may be variously interpreted as evidence of one who is willing to change in the light of new investigation (Jensen's own claim, 1974a), or of one whose ideas are in the process of forming, or, I suppose, simply of one whose notions are not very well thought out. Whatever the interpretation, however, these statements of Jensen are hardly consistent with the rather intractable ideas commonly supposed to characterize prejudice. On this basis, I take as my starting-point the assumption that Jensen's views cannot be simply dismissed as racist and, therefore, unworthy of deeper attention.[4]

In general, Jensen makes a plea for the consideration, at least, of genetic factors in disadvantage. In the 1969a paper, he points to the ignorance of the possible importance of genetics and the general unwillingness to admit it to the discussion at all. Later (1973) he reiterates the need to investigate what has been a 'taboo' research topic. I have already noted that we *do* live in an era in which environmentalism is stressed and so, to the extent to which prevailing attitudes hinder research into genetic determinism, Jensen is scientifically quite correct. But it has also been pointed out that science and society often interact; consequently, it is possible for an impersonal investigation to stir up strong feelings and thereby have negative implications for the topic under study. Clearly, this view is rejected by Jensen. The scientist must be allowed to get on with his work trusting that, in the long run, the results will be positive (i.e. lead to greater understanding). But not everyone would agree with this view. Many would no doubt concur with Hudson's (1973) comment on Jensen's work—it is 'the stuff of racist propaganda' (120). Cronbach (1975), for example, notes the general concern that Jensen's views on the failure of compensatory education might be used as justification for reducing financial support, in general, of programmes directed largely at black children. The fact that Jensen claims that his work is tentative and open to further investigation and interpretation is thus objectively laudable but, given the subject matter, perhaps quite irrelevant to its potentially harmful consequences.

This large and vexing issue is one which cannot be settled by appeal to scientific method. My own view is largely to agree with Jensen on the matter—although

[4] It should be obvious that the use of 'racist' is given here to imply not only characteristics associated with different races, but also the notion of superiority/inferiority and, in fact, race hatred. This extension of the term is now commonly found in dictionary definitions.

I have serious reservations concerning the manner in which he often treats his topic. Jensen admits, for example, that in his interpretations of the data he is 'somewhat less conservative than ... some other students' (1973, 3). In an area of great controversy, conservatism of expression is perhaps not a bad thing. Statements such as

> Is there a danger that current welfare policies, unaided by eugenic foresight, could lead to the genetic enslavement of a substantial segment of our population. (1969a, 95)

seem somewhat ill-advised, despite their interrogative phrasing.

In spite of the fact, mentioned above, that Jensen constantly refers to his findings as mainly suggestive, and most directly valuable in simply bringing genetics into the realms of discussion, there is little doubt that he has a strong personal commitment to the validity of genetic determinism. This is based, of course, upon his interpretation of the data. Thus, it is to his arguments that we must now turn.

1.1.1.1 The failure of compensatory education

To begin with, Jensen feels that compensatory education for disadvantaged children has failed because it has ignored genetic group differences. That is, he considers that the environmentalists, through their many and varied programmes, have had ample opportunity to prove their case but have been unable to do so. Hence the causes of disadvantage must be looked for elsewhere. Jensen's view in this regard has been criticized by environmentalists like Deutsch (1969), Kagan (1969) and Stinchcombe (1969), basically on the grounds that he much oversimplifies environment and its measurement (see also Swift, 1972). I shall be considering programmes of compensatory education more directly in chapter 2; here I wish to make the general point that Jensen cannot dismiss the environmentalist position as he does, simply because insufficient attention has been paid to specific environmental variables and their possible links to educational disadvantage.

Many intervention programmes were hastily conceived and set in motion, using only the most cursory cues to disadvantage in the selection of their subject populations. One may read elaborate reports, statistically highly sophisticated, which employ many tests, treatments and instruments. Yet very often a large degree of homogeneity is assumed to exist in the backgrounds of the participants—an assumption based upon observations of physical correlates of poverty which may obscure many subtle factors. This is not to say that more fine-grained information about disadvantage is absent from the psychological and educational literature; such information is, however, not often brought to bear on actual intervention programmes (see Edwards, in press). I suggest, therefore, that before we could accept Jensen's argument concerning the reason for the failure of compensatory education, a great deal more work would be necessary in making intervention programmes more specifically attuned to the characteristics and needs of the children for whom they are designed. At the moment, the 'enormous variety of compensatory education programs' (Jensen 1973, 23) is, unfortunately, quite homogeneous in terms of approach to disadvantage.

1.1.1.2   Intelligence and IQ scores

The most central part of Jensen's work is his investigation of genetic differences supposedly obtaining between social class and racial groups. There are several aspects to this which should be looked at here. Most basic is Jensen's reliance upon intelligence tests and IQ differences. Well aware of criticisms of tests biased in favour of certain groups, Jensen notes that

> environmentalists who criticize intelligence tests usually give as examples those tests which are most obviously loaded with what is presumably white, middle-class factual knowledge, vocabulary, and the like. (1973, 360)

He accordingly bases his observations not on the results of tests such as these (which are seen to reflect highly specific abilities) but rather upon tests tapping more general mental ability.[5] In fact, Jensen claims that it is on tests which are the least culture-biased (i.e. which have the highest 'g' content) that blacks do most poorly. Tests which are more obviously culture-specific, often necessitating considerable use of verbal skills, are those on which blacks do best (thus, incidentally, Jensen rejects the notion of language deprivation as an explanation of disadvantage: see chapter 2). On all tests, however, blacks tend to score lower than whites.

Clearly, Jensen feels that appropriate intelligence tests are getting at something general and universal. But all tests are devised by someone to measure something; even if the object is to tap highly abstract, nonverbal intelligence, it is difficult to see how sociocultural determination of intelligence can be avoided. That is, tests can obviously be made less directly related to the knowledge and skills available more to one group than to another. But, even tests aimed at elucidating the so-called 'g' factor carry implications concerning intelligence which derive from a given set of values. Kamin (1974), for example, has asserted that the originators of IQ tests were prejudiced against certain minority groups. In general, therefore, it would seem that since IQ tests are constructed within a given psychological space, they must reflect, at least to some degree, certain assumptions about the nature of 'g' itself. The argument that blacks and whites and, in fact, *all* social subgroups share much that is culturally common, and hence should not be discriminated against by tests of 'g', simply does not come to terms with the degree and subtlety of group differences which may exist.

An argument used by Jensen to support the utility of IQ tests is that some groups, more materially disadvantaged than blacks, actually do better on nonverbal tests than do the latter. This, he claims, is difficult for environmentalists to explain, unless they take refuge in 'speculative cultural and attitudinal factors' (Jensen 1973, 360). Yet recourse to these as yet ill-understood variables may be more reasonable than Jensen supposes. Who can say that we comprehend all the complexities and subtleties of environmental difference which may allow some

---

[5] The dichotomy between specific and general ability derives from Spearman's division of intelligence into 's' and 'g' factors (see Spearman 1927, Spearman and Wynn Jones 1950). Deutsch (1969) and others have noted that alternative approaches to intelligence have been proposed, of which Jensen has apparently taken little notice:

groups to do relatively better on IQ tests, and cause others to perform more poorly? This takes on more relevance if we understand that a simple correspondence between material disadvantage (i.e. poverty) and educational disadvantage is over-simplified and may distract attention from more subtle and important factors which may be operating (see, e.g., Crow 1969).

Eysenck (1975) makes an argument similar to that of Jensen in a discussion of the nonverbal test performance of Eskimo children. Apparently they have been found to out-perform black American children, even though they live under much harsher environmental conditions. As a matter of fact, Eysenck notes that the Eskimo scores are at or above the norms established for white children.[6] Again, the argument is that

> if social and sensory deprivation, or other environmental deprivation factors, are postulated to account for IQ deficits in white working-class or coloured populations, then the logic of the explanation requires absolutely that a severely deprived group, such as the Eskimos, should show evidence of IQ deficit; the fact is that they do not.   (Eysenck 1975, 110).

But this is again equating observable and rather gross indices of material deprivation with intellectual disadvantage, when such variables may not in fact be directly relevant. Generally, there may exist all sorts of differences in all sorts of groups, such that some will score better than others on any given test; such differences may or may not be related to poverty of physical environment. It is at least a reasonable assumption, however, that score differences may be related to more specific, less visible variables which exist and operate in the social environment.[7]

Another important factor concerning intelligence tests relates to the manner and context in which they are administered. Jensen presents some evidence to show that having black children examined by black testers makes no difference to scores; neither does the translation of tests into black English. He also states that there is no reason to suppose that blacks are less motivated than others in a test situation. Yet this is by no means a clear issue. Anderson (1969) criticizes Jensen (1969a) on exactly these issues. Watson (1972) reports that situational variables do make a difference in IQ performance. And, perhaps best known of all, Labov (1973a) has demonstrated rather clearly the effects of context in eliciting responses from black children. Since much of interest here relates directly to language perform-ance, I shall defer further discussion on this matter. It might simply be noted that situational determinants of test performance and, more generally, approaches to the whole milieu in which testing occurs, cannot be lightly dismissed. In fact, at

---

[6] More recent investigation of Jensen's hypotheses with regard to Eskimo children can be found in Taylor and Skanes 1977.

[7] In fairness to Jensen and Eysenck, it is true that the environmentalist position which they attack *has* based its arguments essentially upon material deprivation. But this emphasis is a weakness of the usual environmentalist stance on disadvantage, not of the explanatory value of the environment *per se*. That is, as will be seen below, the environmentalist position itself is less than satisfactory. In trying to counter the arguments of Jensen and Eysenck I am, therefore, anticipating somewhat my criticisms of environmentalism.

one point Jensen (1969a) himself adverts to the possibility of depressed scores resulting from children's inhibitions in the test situation.

Much of Jensen's argument concerning group IQ differences rests upon studies of identical twins; since such siblings have identical genetic structure, any intelligence differences observed should be due to environmental influence. Therefore, investigations of such twins who, for varying reasons, have been reared separately (i.e. in different environments) have been cited by Jensen as evidence of the high heritability of intelligence. This is because the measured IQs of such twins are often found to be very similar, a fact which has led Jensen (and others) to assume that environment makes relatively little difference in terms of IQ. The major problem here is that the 'different' environments in which separated twins have been studied are usually not very different at all. Twins put up for adoption, for example, are often placed in homes of generally similar socioeconomic characteristics (see, e.g., Daniels 1973, Hebb 1968). To test properly the heredity-environment hypothesis, Hebb notes, the separated twins should be placed in maximally different environments. This of course is not likely to occur, since ethical constraints quite rightly prevent us from subjecting a twin to a poor environment on an experimental basis.[8]

Even if heredity *could* be shown to be of great importance, difficulties would still exist. Thus, Kagan (1969) notes that 'the essential error in Jensen's argument is the conclusion that if a trait is under genetic control, differences between two populations on that trait must be due to genetic factors' (275). Kagan alludes here to the difficulties involved in generalizing from within-group measures to between-groups measures (see also Hebb 1968, Hunt 1961). This difficulty arises because environments are often markedly different for different groups. Furthermore, attempts to control for environment by matching socioeconomic status (SES) levels across groups are not successful in societies in which such matching does not really imply environmental equality—'equal SES scores still imply more restricted life-chances for blacks' (Light and Smith 1969, 488; see also Bodmer 1972). Lewontin (1976) summarizes the matter neatly: 'Heritability within groups tells one nothing at all about the causes of the differences between groups' (97).

Further to this issue, Hudson (1973) notes that black twins would have to be separated at birth, with one being brought up in a white environment—in which there was no prejudice, and in which the child's blackness was not noticed—before genetic differences in intelligence could be established. Bodmer (1972) also refers to this sort of cross-adoption as the only way to investigate accurately the influence of genetics. Overall, however, because of continuing prejudice against blacks and because of the obvious practical problems in carrying out such work, Bodmer concludes that

> the question of a possible genetic basis for the race-IQ difference will be almost impossible to answer satisfactorily before the environmental differences between US blacks and whites have been substantially reduced.   (111)

---

[8] The high observed correlation between the IQs of twins raised apart has itself been questioned recently; thus, the reader may be aware of the controversy surrounding the work of the late Sir Cyril Burt, whose twin studies Jensen cites in support of his position. For a recent overview of the Burt controversy, see Gillie 1978.

Jensen, on the one hand, claims that the evidence for genetic differences in intelligence is not conclusive, but suggestive. On the other hand, those who are sceptical of genetic influence in this regard admit that genetics cannot be ruled absolutely out of the question. The issue is not one which can be settled one way or the other; as we shall see, however, one might reasonably ask whether the whole enterprise is even worth the candle.

As a final note here, there are technical disagreements with Jensen's data-analysis techniques. Crow (1969), for example, questions the use of analysis-of-variance as the most appropriate statistical tool (see also Fehr 1969, Light and Smith 1969). In addition, there is the question of the degree to which American blacks and whites are separate groups (Anderson 1969). Certainly in his later work at least (e.g. 1973), Jensen refers to racial mixing, claiming that American blacks are racial hybrids. Yet he obviously feels that this does not vitiate his findings. Indeed, Jensen's genetic claims apply not only to racial groups, pure or mixed, but also to different white social-class groups. Here I only wish to point out that, while not denying that genetic factors operate along race and class lines, the genetic 'case' for disadvantage is hardly a strong one, especially bearing in mind the sociocultural nature of intelligence itself.

1.1.1.3   Educational implications

Another major theme of Jensen's work is to suggest ways in which educational policies for disadvantaged children might be altered, on the basis of his data. This is an aspect of Jensen's investigations which, although a natural consequence of his work, has not received a great deal of attention, understandably overshadowed by the more controversial features of the discussion (Cronbach 1975).

Since it was the apparent failure of compensatory education which, Jensen (1974a) tells us, first turned his attention to the whole topic, he devotes some time to outlining the educational implications of his findings (1969a). To begin with, he notes that the observed IQ-score differences along socioeconomic lines are understandable only in terms of two quite different underlying abilities which are differentially represented in different groups. Level I ability is mainly 'associative' in nature; there is little transformation of what is learned, and intellectual functioning is apparently on the level of regurgitation. Tests for associative ability are of the rote-learning, simple memory type. Level II ability, on the other hand, is seen as more conceptual in nature. Here, one is able to elaborate on and transform the basic input, as exemplified in problem-solving tasks. All classes have roughly the same amount of Level I ability, but Level II competence is much more evident in higher socioeconomic status groups. Furthermore, Level II ability presupposes competence at Level I, but the reverse does not hold. Finally, Jensen postulates that different neural structures may underlie the two ability levels.

IQ tests can now be seen as unfair to disadvantaged children because they do not tap what these children are strongest in—Level I ability. Typically, schools emphasize concept formation and problem-solving ability. However, Jensen's argument is that the 'basic scholastic skills' can be learned by children with Level I ability if curricula are suitably altered. Jensen (1970) expands on this by introducing the terms 'educability' and 'trainability', as processes associated with one or other of the two ability levels.

> Educability implies that the learner is already able to act upon the instructional input in order to master it. Trainability, on the other hand, assumes basic learning ability as a prerequisite, but the focusing of the learner's attention, his active engagement in the task, and the immediacy of recognition and reinforcement of correct responses are not entirely left up to him.   (129)

What Jensen appears to suggest here are different methods for teaching the same basic educational goals—methods which are attuned to a child's inherent ability. Later (1973), he seems rather pessimistic about the likelihood of finding appropriate ability/method interactions.

These ability levels can be questioned, however, on the grounds that they greatly oversimplify abilities in general (Cronbach 1969). Also, despite Jensen's claim that either level can lead to mastery of basic skills, with appropriate guidance, there is little doubt that one is of a lower order than the other. Therefore, and especially in the light of arguments which can be made against Jensen's views of genetic difference, differential teaching methods could only serve to increase differences between groups and pull them further apart. Even if genetic differences in intelligence were a factor to be reckoned with, could one reasonably teach some children in ways that might well exclude them from full participation in a society in which conceptual ability is generally more important than rote learning? This approach is surely defensible only if one is dealing with the education of severely subnormal children whose genetic disabilities are pronounced and obvious.

Discussion of Jensen's Levels I and II leads directly to the more general question of the practical implications of his work as a whole for the education of disadvantaged children. It is hard to see that there are any. Whether or not genetic factors influence intelligence it is not clear that this is of any concern to the teacher. Let us assume that a difference of 10 to 15 IQ points *does* exist between black and white children, for example; further assume that this difference *does* reflect something of underlying intelligence. This is not so large a difference as to make for great problems in schooling, and is certainly not sufficient to warrant differential treatment of children along the lines proposed by Jensen (see Anderson 1969). Kagan (1969) notes that

> genetic factors are likely to be most predictive of proficiency in mental talents that are extremely difficult to learn.... Learning to read, write or add are easy skills, well within the competence of all children who do not have serious brain damage.... Ninety out of every 100 children, black, yellow or white, are capable of adequate mastery of the intellectual requirements of our schools.   (277).

Thus, even allowing Jensen's claims (which, obviously, has not been my intention here), it is difficult to see their relevance. It may or may not be admitted that Jensen's work is of academic interest; educationally, however, 'it is pointless to stress heredity' (Cronbach 1969, 345). The teacher's job is to work with every child, regardless of the aetiology of any problems he may have; a similar, although perhaps more complicated, task confronts the clinician (see chapter 3). In addition, the practical view dictates that since we can work only with the environment, it is the environment which should be stressed. Bloom (1969) thus notes that the teacher must be an environmentalist—'If heredity imposes limits—so be it. The educator must work with what is left' (421). Wiseman (1973) states that

> the fierce controversies over the precise proportion of influence exerted by nature as opposed to nurture are of importance to the geneticist and the psychologist, but for the teacher I suggest that they are largely irrelevant.   (87)

Finally, a recent article by Perney, Hyde and Machock (1977) questions the very basis of arguments concerning black-white IQ differences. Using the Kuhlmann-Anderson Test of Intelligence, the IQ scores of 1119 black first-grade children in Ohio were found to be slightly but significantly *higher* than national norms. The authors point out that these findings suggest, at the least, that the matter of black intelligence is by no means settled.

Overall, therefore, it would seem that even if one assumed Jensen (and the genetic argument in general) to be correct, there is little of interest here in any practical sense. Thus, the relevance of the genetic argument to classroom practice is doubtful.[9] Nevertheless, it has merited consideration here because it is a controversial and often poorly-understood viewpoint. As an explanation for disadvantage, however, it has little value.[10]

1.1.2   Environmental deficit

In this view of disadvantage, genetic determinants are rejected in favour of environmental factors which are seen as the principal causes. The disadvantaged child arrives at school unprepared for the demands and challenges which it will present to him. His deficiencies in school and, by extension, in later life, derive largely from the unsatisfactory nature of his early physical, social and psychological background. This general view has been prevalent for some considerable time. Not all environmentalists reject completely, however, the importance of genetic factors.[11] They tend rather to stress the potency of the interaction of genetics and environment and, being mainly of a practically-minded bent, emphasize the environmental contribution. That is, there exists the realization that one can do little with genetic factors (short of eugenics), even if they are found to have some impor-

---

[9] Hudson (1973) suggests, in fact, that despite Jensen's alleged motivation, stemming from the failure of compensatory education, his real purpose is to refute environmentalism *per se*. Jensen himself (1973) is highly critical of what he terms 'egalitarian environmentalism' (8). Finally, Jensen has recently suggested that cumulative environmental factors may *contribute* to lower black IQ scores, especially in the rural southern United States (1977); related work, however (Jensen 1974b), makes it clear that he has by no means abandoned his earlier position on the importance of genetic factors in this regard (see also Kamin 1978).

[10] A recent collection of essays on genetics and IQ is that of Block and Dworkin (1976). Many of the notable figures in the field are represented, and a long essay by the editors themselves (410–540) is of particular interest.

[11] Henceforth, the term 'environmentalist' will refer to one supporting the view that environmental deprivation leads to educational disadvantage.

tance, and rather more with the environment. Consequently, it is the environmental-deprivation approach to disadvantage which has provided the impetus for most of the compensatory education programmes aimed at helping the disadvantaged child.

As was mentioned in the preceding section, there are some difficulties with the environmentalist position which should now be considered further here. If Jensen's claims of the environmental failure to explain disadvantage have been seen as less than satisfactory, it is equally true that aspects of the environmentalist position itself are open to question. Because there are several variants of the environmental deprivation approach to disadvantage, discussion of it as a general stance is inappropriate. Hence I have attempted, in what follows, to isolate the two major themes of the position. It must be kept in mind, however, that simplifying viewpoints for the ease of presentation always implies the possibility of introducing inaccuracy. Nevertheless, I think it fair to say that all varieties of environmental deprivation theory assume that disadvantage, educational and social, is an inevitable consequence. They differ in explaining *how* this disadvantage arises.

1.1.2.1 Sensory deprivation

It is well known that animals reared in severely abnormal conditions develop in inappropriate ways. Aberrations in normal developmental patterns may be permanent, depending upon the length and severity of the deprivation. Deprivation itself may involve only one sense modality (e.g. vision), or it may take the form of general restriction of all sensory input. Many studies, in fact, involve animals reared in isolation from others (Konrad and Melzack 1975), often in darkness. Such deprivation may interfere with the development of species-normal learning ability, social and sexual behaviour or reactions to noxious stimuli, and indeed may entail substantive neural degeneration.

Among human beings, the effects of sensory deprivation (or, perceptual isolation) were demonstrated in experiments at McGill University during the 1950s (Bexton *et al.* 1954, Hebb 1968, Heron 1957, 1961). Well-paid subjects were required to lie on a bed with no visual, somaesthetic or auditory stimulation. Few subjects could endure this monotony for more than a few days, and the maximum was six days. Hebb (1968) describes some of the effects:

> The subjects in isolation complained of being unable to think coherently.... they began to have hallucinations.... The subjects' very identity had begun to disintegrate. (252)

These experiments indicate that the absence of normal sensory input is extremely disturbing to adults. Naturally, for human analogies to the infantile deprivation of animals, no experiments are possible. Here, evidence for the importance of early stimulation derives largely from studies of children in orphanages, or who are in some other way institutionalized. Such children, often receiving adequate physical care, nevertheless may be deprived of a great deal of attention, and may be more or less isolated in dull and unchanging environments. They often exhibit apathy and poor motor and mental performance (see, e.g., Skeels and Dye 1939). Developmental retardation, and so-called 'anaclitic depression'—which includes withdrawal, weepiness and increased susceptibility to illness—have been described by Spitz (1946) as due to the lack of attention given to institutionalized children.

An often-cited study in this connection is that of Dennis (1960). He investigated infants, ranging from one to four years of age, who were being cared for in three institutions in Teheran. Two of these were state-run and provided only the minimum of physical care; each attendant looked after several children, and none was specifically assigned to particular children. The other institution was privately run, and provided much more individual attention. Toys and games were available for the children's use. It was found that investigations of the children's motor development (sitting, standing and walking) revealed great retardation among the children cared for in the two state institutions. Dennis ascribes this to the lack of handling and attention received by the children there. Overall, the study suggests that quite unambiguous effects may be brought on by early deprivation. Such work clearly points to the importance of adequate environmental stimulation.

Much of the work in the area has been reviewed by Hunt (1961). In gathering together data from animal studies and from experiments and observations on human beings, Hunt proposed that the old concepts of fixed intelligence and predetermined development were inadequate; he stressed the importance of the environment and the need to consider its effects upon the developing child. In pointing to the importance of the social context for all children, Hunt expanded the scope of previous work on sensory and/or social deprivation; in particular, it appeared to some that the cause of disadvantage might be sought in a sensorily-deprived environment.

Hunt (1961) himself says nothing directly to suggest a link between sensory deprivation and educational disadvantage, although he does express the 'hope of increasing the average level of intelligence by proper manipulation of children's developmental encounters with their environments' (346). In fact, Bereiter and Engelmann (1966), in discussing sensory deprivation as a possible cause of disadvantage, suggest that Hunt has been misinterpreted by those caught up in what they term 'the sensory deprivation fad' (27).[12] Deutsch (1967a), for example, seems to consider that sensory deprivation may exist among lower SES children. Interestingly, in supporting this view, Deutsch quotes the work of Bruner (1961) who nowhere mentions disadvantage; in fact, the section of Bruner's article most directly referred to by Deutsch is based upon a hypothetical animal study of deprivation.

In later work, Hunt (1964) does appear, however, to attach more importance to sensory deprivation as a factor in disadvantage. He notes that

> the difference between the culturally deprived and the culturally privileged is, for children, analogous to the difference between cage-reared and pet-reared rats and dogs. (236)

[12] To bolster their claim, Bereiter and Engelmann note that in his later work, Hunt (1964) actually suggests that in the vital first year of life, lower-socioeconomic-status children, living in crowded conditions, may receive *more* stimulation than their middle-class counterparts. They neglect to point out, however, that the general tenor of Hunt's article is quite different. In fact, on the subject of crowding, he goes on to remark that it may have very serious effects in the *second* year of life—still a fairly important age, one would think.

Hunt also relates disadvantage to the early work with institutionalized children:

> I have viewed the effects of cultural deprivation as analogous to the experimentally-found effects of experiential deprivation in infancy. (242)

Perhaps, as Bereiter and Engelmann (1966) suggested, Hunt (1961) was rather overinterpreted; Hunt (1964), however, appears to link sensory deprivation with disadvantage (or, as he terms it, cultural deprivation; see below). This view of Hunt's work is supported by Katz (1970).

Later still, Hunt (1969), in a comment on Jensen 1969a, reiterates the importance he attaches to early stimulation (see also Hunt 1972, 1975). Overall, however, it appears that the analogy between sensory deprivation in experimental animals and in institutionalized children, on the one hand, and in lower-class children on the other, is very weak. Lower-class environments are surely not at all similar to those obtaining in institutions, for example and, as Jensen (1969b) points out, 'culturally disadvantaged children are obviously not reared in the dark' (471). A comparison between the sensory stimulation in lower-class homes and that in middle-class ones may reveal some interesting differences, but there is little to suggest that the *amount* of stimulation is markedly different or, at least, so deficient in given environments as to even approach a state of sensory deprivation.

Jensen (1969b) goes on to suggest that, in fact, the greater stimulation which Hunt (1964) concedes to the lower-class child up to one year of age may well continue beyond that first year (see footnote 12). To cite Bereiter and Engelmann (1966) once again:

> It would seem that those who have attributed sensory deprivation to lower-class children have not seriously considered what the term implies. It has nothing to do with the educational quality of the stimuli available, but only with their variety, intensity, and patterning. On these purely quantitative bases, automobiles passing in the street are as good as story books, old shoes are as good as dolls, and trash cans are as good as toy drums. (27)

I need hardly point out that using Jensen's arguments against sensory deprivation as a factor in disadvantage does not imply acceptance of his own position (section 1.1.1). Equally, Bereiter and Engelmann's position on disadvantage will be criticized later. Nevertheless, in their criticisms of Hunt in particular, and the sensory deprivation approach to disadvantage in general, they are essentially correct. In short, it seems rather unreasonable to view sensory deprivation as a factor in disadvantage.

1.1.2.2 Social/cultural deprivation

Proponents of this view of disadvantage claim that the early physical and psychological environment of lower-class and minority group children is deficient with respect to that of the middle class. It is, in fact, from this viewpoint that the deficit stance on disadvantage most often arises. That is, most who feel that the problems of disadvantaged children are actual deficiencies do not emphasize either genetic factors or sensory deprivation in their explanations. Rather, they stress the inadequate aspects of early socialization practices which lead to cognitive and emotional defects in children—defects which show up most clearly in the early school years.

Deutsch (1967b) notes that lower-class children's culture is different from that reflected in the school system. Further, the differences in lifestyle are such that deficiencies in cognitive and intellectual functioning result. Thus, 'the lower-class child enters the school situation so poorly prepared to produce what the school demands that initial failures are almost inevitable' (39). Deutsch goes on to mention the 'invidious influences' of slum life.

Whiteman, Brown and Deutsch (1967) describe a procedure by which they attempt to come closer to the concept of social deprivation. Six variables appeared important in this respect, and a child could receive a score of either 1 or 2 on each. Information from about 300 first and fifth-grade children was collected, and a child's score on the 'deprivation index' simply results from the addition of his six individual scores. The variables, and the manner of assigning scores, are as follows (see also Whiteman and Deutsch 1967):

1   Housing dilapidation (1 = less than sound; 2 = sound, with complete plumbing)
2   Educational aspirations of parents for children (1 = college or less; 2 = graduate or professional training)
3   Number of children at home who are less than 18 years old (1 = three or more such children; 2 = two or fewer)
4   Dinner conversation (1 = child takes no part in such conversation; 2 = child does take part)
5   Number of 'cultural experiences' to be engaged in during the coming weekend, including family visits, trips to zoos, libraries etc. (1 = none; 2 = one or more)
6   Kindergarten attendance (1 = child did not attend; 2 = child did attend)

Although the authors note that each deprivation variable may be relevant to any class, high scores (which are related to lower-school achievement) are pretty well confined to those at the lower end of the socioeconomic continuum. Variables 1, 3, 5 and 6 are, for example, clearly going to discriminate between middle- and lower-class children. In this sense, it is hard to see that the index throws any new light on the environment. Variable 4—conversation over meals—is related to perceived language differences in home environments, but here there are obviously difficulties in accurate measurement and interpretation. Variable 2 is interesting; in order for a child to score as relatively undeprived, parents' educational aspirations have to be very high indeed. Labov (1973a) has called attention to this variable as representing, at the very least, a rather curious view of deprivation. Overall, it appears that the 'deprivation index' is but a slight refinement of more general descriptions of disadvantage and poverty.

The very existence of such an index is telling, however, for it points to what is perhaps the major thrust of the social/cultural deprivation position. This is the continuing effort to isolate factors in a child's early environment which are important for the lack of adequate development of cognitive skills. Thus, for example, Deutsch and Deutsch (1967) note that a task of importance is

> the identification of the stimulation lacks in the environment; the diagnosis of the areas of retardation ... the prescription of particular stimuli, strategies, and techniques ... and the evaluation of the efficiency of the techniques used. (381)

We can now see that it is not surprising that it is this environmentalist view of disadvantage which most directly leads to intervention programmes of 'enrichment' or compensatory education. The very deficiencies which for so long branded the poor as inferior in the school system (which placed the onus for change upon the poor themselves, if they wished to benefit from formal education; see Edwards, in press), now provide the greatest impetus for various sorts of educational adjustments to meet the needs of the poor.

It may be instructive here to consider briefly some of the characteristics of the disadvantaged child that are commonly seen as deficiencies. I should point out here, however, that as I shall be dealing specifically with language in the following chapters I shall not mention it here; nevertheless, the reader should bear in mind that language is generally considered the single most important aspect of presumed deficit. For much of what follows, I draw upon the reviews by E. Gordon (1965) and J. Gordon (1968).

The frequently-cited characteristics of disadvantaged children can be seen to fall roughly into two categories—those relating to the home environment in general, and those more particularly descriptive of the disadvantaged child himself.

As Morrison and McIntyre (1971) and Musgrove (1966) have indicated, home life may have much to do with school performance. Thus the Plowden Report, in its survey of children and schools, stressed the importance of low socioeconomic status, large family size, receipt of state supplements and generally poor, overcrowded living conditions for disadvantage (Great Britain: Department of Education and Science 1967; see also Ferguson et al. 1971). Others have noted the relevance to disadvantage of incomplete or disorganized families (Gordon 1965, Klaus and Gray 1968, Passow and Elliott 1968); families of immigrant or ethnic minority origin (Gordon and Wilkerson 1966, Stodolsky and Lesser 1967); low value placed upon formal education, and absence of books and other cultural or educational materials in the home (Gordon 1965, Havighurst 1970). Lower-class parents are presumed to respond poorly to children's questions, and to place little value upon the child's natural curiosity (Gordon 1965, Hess and Shipman 1965, 1968a, Hunt 1969). Generally, the whole area of adult/child interaction and communication (especially between mother and child) is seen to be one in which the lower-class child is at a disadvantage, both quantitatively and qualitatively.

The home environment, in short, is viewed as one of noise, crowding and physical discomfort, in which children have little opportunity to learn and develop, and in which the usual (i.e. middle-class) parental role of tutor and guide is largely lacking. Such factors are seen to lead to deficits in the child's perceptual and conceptual abilities and, as we shall see, in his verbal development.

Characteristics of the child himself presumably derive from the home background, and many specifics have been discussed. The disadvantaged child is seen to be more 'activity-oriented', for example, putting greater emphasis upon motor behaviour than upon conceptual processes. This, as Gordon (1968) notes, is seen as particularly unfortunate for the child in the school situation which typically stresses thought rather than action (see also Passow and Elliott 1968). Gordon (1968) also points out that the disadvantaged child is more concerned with the here-and-now, is less likely to anticipate or think about the future, and is hence unwilling to delay gratification. The emphasis is upon immediate reward; again, the school's typical concern with knowledge for its own sake, and with sequential learning leading to mastery of a subject, is considered to be unappealing to the disadvantaged child.

Other characteristics include fear and insecurity, less regard for 'conscience' and greater aggression and hostility (Barbe 1967, Gordon 1968). Also, the disadvantaged child is seen to possess little self-esteem (Deutsch 1967b, Gordon 1968, Passow and Elliott 1968) and to have lower academic motivation and aspirations than his middle-class counterpart (Deutsch 1967b, Gordon 1965). Virtually *all* writers comment on the poor language ability of the disadvantaged child (see chapter 2).

The list of characteristics given above is by no means exhaustive and the interested reader can easily add to it. I am concerned here only to point to some of the more commonly-held views concerning specific deficits supposedly attaching to life in lower-class society. On the surface, it would appear that many problem-causing factors have been elucidated. There are, however, some difficulties here.

The first of these concerns the use to which knowledge of these characteristics, such as they are, is put. Although many writers have called attention to the need to consider more closely details of the lifestyle of disadvantaged children, the fact remains that simple socioeconomic status variables are most often referred to in discussions of disadvantaged children. Thus, despite the more detailed information available, there still exists, for practical purposes, an equation of material disadvantage with educational disadvantage (see Edwards, in press).

Chazan, Laing and Jackson (1971) note that 'it is necessary to be cautious in generalizing, on the basis of the area in which they live, about the disadvantages children suffer' (153; see also Chazan 1973, Kellaghan 1977). Swift (1968) has cautioned that social class is merely a summarizing variable, and Wiseman (1968) has pointed out that social class, as a category, masks many important differences. Even Deutsch and Deutsch (1967) acknowledge that social-class groups are far from homogeneous (see also Bijou 1975, Booth 1975, Gallagher and Bradley 1972, Messick and Barrows 1972).

Yet despite these claims, environmentalists often fall back upon rather gross variables when dealing with disadvantaged children. A language programme designed by Blank and Solomon (1968), for example, used only a geographical selection procedure, drawing participants from given urban areas. Klaus and Gray (1968), in a well-known programme of compensatory education, did consider individual characteristics but it is unclear whether or not these related specifically to their own subjects. Indeed, the authors described their programme as an attempt 'to offset the deficit *usually* observed in children from culturally deprived homes' (5; my italics). This appears to imply an assumption about the homogeneity of disadvantage which may be quite untenable. More recently, Miller and Dyer (1975) conducted an exhaustive and well-executed comparison of four types of preschool compensatory education. Although some information about the motivational and perceptual characteristics of the participants was provided, along with some data concerning home background, most of the attention was simply given to socio-economic status. I shall return to the topic of compensatory education in the next chapter; here we can simply note that the characteristics of disadvantaged children, as investigated by the environmentalists themselves, are often not given what one might consider their due weight in programmes designed to help these children.

A second difficulty associated with the environmentalist approach relates to the presumed characteristics of disadvantage themselves. We should be cautious, for example, in interpreting studies in which aspects of the home life of individuals are discussed. How was such information obtained? Does it derive from self-report, or from interviews with parents, children or teachers? Data concerning personal background may well be very important, but it is difficult to obtain and measure them with accuracy. Thus, Gordon (1965) notes that much of the effort in this direction is essentially speculative. What is needed, evidently, are patient, longitudinal studies which aim systematically to describe naturally-occurring behaviour. These, of course, are difficult and regrettably rare.

Also, in determining characteristics of the disadvantaged child at school, it is debatable to what extent one can rely upon standardized tests and observations in what is a rather formal setting. As we shall see, in discussing the elicitation of speech samples (chapter 3), the context of testing and/or sampling can be crucial. It is surely not surprising to realize that such difficulties can extend beyond the domain of language *per se*. For example, as mentioned above, lower-class children are often reported to be low in academic motivation (see, e.g., Gordon 1965). Yet Bloom, Whiteman and Deutsch (1967) report extremely high educational aspirations on the part of black parents for their children, higher in fact than those of white parents (see also Labov 1973a). While parental aspirations need not, perhaps, be directly related to children's motivation, there presumably exists some sort of relationship between them; parental attitudes among the middle class, for example, are often assumed to be important in children's school performance. Perhaps, therefore, this lack of a close fit between the alleged views of black parents and those of their children indicates that we should look more closely at the context in which such measures are obtained, and at how this context is perceived by lower-class individuals.[13]

A further important issue with regard to the characteristics of disadvantage is that we do not know the relationship between early environment and such characteristics, nor are we on firm ground when considering possible links between

[13] There is evidence suggesting that ethnic minority groups have higher educational aspirations now than before (see, e.g., Ovando 1978). Thus the whole area may be more dynamic than is sometimes assumed.

these characteristics and school success (or lack of it). Mere classification and description are not sufficient. How can we account, for example, for the success of many children who live in disadvantaged areas, whose homes are physically inadequate and whose early life is, in the environmentalists' terms, disorganized (Robinson 1976, Wiseman 1968)? I have already mentioned Wiseman's comment that there are many 'good' homes in the working class, and many 'poor' ones in more affluent surroundings. He goes on to note that 'bad homes and neighbourhoods are more effective in preventing the emergence of brightness than they are in producing backwardness' (268). Thus, it seems fair to say that our detailed knowledge of what constitutes educational disadvantage is rather meagre. This is not so much a criticism of the environmentalist position in principle as it is of the lack of the necessary detail which that position really requires.

An additional point, however, *is* a criticism of the environmental-deficit position *per se*. It is that behind the environmentalist view, as it were, is a profound and overwhelming middle-class bias. Gordon (1968), in a review of the characteristics of disadvantage, notes that virtually all 'deficits' might well be seen as strengths if the immediate context of the disadvantaged child were kept in mind. Thus:

> For example, instead of discussing the supposed short-term gratification pattern of the disadvantaged youth ... it would be possible to discuss the long-term gratification pattern typical of the middle class, with *its* consequences (e.g., inability to enjoy the present moment, generation of guilt over immediate pleasures ...).   (70)

Because of the *comparison* implicit in all discussions of the characteristics of disadvantage, Gordon makes it quite clear that such characteristics must be viewed only descriptively, and not as 'imputations of pathology' (70). A similar point is made by Gordon (1965) who again notes that deficits are so perceived only insofar as they are deviations from middle-class norms (see also Tulkin 1972). In fact, characteristics such as a poorly-developed sense of conscience, or aggressive behaviour, could be seen quite easily as not only appropriate but eminently sensible for certain environments (see also Edwards 1976a).[14] In general, the thrust of this argument is not to deny that the described characteristics of disadvantage exist, but rather is to point out that it is incorrect to view them as substantive deficits. This, in fact, is the essence of the *difference* position on disadvantage, to be discussed below.

A final point is in order here. If, as the environmentalists believe, the differences characteristic of disadvantaged children are, in fact, deficits, then it is understandable that the remedy is seen to lie in compensatory education. The school, while being willing to adapt its procedures somewhat to the requirements of the disadvantaged child, must nevertheless retain fairly traditional goals. This is the rationale behind the American *Head Start* and other types of intervention programmes. Thus the educational amendments sometimes suggested by programmes

---

[14] Entwisle (1968) conducted a study in which inner-city children were seen to be *more* advanced on some language measures than surburban children. The crowding, noise and ever-present television, cited by deficit theorists as interfering with the development of the disadvantaged child, are considered by Entwisle to be potentially enriching aspects of the verbal environment (see also Entwisle 1970).

of compensatory education do not go quite as deep as is often professed. It is hard to escape the conclusion that there is a strong sense of the correctness of middle-class standards, as reflected in the educational system. Before commenting further on this, however, it is just as well to consider the *difference* approach to disadvantage. This is because the two points of view—difference and deficit—generally deal with exactly the same information—the observable characteristics or correlates of disadvantage—but interpret it rather differently.

1.1.3 Disadvantage as difference

The so-called difference view of disadvantage does not deny that children from the lower classes perform poorly in school, nor that such children may have different attitudes and values than their middle-class schoolmates. But, for proponents of this view, such social-class differences are just that—differences. Invoking the charge of middle-class bias, difference theorists claim that the social or cultural deprivation approach unfairly translates difference into deficit. Much of the support for the difference position comes from studies of lower-class language, which is considered a central issue by *all* concerned, and which I shall discuss later. The reader should bear in mind here, therefore, that the criticisms of the cultural deprivation approach in general spring most directly from investigations of language. In this section, it is the more general criticisms with which I am concerned. Furthermore, as will be seen, the difference position is defined most clearly as a reaction *against* the cultural deprivation interpretation of disadvantage.

We can begin by considering the charge that the very term *cultural deprivation* implies a middle-class bias. The general claim is that, since it is ludicrous to describe a group as being deprived of its own culture, the term really indicates that the culture in which certain groups are seen to be deficient is that of the middle class. Even Riessman (1962), although he entitled his well-known book *The culturally deprived child*, acknowledged that the term was inaccurate. Similarly, Bereiter and Engelmann (1966), clearly proponents of the deficit position on disadvantage, note the objections to the term.[15] It is felt, generally, that an invalid comparison is being made, in which the norms and standards of one group (the middle class) are being applied to the lifestyle of another group. The notion of cultural deprivation has come under strong attack from Ginsburg (1972) and, most recently, from Keddie (1973). She notes that the term is

> a euphemism for saying that working-class and ethnic groups have cultures which are at least dissonant with, if not inferior to, the 'mainstream' culture of the society at large.... The argument is that the school's function is to transmit the mainstream values of the society. (8).

The difference view of disadvantage claims that, to the extent to which lower-class society does *not* possess the same values, attitudes etc. of the mainstream

[15] They justify its use, however, by claiming that although groups within a larger society may differ, they do share many aspects of a common culture. To the extent to which values, attitudes and behaviour *are* common, 'it is both legitimate and useful to speak of *cultural deprivation*' (24).

society, its members will be on a less than equal footing. Since it is assumed that there are no substantial or important inter-group differences in basic cognitive ability, any differences simply reflect varying adaptations to environments, most particularly in terms of early socialization. Inherent in the difference position is a respect for social differences; cultural and social pluralism is seen to represent an enriching aspect of the larger society, and not something to be eradicated.

It is important to realize, however, that difference theorists are aware that although social and cultural differences do exist among subgroups in society, one is not dealing with separate cultures in the commonly-understood sense (in which, say, we can differentiate between English culture and Pacific Islands culture). The disadvantaged *share* much in common with society at large, and are constantly in touch with it. This is really the heart of the matter—disadvantage can only be seen to arise when groups which have much in common, and yet which differ in some respects, come into contact. Are we entitled, in such situations, to see these subcultural (perhaps a more appropriate term here than cultural) differences as deficits precisely because of the larger common involvement? Or should we view them as valid differences to be treasured, lest they disappear to the impoverishment of all? We can perhaps begin to be aware here that philosophical differences in how people view society, and in how culture is defined, may greatly influence perceptions of difference or deficit.

One recent interpretation of culture has greatly exercised those holding the difference view. It is the *culture of poverty*—essentially a view of the poor that is seen to buttress a deficit position on disadvantage (Cole and Bruner 1972). Lewis (1966) argues that those who have been poor for generations develop a lifestyle which is

an adaptation and a reaction of the poor to their marginal position in a class-stratified, highly individuated, capitalistic society.   (21)

Such a lifestyle becomes a culture, which perpetuates itself as do all cultures by passing on to its children group values and attitudes. In short, Lewis believes that the poor, if denied full participation in the larger society over a long enough period of time, develop a culture of their own. That is, only those who are at once poor and yet surrounded by a more affluent society, create a culture of poverty.[16] It is a rather curious urban phenomenon which Lewis suggests may be restricted to capitalist countries. Once established, a culture of poverty is not necessarily susceptible to changes aimed at eradicating or lessening poverty *per se*; the values and attitudes previously forged now have a life of their own, as it were. Some of the characteristics of such a culture, as outlined by Lewis, are very similar to those we have already noted, and include strong fatalistic feelings, sense of inferiority, parochial outlook on life, little opportunity for privacy and different patterns of parent/child interaction.

[16] There is a strong sense here of people living a 'marginal' existence, seeing affluence around them, yet unable to benefit from it. Terms such as 'the disinherited' (Rainwater 1970) and 'the urban villagers' (Gans 1962) are implied in Lewis's writings, although it is by no means clear that either Rainwater or Gans subscribes to the culture of poverty thesis.

The culture of poverty has been most systematically criticized by Leacock (1971). She points out that 'culture' is used here to mask what are essentially distorted characterizations of the poor, in which negative aspects of life are emphasized. She is critical of the excessive importance accorded to early life, with the implication that after the age of six or seven, poor children are firmly 'set' in terms of their attitudes and values, and of the assumed homogeneity of life within the culture of poverty. For example, Leacock cites data stating that 23·2 per cent of black families are matrifocal—apparently nearly three times the percentage obtaining for white families. But to jump from this to say that the black family is matrifocal is, in Leacock's words, 'quite a trick ... when 76·8 per cent of the families are not' (26). Leacock also makes the familiar point that a strong sense of *comparison* with the middle class runs through the 'culture of poverty' approach—a process not generally applicable in crosscultural studies. Overall, the culture of poverty idea is seen as an attempt to systematize the deficits of the poor into a self-perpetuating pattern (see also Robinson 1976). The difference theorists claim that, in fact, many characteristics of poor people may represent optimal solutions to problems presented by their environment.[17]

Another criticism of cultural deprivation has been provided by Wax and Wax (1971) in their studies of American Indian life. They report that official evaluations of Indian life emphasize its presumed deficiencies; for example, the home

> has no books, no magazines, radio, television, newspapers—it's empty! ... The Indian child has such a *meager* experience.   (129–30)

Wax and Wax summarize this and similar views as constituting a 'vacuum ideology'. Thus, the child is seen as lacking many important things which it is the role of the school to compensate for. Here the stress is not so much upon replacing inappropriate skills, attitudes and values as it is upon filling a void. Wax and Wax's last paragraph is worth citing here, since it represents well the criticisms made of cultural deprivation. For 'Indian child', we could also read 'black child', 'immigrant child', 'lower-class child' etc.

> If the Indian child appears as 'culturally deprived', it is not because he is lacking in experience or culture, but because the educational agencies are unwilling to recognize the alienness of his culture and the realities of his social world. It is not that the child is deprived of culture, it is that the culture which is associated with his parents is derogated because they are impoverished and powerless.   (138)

This leads us to a brief consideration of the role of education generally from the difference viewpoint. Clearly, the notion of compensatory education is rejected, since it implies that there is something deficient to be made up or replaced. Even Bernstein (see chapter 2), whose early work on the language of working-class children provided much fuel for the deficit position, notes in a recent article (1972) that the term 'compensatory education' is inappropriate, since it stresses deficiencies in the child rather than changes which may be required in the school. Similarly,

---

[17] Thus Rodman (1977) has noted that, if one were to look at the positive and useful aspects of poverty, it is possible that 'culture of poverty' might be a worthwhile term.

Labov (1973a) points to the danger of a position which attends to imaginary defects of children rather than to the real deficiencies in education for them.

Thus the difference position emphasizes above all the need for schools to change, and to accommodate to the needs of the disadvantaged child. This does not involve *replacement* of what a child brings to school, but an acceptance of the value of all backgrounds. But, if the school adopts a more enlightened view of disadvantage, might not this actually do a disservice to the child, who will be in for a rather rude awakening upon entering the larger society after school? For this reason, a difference position also often advocates large-scale social change. To eradicate disadvantage is, in part, a matter of changing traditional social views of the poor; it is also, however, necessary that society itself be changed so that poverty itself can be more successfully attacked. Thus, unlike the environmentalists who focus upon school as an agent for the integration of the disadvantaged into society at large, the difference proponents see the school as but one part (albeit a very important one) of a much larger and more radical alteration of society. For example Rainwater (cited in Leacock 1971) states that 'the only solution of the problem of underclass is to change [the] economic system' (36). Ginsburg (1972) talks of the revolution needed in education. Even Lewis (1966) feels that external social forces will, in the long run, outweigh the self-perpetuating aspects of the culture of poverty (see also Leacock 1971, Robinson 1976). In general, I find it unsurprising that a view which stresses *difference* rather than *deficit* leads more or less directly first to respect for such differences and second to the perceived necessity for school and society to change.

Many proponents of difference, however, acknowledge that while waiting for large-scale change, some more immediate steps need to be taken to help the disadvantaged child. This is because the differences which lead to poor scholastic performance are not perceived as such by teachers and others; consequently, the appropriate responses are not made. In other words, one can reject the notions of cultural deprivation and deficit while still admitting that differences may constitute *social* deficits (see, e.g., Cazden 1968a, Day 1974, Stubbs 1976). Kellaghan (1977) states that, 'on the basis of a "difference" model, one is not precluded from providing special means to help a child function in two types of environment or subculture—his own and that of the school' (18). Again, this is an area of most direct concern for the speech of disadvantaged children, and so I shall be brief here (see chapter 5).

If teachers react negatively to disadvantaged children, and expect less of them than of others, then the children's differences become, in effect, deficits. It is this 'self-fulfilling prophecy' (Rist 1970) which poses the most pressing problem for those who do not believe that disadvantaged children suffer any substantive intellectual disabilities. A child whose teacher expects he will do poorly may, being sensitive to differential treatment received, come in time to fulfil this expectation. The most well-known demonstration of this process is found in the work of Rosenthal and Jacobson (1968), whose explanations for the phenomenon go considerably further than my brief outline here.[18] The net result is that teachers may

[18] Rosenthal and Jacobson's work has been extensively criticized, and attempts to replicate the

treat children unfairly, on the basis of stereotyped (and possibly erroneous) views of their likely capabilities.

To break this vicious circle, difference theorists advocate the provision of psychological and linguistic information to teachers in order to lessen the perceived negative consequences attaching to certain characteristics of disadvantage—consequences which are seen to commence as soon as a child enters school (see Edwards 1976a, in press).

Nevertheless, difference theorists also emphasize larger social change because they realize that social deficits which become especially evident at school also exist in the larger society. It is thus only when society alters its views that such deficits will disappear. For despite changes which may be made in school, including changes in teachers' attitudes towards disadvantage, it must be borne in mind that, upon leaving school, a child may discover that, in the words of Cole and Bruner (1972),

> the great power of the middle class has rendered differences into deficits because middle-class behavior is the yardstick of success.   (176)

This problem is a thorny one indeed because it points to the fact that, in society at large, differences often *are* deficits. At some point, it may be mere semantic quibbling to insist on any distinction between the two since they may well be, to all intents, synonymous.

1.2   Poverty without disadvantage—disadvantage without poverty

Any view of disadvantage which employs a geographical approach to the issue, or which stresses homogeneity within disadvantaged populations, finds it more difficult to account for the fact that not all children living in disadvantaged areas are educationally disadvantaged (see, e.g., Kellaghan 1977, Robinson 1976, Tizard 1975). At the least, this argues for more specific knowledge of presumed links between certain characteristics and lack of school success; it probably also means that any factors of scholastic significance are considerably more subtle than those commonly measured. Here, therefore, the equation of material disadvantage with educational disadvantage may do a great disservice to many children. Wiseman (1968, 1973) calls for much greater attention to the talent hidden away behind the labels. Social-class labels obscure much heterogeneity, and differences *within* classes may in fact be greater than those *between* classes. Simply on this basis alone we would expect that numbers of children living in poor conditions would *not* be educationally disadvantaged. The general point here is that although poor areas provide the greatest concentration of disadvantaged children, many within such areas will not be disadvantaged.

---

findings have not always been successful (Cronbach 1975, Dusek and O'Connell 1973, Elashoff and Snow 1971, Mendels and Flanders 1973, Rubovits and Maehr 1971). Dusek (1975) provides a useful review of the area. In general, although Rosenthal and Jacobson's results may be questioned, there is little doubt that teachers' expectations (especially those based upon speech patterns) are important for disadvantaged children (see also Brophy and Good 1974 and chapter 5 below).

In this connection, consider the issue of educational aspirations of parents for their children. As was noted above, Labov (1973a), in examining the data of Bloom, Whiteman and Deutsch (1967), pointed out that such aspirations appear to be higher among black parents than among white parents. In mentioning this point again, I want to note that, although some lower-class parents may see little value in formal education, do little to assist their children in schoolwork, and generally have a low regard for school, the opposite is equally possible. That is, parents may perceive the school to be an avenue (perhaps *the* avenue) of upward mobility for their children (see Edwards 1977a). The obvious material disadvantages which often attach to lower-class life may prove a powerful motivation to seek something better for one's children.

Disadvantage can also be understood to exist in more affluent, middle-class surroundings. In fact, it has been pointed out that more children at educational 'risk' live outside areas of visible poverty than within them. This is not difficult to comprehend; if such factors as family stability, parental guidance and aspirations are seen to be important for a child's success at school, then clearly many middle-class homes are disadvantaged (see e.g., De Coster 1974, Schools Council 1970, Yates 1970). Coles (1977), for example, remarks that

> we blame the alcoholism, insanity, meanness, apathy, drug usage, despondency, and, not least, cruelty to children we see or are told exists in the ghetto or among the rural poor upon various 'socio-economic factors'. All of those signs of psychological deterioration can be found among quite privileged families, too. (54)

Coles goes on to comment that material affluence is no proof against frustrations and unhappiness which can lead to problems at school.

Fantini and Weinstein (1968) broaden the argument considerably by claiming that we are *all* disadvantaged. Anyone, at any level of society, can be blocked from successful self-actualization by faults in our social institutions (especially the school). Thus, while not denying that some degrees of disadvantage are worse than others, Fantini and Weinstein point to the failure of the school as a problem of greater generality than is often supposed. Thus they state that

> the middle-class child who comes to school prepared to succeed in a mediocre, outdated educational process may also be crushed; he too is disadvantaged. (38)

The acknowledgement that poverty and disadvantage are not synonymous has been made very briefly here. However, it is an extremely important point, especially with regard to the description and classification of the characteristics of disadvantage, which should now be seen to extend across class lines. The justification for the brevity here is that, concerning language, it is the large overlap between disadvantage and poverty which provides the major interest. Language differences among middle-class disadvantaged children do not constitute the main focus of their difficulties. For poor children—especially black children, immigrants, ethnic minorities and inner-city children generally—language differences are, on the other hand, the most salient and observable characteristics of their educational disadvantage. Consequently, the large part of what follows is concerned with the language of those who are both disadvantaged and poor.

1.3 Summary and implications

In discussing the major approaches to disadvantage I have been intentionally critical. Here I should like to gather together the threads of what has been presented, to offer my conception of what disadvantage is and is not, and thereby to provide a perspective for what is to follow.

Concerning the genetic deficit model of disadvantage in general, and Jensen's views in particular, two points should be made. First, we are far from having clearcut evidence that would support the position that innate differences are the major cause of educational disadvantage. Second, even if we were to accept completely Jensen's arguments, the practical implications are virtually nonexistent. For it is the case that Jensen himself claims that the difference under discussion is only of the order of 10 IQ points (whatever IQ may signify) and, as we have seen, such a difference need not create untoward problems in the acquisition of basic educational skills. Thus, Jensen's solution—different curricula for different students— is not only unpalatable, given our aspirations to equality of education, but simply unnecessary. It is also interesting to consider here that, even if *large* intelligence differences between races or social classes could be shown to exist, it is still uncertain what action, if any, would be warranted. In fact, it is difficult to visualize the sort of evidence that could be adduced to obtain general endorsement for widely varied educational treatments directed towards different racial or class groups. This position does not, I think, derive merely from the current liberal *zeitgeist* but also reflects fairly well our knowledge of genetics. The most extreme response to any 'problem' of genetic differences—eugenics—is therefore quite inappropriate.[19]

It seems clear that disadvantage is a product of environment. Those who argue, however, that the characteristics of disadvantage represent substantive deficiencies in intellectual functioning (as a consequence of inadequate patterns of early socialization) are, in my view, misguided. The middle-class bias and the assumed correctness of certain norms which underlie such a position are clear. Even from the brief treatment of the issue here the reader will be able to see how easy it would be to term lower-class characteristics as good, and middle-class ones as deficient, simply by shifting one's point of reference.[20] It would appear, therefore, that the *difference* position on disadvantage is the most appropriate. In this conception, disadvantaged children are so, not because of cognitive deficiencies, but because certain aspects of their behaviour, attitudes etc. are *viewed* as deficits by middle-class society, of which the school is generally, and most importantly, representative. This does not make any the less real, of course, the difficulties encountered by disadvantaged children; rather, it changes the direction of the issue from one in which deficits must be remedied to one in which social prejudices must be broken

[19] It is not without its supporters however. Shockley (1970), for example, pointed to the need at least to consider whether eugenic measures might be appropriate to counter declining intelligence in America. Elsewhere (cited in Zimbardo and Ruch 1977), Shockley advocates financial compensation for black people willing to undergo voluntary sterilization. Daniels (1973) provides some further comment on Shockley's ideas.

[20] This assumes that important characteristics can be readily identified and measured.

down and, in the shorter term at least, the disadvantaged child should be assisted to become more adept in the ways of the important, middle-class world.

While agreeing with the difference position in principle, I cannot conclude here without noting one or two difficulties to which it sometimes gives rise. The first is that difference theorists sometimes tend to gloss over real problems and to over-romanticize the poor (see Robinson 1976). Although many of the characteristics of disadvantaged children themselves are best seen as differences and not deficits, there is no doubt that such children do suffer from actual deficiencies, including poor housing, overcrowding, ill-health or inadequate nutrition. In doing justice to their basic cognitive skills, we should not forget that these arise despite, not because of, poor physical backgrounds. Surely not even the most passionate advocate of cultural difference could claim that such factors are anything but deficiencies. There is no virtue in poverty and squalor *per se*. Thus Deutsch (cited in Robinson 1976) cautions against

> a respect for slum life so extensive that efforts to eradicate slums ... would be halted.   (42)

A second point refers to the notion of 'social deficit'—the acknowledgement that, although disadvantaged children do not necessarily have intellectual deficiencies, their differences are seen in this light by society at large. Is there some point at which differences *are* deficits? What does it matter, if the insights of difference theorists do not penetrate to the mainstream society, if one's problems are called differences or deficits? They are still handicapping. I do not mean to suggest here that the difference position is wrong, only that its proponents may sometimes be rather naïve.

A final point is the emphasis upon the school as an agent of social change. Clearly, the deficit theorists, with their programmes of compensatory education, place more stress on the school than do those supporting cultural difference. Thus Deutsch (1967c) speaks of the perceived 'pivotal role of education in "solving" major social problems' (371). Even among difference theorists, however, much energy is directed towards informing the teacher, attempting to change his or her views on disadvantage, and lessening the misperceptions about the characteristics of disadvantage generally. In this connection it is worth pointing out that schools tend to follow the larger society rather than lead it, and stereotypes and prejudices in this larger society are deep and unlikely to be changed easily or quickly.

This might be taken to indicate that widespread social revolution, redistribution of wealth etc. are the ultimate solutions. But although such agitations often dislocate social classes, one often observes in their aftermath that new inequalities are created. Thus, although the characteristics may differ, disadvantage itself may well remain. I do not wish here to be overly pessimistic, and certainly one would hope that amelioration of difficulties can be achieved. Nevertheless, when discussions of disadvantage lead to suggestions of large-scale social change, it is as well to bear in mind that relativism of one sort or another seems a long-enduring aspect of society.

2

Deficient language

'Speech is a mirror of the soul: As a man speaks, so is he.'   Publilius
Syrus

'... the operative class, whose massacre of their mother tongue, however
inhuman, could excite no astonishment.'   Thomas Hamilton

It is clear from the previous chapter that the general view of those espousing a
deprivation position is that disadvantaged children suffer various deficiencies
caused by their early environment. It is not an overstatement to say that, of all
the characteristics of disadvantage, the single most discussed is language. In this
chapter I wish to turn directly to language and, particularly, to the view of disadvantaged language as deficient language. My conclusions here can be easily anti-
cipated from the general rejection of the deprivation position in chapter 1. However, because of the centrality of language in any investigation of disadvantage,
the environmentalist stance on it should be made clear. Language is at once
the main pillar of the deprivation position and, at the same time, the major issue
with regard to which the *difference* attack on the former position has been most
successful.

In the sense that class and regional differences in accent and dialect have, traditionally, been the source of comment, imitation and sometimes derision, it is not
difficult to understand that a deficit view of certain speech styles should be appeal-
ing to many. A pleasant overview of what might be termed the traditional anec-
dotal reactions to speech variations will be found in Pear 1971. Regional and social
dialects, pronunciation differences, U and non-U speech etc. are all briefly considered and illuminated with examples. A more recent, comprehensive treatment
of the topic will be found in Giles and Powesland 1975.

One of the first attempts (perhaps the first; see Dittmar 1976) systematically
to investigate class differences in speech was that of Schatzman and Strauss (1955).
Their study took the form of interviews with lower- and upper-middle-class people
in Arkansas who had been present during a tornado, and the authors were concerned to investigate differences between the classes in their descriptions of this
frightening event. Overall, the lower-class respondents were found to transmit
much less information about the occurrence than were those of the middle class.
There was little attempt to set the scene, as it were, for the interviewer, and respondents were apparently able to do little more than reconstruct the event as it had

appeared to them directly and personally in 'particularistic or concrete terms' (333). There was much digression which, though perhaps meaningful for the speaker, was irrelevant and/or confusing for the listener. This often resulted in spatial and temporal ambiguity, and it proved difficult for the interviewer to obtain a rounded picture of what had happened. People were mentioned in the narratives who were not known to the interviewer, and whose roles were unclear, and yet little attempt was made properly to identify and integrate such persons. The authors note that lower-class respondents appeared to assume that the interviewer shared much contextual information when, in fact, this was not so. One is reminded here of Joos' (1967) description of language styles, in which he points out that it is only among friends, or persons who have shared experiences, that the deletion of background material is reasonably possible. This was not the case in Schatzman and Strauss's study of course, and to the extent to which respondents took such shared information for granted their communication suffered. Thus the authors state that some lower-class respondents 'literally cannot tell a straight story or describe a simple incident coherently' (336).

Middle-class interviewees, on the other hand, were generally able to reconstruct the event in a logical and meaningful way, such that the listener was more fully informed; thus, the differences between these descriptions and those of the lower-class respondents were marked. Part of this Schatzman and Strauss ascribe to the fact that the lower-class respondents were communicating across class lines to a middle-class interviewer and were more unfamiliar with the requirements of the task (an important point, as we shall see). Nevertheless, the authors feel that the lower class have an inferior capacity for perceiving and communicating abstract thoughts, unlike the middle class whose speech is rich in abstract conceptual terminology.

In a later paper, Strauss and Schatzman (1960) elaborate further on class speech differences, as revealed in interview data. Lower-class respondents are described as less sensitive to the needs of the questioner who, therefore, 'must accept greater responsibility for strong control in the lower-class interview' (212). Again they allude to the possibility that the obvious differences in background and education between the interviewers and the respondents may account for the results; however, as their intent in this second article is to comment upon interviewing as a method they are more concerned with description than with explanation.

Another relatively early study was that of Templin (1957). She investigated the development of language skills in lower and middle-class white American children across eight age levels (from 3 to 7 years). Speech samples were obtained for all the children, and these were analysed in several ways. In terms of complexity of utterance, for example, differences between lower- and middle-class children were small. Although there was some tendency for lower-class children to use simpler sentences (i.e. sentences with few phrase or clausal constructions), it was not the case that such children *never* used more complex expressions. Thus one could not deduce, from Templin's evidence, that lower-class children were *incapable* of certain forms, only that their usage of them was somewhat less than that of their middle-class counterparts. To anticipate a bit, this raises the problem of inferring linguistic *competence* from linguistic *performance*. Even if a lower-class child, over 100 sentences, were to use a subordinate clause only once, this would be sufficient to show that he has some basic capability. The question of interest, therefore, is why the child's *habitual* performance is as it is—which is somewhat different from talking about basic abilities and disabilities in language.

Similar conclusions may be drawn from a study which followed Templin's. Loban (1963) carried out a longitudinal investigation (over a period of six years) with 338 black and white American elementary-school children. Again, one notes a tendency for lower-class children to produce fewer complex sentences than their middle-class schoolmates; however, they did produce some. Further to the point raised in the last paragraph, Dittmar (1976) has noted that even if *no* complex sentences had been produced by the children, one could still not be certain that they were unable to do so. Thus, 'it could be that they readily understood sentences of this type, yet lacked a disposition towards producing them' (49). As we shall see in chapter 3, there is in fact strong evidence that this is exactly what is occurring. Perhaps the results of studies such as Templin's and Loban's tell us more about the child's state of ease in a formal school situation than they do about his linguistic abilities.

2.1   The work of Bernstein

There is little doubt that Bernstein's work has been extremely influential in socio-logical and educational circles, and his views of working-class and middle-class language are widely discussed. Bernstein is not easy to interpret, however, since his work has extended over a period of 20 years and his theoretical stance has not always been completely clear. In his earlier work, Bernstein appeared to sup-port the environmentalist-deficit view of lower-class speech, but more recently he has been careful to note that this is not the import of his studies.[1] In one sense, therefore, it may not be entirely correct to discuss Bernstein's work under the general heading of language deficit.[2] Nevertheless, whether through his own ambi-guity or through misinterpretation of his work by others, it seems fair to say that Bernstein has popularly been associated with a language deficit approach to dis-advantage; certainly his studies have been much quoted in the environmentalist camp. For present purposes, therefore, I want to consider the general tenor of Bernstein's arguments, and their relevance to the issue of disadvantage.[3]

Bernstein, a British sociologist, presented his initial theoretical position on lan-guage in two early papers (1958, 1959) in which he introduced the terms 'public' and 'formal' language. The former is characterized generally by its emphasis upon

[1] Some of Bernstein's own comments on his work can be found in the introduction to his (1971) book; he notes that his initial studies were obscure, ambiguous and conceptually weak. As Rosen (1972) points out, it is therefore not surprising that Bernstein should have been misinterpreted.

[2] A. D. Edwards (1974), however, notes that Bernstein 'through all the revisions ... is still offering a sophisticated 'deficit' theory' (76).

[3] There exist several useful overviews of Bernstein's work; these include Coulthard 1969, Dittmar 1976, A. D. Edwards 1974, Lawton 1969, Lee 1973, Rosen 1972, Stubbs 1976 and Trudgill 1975.

'the emotive rather than the logical implications' (1958, 164) of language; more particularly, Bernstein (1959) provided a list of ten attributes of public language. With some simplification, they are as follows:

1   short, simple, often unfinished sentences, with poor syntax
2   simple and repetitive use of conjunctions
3   frequent use of commands and questions
4   rigid and limited use of adjectives and adverbs
5   infrequent use of impersonal pronouns as subjects
6   statements in the form of implicit questions (e.g. 'It's only natural, isn't it?')
7   reasons and conclusions confounded to produce a categoric statement (e.g. 'Do as I tell you')
8   frequent use of idiomatic phrases
9   low-order symbolism
10   much of the meaning is implicit

The traits listed above suggest that users of public language have few syntactic and lexical alternatives and are restricted to concrete, non-symbolic modes of expression in which much is taken for granted (i.e. implicit).[4] Public language, so defined, is seen to be available to both lower and middle classes. However, for the former group, it is often the *only* language used; thus, Bernstein notes that linguistic limitations apply to working-class speakers.

On the other hand, members of the middle class have, in addition to public language, access to formal language, with a greater range and variety of expressive techniques, and greater symbolic power. Relative to public language, Bernstein (1959) listed eight characteristics of this formal language, as follows:

1   grammatical and syntactic accuracy
2   sentence complexity via the use of conjunctions and clauses
3   frequent use of prepositions to indicate logical, temporal and spatial relationships
4   frequent use of impersonal pronouns
5   a range of adjectives and adverbs
6   ability to organize experience conceptually
7   use of expressive symbolism
8   much of the meaning is explicit

With the subsequent translation of public and formal language into the now well-known 'restricted' and 'elaborated' codes (Bernstein 1962a), one can understand how Bernstein's early work was easily associated with the deficit theory of the speech of lower-class children. This is especially so since, in the 1958 paper, Bernstein refers to characteristics of lower-class children which are often cited by the environmentalists—e.g. difficulty of delaying immediate gratification and of planning for the future, and more 'volatile' expressive behaviour. In addition,

---

[4] The reader will note the similarity between this description and that of Schatzman and Strauss (see above); Bernstein was clearly aware of their work, and cites it in his 1959 article.

Bernstein (1959) relates the development of the codes to the social milieu in a manner similar to that of the environmentalists (see below).[5] Further, Bernstein (1960), in presenting data showing substantial differences (for working-class children) between verbal and nonverbal test scores, notes that

> one mode [i.e. of speech], associated with the middle-class, points to the possibilities within a complex conceptual hierarchy for the organization of experience, the other, associated with the lower working-class, progressively limits the type of stimuli to which the child learns to respond.   (276)

Although not crystal clear, this statement certainly has an environmentalist-deficit flavour to it.

Bernstein's early experimental data to support his theory are found in four articles (1958, 1960, 1962a, 1962b)—although all these investigations really form one study, as will be seen below. First, Bernstein (1958) administered two intelligence tests to a group of 309 working-class messenger boys between the ages of 15 and 18. One test was the Raven's Progressive Matrices (a nonverbal intelligence test); the other, verbal, test was the Mill Hill Vocabulary Test. The general finding was that nonverbal scores were higher than verbal test scores.

In the second study (1960), Bernstein wished to compare working-class test performance with that of the middle class. He therefore assembled two divergent social groups; messenger boys (N = 61) again constituted the working-class group, while senior public-school boys (N = 45) provided the middle-class comparison group. Once more Bernstein administered the Matrices and the Mill Hill tests and found, as hypothesized, that the working-class scores on the nonverbal test were higher than scores obtained on the Mill Hill scale (especially at higher score levels). The middle-class boys, on the other hand, performed very similarly on both tests. Bernstein offers two possible explanations for these results: either the lower working class are genetically deficient with regard to ability to express complex verbal relationships, or the expression of intelligence (either verbal or nonverbal) is a function of culture. Bernstein rejects the first possibility and favours the second, environmental, explanation for the depressed verbal scores of the working-class boys because 'the normal linguistic environment of the working-class is one of relative deprivation' (1960, 276).[6]

In the third study, Bernstein (1962a) employed smaller groups, selected from the 1960 investigation, to consider differences in speech forms used by the working class and the middle class. Two groups of middle-class boys and three of working-class boys (N = 5 in each group) were recorded discussing the topic of the abolition of the death penalty. The overall findings (i.e. without regard to the test scores

---

[5] It is worth noting however that even at this early stage Bernstein does note some strengths of public language, and in the following statement seems to lean more towards an addition (i.e. difference) position than to a replacement (deficit) one: 'The problem would seem to be to preserve *public* language usage but to create for the individual the possibility of utilizing a *formal* language' (1959, 323). Such statements give some weight to Bernstein's later assertions (e.g. 1971) that his work has been misinterpreted.

[6] The reader will note that statements such as this make it difficult for some to believe that Bernstein is not (or was not) an upholder of the deficient language viewpoint.

previously measured) were that the working-class boys used shorter words, longer phrases and spent less time pausing. This last index derives from the work of Goldman-Eisler (1954) in which more abstract symbolic speech was found to contain longer and more frequent pauses.[7] On the basis of these results (and especially those relating to pausing), Bernstein concluded that the working-class speech was 'restricted' and the middle-class 'elaborated'.

The fourth study (1962b) analysed these same speech samples for their grammatical elements. No class differences were found with the use of finite verbs, adverbs, nouns and prepositions, but the working-class boys used relatively more personal pronouns, and the middle-class subjects used relatively more 'uncommon' adverbs and adjectives, subordinate clauses and passive verbs. Again, Bernstein concludes that the middle-class speech was more elaborated than that of the working class.

Before mentioning further work by Bernstein or his associates, we might consider the results of the four studies just presented. They represent Bernstein's earliest investigations in the field which, as has already been noted, he subsequently wishes had been better put; nevertheless, these studies were among the most influential, especially in compensatory education circles (see section 2.3). The most general comment to be made on them is the same as was made on the environmental-deficit position in the last chapter—that it is possible to view differences found *as* differences, attributable to variations in early lifestyle, rather than as deficits in working-class speech. Again, therefore, one is faced with the difficulty of interpretation. Bernstein himself now rejects the deficit viewpoint of lower-class language and, indeed, there are hints in his earliest work of this.[8] However, one can also find statements that seem to show support for a language-deficit point of view (see for example the quotations on p. 35 above). The most unfortunate aspect of this lack of clarity is that, regardless of whether or not Bernstein *is* a deficit theorist, *was* a deficit theorist, or was always a (misunderstood) proponent of language *difference*, his early work had the potential to fuel the environmental-deficit argument concerning the speech of disadvantaged children.[9]

Another study, by Bernstein and Henderson (1969), investigated the perceived importance of the role of language in socialization practices among middle-class and working-class mothers (N = 50 each). Each mother was presented with eleven statements relating to socialization processes (helping children to make things, disciplining children etc.) and was asked, for each one, to assess how difficult she

[7] This is not always found; see Jones and McMillan (1973), in which middle-class subjects paused *less*. Generally, it is interesting that lengthy pauses are often associated with elaborated or 'abstract' language (see Labov's criticisms of middle-class language in chapter 3; see also the work of Williams (1970b), discussed in chapter 5).

[8] In his 1959 article, for instance, Bernstein notes that 'a *public* language contains its own aesthetic, a simplicity and directness of expression, emotionally virile, pithy and powerful and a metaphoric range of considerable force and appropriateness' (322–3).

[9] Rosen (1972) feels that the bulk of Bernstein's work must be seen as supporting a deficit position (see also A. D. Edwards 1974). Dittmar (1976) makes the rather pointed assertion that Bernstein has attempted to retract the deficit viewpoint he once represented because of the failure of compensatory education in the United States (which his work was popularly taken to support; see below).

thought it would be for parents *who could not speak* to deal with such situations. This curious procedure was used to focus the mother's attention upon language skills while, at the same time, not challenging her own characteristic ways of dealing with her children. For both classes social control situations were seen as more difficult to handle without speech than were situations involving the teaching of skills. However, the middle-class mothers emphasized language more than the lower-class mothers with regard to situations involving social control and personal relations (like discipline), while the reverse held for situations dealing with skill transmission. Drawing upon other work demonstrating the greater passivity of the working-class child, Bernstein and Henderson claim that the working-class mother stresses language for the transmission of concrete and specific skills whereas her middle-class counterpart, with a more autonomous and active child, need not do so. The more abstract area of social control/personal relations, on the other hand, *is* stressed by the middle-class mother, with much more careful and detailed explanations given. Thus, in the more general and important areas of early socialization, the middle-class child is at an advantage. This advantage will be most apparent when the child enters a school situation which stresses autonomy in skill-learning *and* verbal facility with symbols and abstractions.

Again, Bernstein's work can be criticized on several counts. First, the mothers in this study had to address themselves to a hypothetical situation which may or may not have reflected anything about their ways of dealing linguistically with their children. Second, interviews from which these data come may well have been more intimidating for working-class than for middle-class mothers. Third, as was noted in the last chapter, causal links between class differences (or alleged deficiencies) and children's cognitive development have not been satisfactorily demonstrated.

In a paper originally delivered in 1970, Bernstein (1972a) refers to a study by Hawkins (1969) which has become fairly widely quoted. As part of this study, Hawkins asked middle-class and working-class children to construct a story after looking at a series of four pictures in which three boys are playing football and a window is broken. He then provides two stories which he (Hawkins) constructed on the basis of responses obtained. The middle-class version is as follows:

> Three boys are playing football and one boy kicks the ball—and it goes through the window—the ball breaks the window—and the boys are looking at it—and a man comes out—and shouts at them—because they've broken the window—so they run away—and then that lady looks out of her window—and she tells the boys off.

The working-class sample:

> They're playing football—and he kicks it—and it goes through there—it breaks the window and they're looking at it—and he comes out—and shouts at them—because they've broken it—so they run away—and then she looks out—and she tells them off.

Bernstein comments that the first version takes little for granted, the reader does not have to see the pictures in order to understand the story, and the story is, thus, 'free of the context which generated it' (1972a, 167). This is not so for the working-class version, where the meaning is implicit and where the reader must have access to the pictures before being able to understand the paragraph.[10] Thus Bernstein sees the importance of this work lying in the demonstration of class differences in responses to the same stimuli. There are some difficulties here, however.

First, the stories are hypothetical; that is, Hawkins himself made them up, rather than presenting actual examples produced by the children themselves.[11] More important, however, is the fact that the lower-class version is seen by Bernstein and Hawkins as less than ideal insofar as it seems to assume that the reader shares background information with the teller—i.e. has seen the pictures. But, as Stubbs (1976) and Trudgill (1975) have pointed out, the experimenter was present when the children constructed their stories, and thus *did* see the pictures. Therefore one might argue that, in fact, the working-class version is more appropriate in a context in which both speaker and listener have the same information available to them. In any event, it is hard to see that the working-class version is any worse than the other, unless one assumes the correctness of middle-class style.

In considering the general impact of Bernstein's experimental and theoretical work, it seems only fair that some of his more recent observations be taken into account. Clearly wishing his work to be disassociated from any deficit view of working-class language, Bernstein notes, for example, that less misunderstanding might have arisen had he labelled his codes as 'sociolinguistic' rather than 'linguistic' (1972a). In the same paper he points out that, although it is more likely that working-class speakers will use the restricted code, this does not mean that they will never use more elaborated speech patterns. That is, Bernstein is stressing context; since environments for working-class and middle-class children differ, it is not surprising that customary language usage will differ also. He clarifies this further by stating that

> at no time did I ever consider that I was concerned with differences between social groups at the level of competency, that is, differences between social groups which had their origin in their basic tacit understanding of the linguistic rule system. I was fundamentally concerned with *performance*. (1973a, 70)

Bernstein (1972b) also considers that the term *compensatory education* is an unfortunate one since it implies that 'something is lacking in the family, and so in the child ... the children become little deficit systems' (137). Again, therefore, he rejects the notion that language difference is language deficit which requires treatment by way of remedial education programmes. In fact, given Bernstein's recent pronouncements concerning the sociolinguistic nature of the codes, and the importance of the context in which they arise (and in which investigations of them occur), his work could now actually be seen to support a radical *difference* point of view—that is, that schools in which working-class children fare badly must change in order better to accommodate these children, and not the reverse (see Trudgill 1975).

[10] See the study by Schatzman and Straus (1955) above.

[11] Bernstein himself constructs hypothetical data which he then analyses (1972a). This curious process is criticized by Rosen (1972).

Overall, then, the reader will understand my introductory remarks about the difficulty of discussing Bernstein's work under the heading of language deficit. It may be the case that Bernstein's early work was taken to imply something about working-class children's linguistic *competence* as well as their *performance*, and that Bernstein himself never intended this—that he was, in fact, a difference theorist from the start. This, of course, is by no means universally accepted; many would claim that Bernstein has changed his point of view, and some would say that Bernstein's work still equates working-class and deficient language. Whatever the case, there is no doubt that Bernstein's work has been widely assumed to deal with language deficiency.

Bernstein's early work, and the difficult, often obscure nature of his writing have made linguists and others very cautious in their approach to it. One, however, who seems more favourable is Halliday (1973b). In a foreword written for Bernstein's second book (1973b), Halliday sketches his understanding of Bernstein's work and its relevance. He begins by noting that Bernstein has never supported a deficit view of working-class language, nor pointed to the greater intrinsic value of elaborated codes of speech.[12] In short, Halliday points to the fact that linguistic disadvantage is an incorrect labelling of what is, in fact, social disadvantage— that the educational difficulties of certain children derive from attitudes towards their speech styles. But he also goes on to note that attitudes towards language do not tell the whole story. One must also consider the different 'orders of meaning' that different groups emphasize, such that the *functions* of language may vary considerably. Thus:

> Just as the language element in educational failure cannot be reduced to a question of linguistic forms, so also it cannot be wholly reduced to one of attitudes. ... It is necessary to think of language as meaning rather than of language as structure. (1973b, xvi)

Thus Halliday feels that Bernstein's work is of great importance since it points to the sociological bases of language differences and, in particular, to functions of language, some of which are more accessible to some groups than to others (see also Halliday 1969).[13]

A good general summary of Bernstein's work and its implications is provided by Trudgill (1975). He outlines five important criticisms of Bernstein, most of which have already been touched upon. First, the notion of elaborated and restricted codes as *linguistic* phenomena is now suspect; they are better seen perhaps as different language styles (see chapter 4) or, as Bernstein himself now states, as sociolinguistic variants. Second, given that class differences in customary language use exist, it is not clear how such differences operate to produce educational problems. Here Trudgill refers to the differential frequency of usage of certain

---

[12] Halliday acknowledges, however, that 'formal education may demand the elaborated code' (1973b, x).

[13] Halliday's work has been quite influential, and I have hardly done his views justice here. The interested reader may wish to consult Halliday 1973a, 1975, 1978, especially with regard to his call for the study of class differences in language *functions* rather than language *structures*.

grammatical elements, and not of course to the very real and easily demonstrated attitudinal prejudices directed towards lower-class language (see chapters 4 and 5). A third, and related, point is that any school requirements of elaborated speech are therefore best considered as social conventions only. Fourth, Trudgill notes the distressing effects that Bernstein's work (or the misinterpretation of it) has had upon teachers and others who often equate working-class language with inferior language. This equation is especially unfortunate given Trudgill's fifth point—that working-class children *can* use elaborated code under some circumstances. Robinson (1965), for example, found that working-class children writing formal letters did not show grammatical use markedly different from that of their middle-class counterparts. Rushton and Young (1975), also eliciting writing samples from working-class and middle-class subjects, report that class differences were influenced by the context of the task (in their study, different essay topics: imaginative, opinionative or technical). These studies demonstrate above all the importance of the context in which language is observed and recorded, and also the danger of simply equating working-class language with the restricted code.[14]

Overall, it appears that Bernstein can now be reasonably placed in the *difference* camp, although the greatest impact of his work has been to support the language-deficit view of lower-class language. After 20 years of apparent misunderstanding (much of it due to Bernstein's own rather tortuous style) then, can one simply conclude that Bernstein has pointed out that there are class differences in speech which operate to the detriment of working-class children because of unfavourable attitudes? Trudgill (cited in Stubbs 1976) states, for example, that linguistically Bernstein's work only demonstrates that

> in situations more artificial and alien to them than to middle-class children, working-class children use a higher proportion of pronouns. Is this what it has been all about? (47)

As has been hinted above, there is perhaps somewhat more to it. Halliday (1973b), for example, has drawn attention to possible differences in *functions* of language for the working class and middle class. The elaborated and restricted codes could then be seen as manifestations of alternative ways of looking at, and reacting to, the world. At this point, we should realize that Bernstein, from his earliest work (e.g. 1958) has acknowledged the influence of Whorf. The latter (whose major writings are most easily accessible in Carroll 1972) formulated the linguistic relativity hypothesis that any given language influences the ways in which a speaker perceives the world and, hence, his cognitive functioning. This so-called 'strong' form of Whorf's hypothesis is not, by and large, accepted. In asking why different languages, or language varieties, differ, the most obvious answer is that they reflect the environments in which their speakers live. Thus, the fact that Eskimos may use many different words to refer to varying types of what we simply term *snow* can be seen as an indication of the greater importance of one concept

---

[14] One might recall here that Bernstein's own early work involved a rather formal experimental context—not one in which working-class children might be expected to be as comfortable as middle-class subjects.

in one given environment. However, anyone *could* expand their lexicon if the situation demanded it. There are, as well, more complicated examples of language difference, ones which are not so visibly linked to the external environment—e.g. the presence or absence of gender in nouns, or the manner of indicating tense. Nevertheless, whatever synchronic or diachronic linguistics tells us about the reason for such differences, there is no sense in which one mode of expression can be judged better than another, nor are concepts dealt with in one language inaccessible to another; if this were so, translation would not always be possible.[15]

A 'weaker' Whorfian hypothesis—that language influences our customary or habitual ways of thinking—has some validity, however. Thus the Eskimo will tend to view his environment in a manner different from that of the outsider, and the tense system of the Hopi Indian will doubtless influence his usual way of conceiving of time (see Carroll 1972). It seems reasonable to accept that language will thus influence our habitual views of our environment, although not to the extent of determining basic cognitive functioning. But, as noted above, the environment also influences language.[16] In fact, language on the one hand, and the sociocultural environment on the other, are part of a circular and mutually reinforcing process.

On the basis of this little digression we can note that, in this process (in which Whorf clearly emphasized the larger importance of language), Bernstein has tended to emphasize the primacy of society or, as Dittmar (1976) points out, the social structures which influence language which, in turn, reinforces the social structures.

Thus Bernstein might be thought of as stressing the circularity of the society-language relationship, and assigning to society a more important role, perhaps, than did Whorf. Further, Dittmar (1976) notes that, unlike Whorf, Bernstein has transferred the enquiry from differences between languages to differences within the same language (hence the codes). Gumperz and Hymes (1972) point out, too, that Bernstein has given 'Whorf's insight new life and sociological substance' (471; see also Hymes 1974).

With the benefit of recent writings, then, Bernstein's position can finally be seen as one which directs our attention to class differences in language; it is suggested that the problems of disadvantaged, working-class children derive not only from middle-class attitudes towards their speech styles, but also perhaps from functional language differences (see Halliday 1973b).[17] I think that this last point—which might be viewed as an extension of the basic difference position, and a useful resuscitation of Whorf—is an important one which deserves more attention. One important issue, for example, in the light of work demonstrating that working-class children can use elaborated code in certain contexts (Robinson 1965, Rushton and Young 1975), is the disentangling of contextual constraints on working-class speech (e.g. unfamiliar surroundings, middle-class investigators—elements present

[15] An interesting, though somewhat controversial, discussion of Whorf will be found in Steiner's recent thesis on language and translation (1975; see also Slobin 1974).

[16] Whorf himself mentions this, noting the constant interplay of language patterns and cultural norms (Carroll 1972).

[17] For a useful paper on a similar theme, see Robinson 1975. For comments on Bernstein as 'sociologist of education', see Cherkaouï 1977 and Swartz 1977.

in Bernstein's own work) from any real language-function differences which may operate. Nevertheless, the fact remains that since no one who is concerned with class differences in accessibility to, or use of, speech variants, could (or should) claim that such differences represent basic deficiencies, any difficulties encountered by disadvantaged children can still legitimately be considered as social in origin.

2.2 Work influenced by Bernstein

A common observation is that, apart from its own intrinsic worth, the extent to which a research programme or a theoretical position provokes further investigation is a measure of its success, sometimes referred to as its 'heuristic' value. On this count, Bernstein's work has been most successful, in its influence upon those concerned with the educational and (presumed) linguistic difficulties of disadvantaged children.

Naturally, Bernstein's own colleagues have been most directly influenced by his investigations, and many have attempted to expand upon his own work. Lawton (1969) provides a useful summary of Bernstein's early studies, and goes on to present data from his own investigation of the speech and writing of middle-class and working-class boys. The findings generally support Bernstein's ideas concerning the restricted and elaborated codes. Hawkins (1977) has followed up his earlier work on class differences in patterns of communication, and Brandis and Henderson (1970) present further information on the same issue. Other work, to be discussed more fully below, includes that of Cook-Gumperz (1973) and Robinson and Rackstraw (1972) on intra-family patterns of speech, Brandis and Bernstein (1974) on teachers' reactions to infant-school children, and Gahagan and Gahagan (1970) on a language programme for working-class children. A recent book by Adlam (1976) considers many of the implications of Bernstein's theory of codes. Finally, Bernstein himself has collected many of his earlier papers (most discussed in the previous section) in his *Class, codes and control*, volume 1 (1971). A second volume (1973b), edited by Bernstein, brings together articles by several of his colleagues; the third volume (1975) goes beyond language *per se* and concerns general issues in the sociology of education.

One of the earliest American studies to follow upon Bernstein's work was that of Hess and Shipman (1965). They begin by presenting two hypothetical maternal responses to a noisy child. One (the lower-class, restricted medium) involves the mother simply saying 'Be quiet' or 'Shut up'. The imaginary middle-class mother, on the other hand, asks, 'Would you keep quiet a minute? I want to talk on the phone.' The first is seen to imply a status-oriented situation in which the authority of the parent is stressed; the second reflects person-orientation, in which actions are explained, alternatives are possible and the situation is generally more fully considered. Hess and Shipman wonder about the differential effects such orientations have upon children with regard to the development of their own cognitive strategies.

Thus, groups of black mothers and their four-year-old children were selected from four socioeconomic levels, ranging from professional to lower working class.

Mothers were interviewed at home and also attended testing sessions in a university setting. In terms of language production, the usual class differences were observed— i.e. the upper-middle-class mothers used longer and more complex sentences. In addition, observing mothers interacting with their children, Hess and Shipman pointed out that the middle-class mothers were more effective teachers. By this they meant that, whereas the lower-class child responds to authority, the middle-class child is reasoned with; hence, the conclusion that the patterns of interaction between middle-class mother and child are more likely to lead to such desirable cognitive strategies as generalization, logical reasoning and future planning.

Hess and Shipman (1968a, 1968b) provide further information on their research into class differences in maternal control. The lower-class family is seen to be characterized by 'imperative-normative' maternal control, with little of the personal and rational elements which typify the middle-class mother/child interaction. The authors summarize their findings as follows:

> The meaning of deprivation would thus seem to be a deprivation of meaning in the early cognitive relationships between mother and child. This environment produces a child who relates to authority rather than to rationale, who may often be compliant but is not reflective in his behavior, amd for whom the consequences of an act are largely considered in terms of immediate punishment or reward rather than future effects and long-range goals.   (1968b, 103)

The reader will note how well the import of this quotation ties in with the general environmental-deficit position presented in the previous chapter. Hess and Shipman go on to suggest that the early life of the lower-class child is such as to limit his mental growth, and therefore they recommend intervention aimed at the 'resocialization' of the child. Although one may speculate that Bernstein himself might have reservations about Hess and Shipman's extension of his early work, it can be seen that there is a clear bridge here between this early work and the programmes of compensatory education of the 1960s (see next section).

The criticisms that can be made of Hess and Shipman are by now familiar. They include the observations that the effects of being interviewed and participating in psychological tasks may be generally artificial and, specifically, unfamiliar and strange to lower-class subjects, that it is difficult to generalize from such experiments to what actually occurs in the home, and that assumptions are made about links between different styles of maternal behaviour and a child's cognitive development which cannot be confirmed. Throughout all the work, of course, there runs a strong middle-class bias. Thus we are left, once again, with data which show class differences (in given circumstances), which may or may not be interesting in themselves, but which can hardly provide convincing evidence of lower-class deprivation.[18]

More recent, and somewhat more sophisticated, work on class differences in the 'language of maternal control' is presented by Cook-Gumperz (1973). On the basis of taperecorded interviews, working-class mothers were observed to employ imperative modes of control, while the middle class utilized a broader and more

---

[18] See also Dittmar 1976, Entwisle 1968, 1970 and Ginsburg 1972.

personal mode. Nevertheless, considerable intra-class variation was also found. Related to the broad tendencies of class differences in control techniques was the use of elaborated code in the middle-class mothers' speech, and restricted code in that of their working-class counterparts. Overall, Cook-Gumperz's study provides a useful extension of Bernstein's studies (although at times it is somewhat ponderous; it is the published version of a PhD thesis) in terms of description of differences in mother/child interaction. The major importance of the work, as noted by Bernstein in the preface to the study, is that it provides a link between the original notion of code and the work of Halliday (see above).

Similar work is reported by Robinson and Rackstraw (1972). In response to various questions, middle-class children were found to give more information and to explain and amplify upon their answers more fully than did working-class children; answers of the latter often involved simple appeals to authority or custom. Between them, Cook-Gumperz and Robinson and Rackstraw provide considerable data on the speech of working-class and middle-class mothers and children (see also Heber 1974, Wootton 1974).

2.3 Compensatory education and verbal deprivation[19]

In the previous chapter I referred to the growth of interest in compensatory education as resulting largely from the view that the home environments of disadvantaged children were deficient in various respects (see, e.g., Deutsch 1967a, 1967b). From this view, it is but a short jump to the idea that intervention is necessary to correct these deficiencies. Although not mentioning language to any extent in the first chapter, I did allude to the fact that it was seen as the central pillar of many programmes of compensatory education for disadvantaged children. Now, having introduced the work of Bernstein, it is possible to comment more directly on the language deprivation aspect of these programmes. For it is undoubtedly the case that the studies of Bernstein have been most important in shaping the ideas of those, especially in the United States, who view educational intervention as necessary to combat verbal deprivation.[20]

In one of the earliest and best-known intervention programmes, Bereiter and Engelmann (1966) begin from the premise that the disadvantaged child (most often black) is retarded in reasoning ability and language skills. Thus, his language is seen as 'immature', he lacks 'the most rudimentary forms of constructive dialog' (39) and has virtually no ability to use language to process information. In fact Bereiter and Engelmann claim, more than once, that the disadvantaged child

[19] There is a vast literature on compensatory education; useful general overviews will be found in Edwards (in press), Kellaghan 1977, Little and Smith 1972 and Van der Eyken 1974a, 1974b. A bibliography with more than 4000 references is provided by the Van Leer Foundation (1971). Additionally, I am dealing here only with compensatory education in English-speaking countries. It extends of course beyond these; useful reviews of the European scene are provided by Kohnstamm and Wagenaar-Hardon 1975, Laurent-Delchet, 1975, Nufer 1975, Ruoppila 1975, Schmalohr 1975 and Thirion 1975.

[20] It is worth stating again that Bernstein now dissociates himself from compensatory education. Indeed, like many others, he considers the very term inaccurate and misleading (see Bernstein 1970, 1972b, see also Halsey 1975).

attempts to get along without language wherever he can. Thus they state that 'language is apparently dispensable enough in the life of the lower-class child for an occasional child to get along without it altogether' (31); some of these children 'manage as far as possible to get along without it' (39–40) and 'language for the disadvantaged child seems to be an aspect of social behavior which is not of vital importance' (42). On this fantastic basis Bereiter and Engelmann, who apparently have never observed lower-class children at play, construct their remedial programme.

Their most immediate problem was to break down what they termed the 'giant word' syndrome. Here it is claimed that disadvantaged children do not recognize single words but, instead, chunk together words to make some larger amalgam. The authors provide the following example:

> Instead of saying, 'He's a big dog,' the deprived child says, 'He bih daw.' Instead of saying, 'I ain't got no juice,' he says, 'Uai-ga-na-ju.'   (34)

The giant-word problem Bereiter and Engelmann see as directly consistent with Bernstein's notion of restricted code and, in particular, with his descriptions of the lack of speech pauses used by working-class boys (see above). Since the child cannot break down these giant words into their constituents, he cannot transform and recombine the elements. Thus, Bereiter and Engelmann's programme consists largely of intensive and highly specific drills in the use of 'correct' English. Detailed instructions are provided for teachers, of which one example will suffice:[21]

A   Present an object and give the appropriate identity statement. 'This is a ball.'
B   Follow the statement with a *yes-no* question. 'Is this a ball?'
C   Answer the question. 'Yes, this is a ball.'
D   Repeat the question and encourage the children to answer it.
E   Introduce *what* questions after the children have begun to respond adequately to the *yes-no* questions.   (140)

Gradually, the disadvantaged child is led through the refinements of 'correct' English so that he proceeds from having virtually no language at all to a position of some mastery. It is apparent, however, that Bereiter and Engelmann's conception of the language of disadvantaged children is very naïve, and most of this derives from a lack of understanding of the linguistic background of black American children. Labov (1973a) notes, for example, that Bereiter and Englemann view the expression 'They mine' as incorrect and, in fact, illogical; in black English (see chapter 3), however, the deletion of the copula (in this case, 'are') is a regular feature and one which detracts not at all from the meaning of the utterance. In addition to ignorance of the norms of black English, however, Bereiter and Engelmann also reject as wrong examples of speech which are more widespread. Thus, Labov (1973a) points to their unfortunate dismissal of

> *In the tree* as an illogical, or badly-formed answer to *Where is the squirrel?* Such elliptical statement are of course used by everyone. ... The reply *In the tree*

---

[21] Most of Bereiter & Engelmann's book is taken up with direct instruction and outline; it is essentially a handbook for teachers. Further examples of the authors' approach will be found in Moss (1973).

demonstrates that the listener has been attentive to and apprehended the syntax of the speaker. (46)

Perhaps it might be argued that, to the extent to which Bereiter and Engelmann's programme aims to inculcate a knowledge of a socially-approved speech style, it could be useful. It is doubtful however that one would wish to approve of a programme built upon such shaky linguistic underpinnings, and which accepts a deficit view of the language of disadvantaged children. It is true that, from a *difference* viewpoint, one may wish to add to a child's repertoire. A policy of addition, however, is philosophically far removed from one which claims children's language to be deficient or nonexistent. Misunderstanding of the linguistic capabilities of a social group, however well-intentioned one's motives may be, can only serve to perpetuate myths.

Another programme designed to repair the language of the disadvantaged child was that of Blank and Solomon (1968). Like the project of Bereiter and Engelmann, the starting-point is the deficiency of the children:

> Their behavior reflects the lack of a symbolic system by which to organize the plentiful stimulation surrounding them. (380)

Lacking a firm 'language base', three- to five-year-old children were provided with short daily sessions of individual tutoring. A general overview of the approach is given by Blank (1970) in which we find that, once again, Bernstein's *early* work was instrumental in the pre-programme planning. Blank's approach is in many ways similar to that of Bereiter and Engelmann (whose work is praised) except that individualized intruction is stressed. The underlying philosophy is virtually identical, however. In order to 'foster the precursors of abstract thinking' (Blank 1970, 73) needed by the young disadvantaged child, the teachers present everyday material and then

> pose many related questions about it which would require the child to reflect, seek information, maintain concentration, examine alternatives, and so on. (75)

In fairness to Blank, a recent publication (1973) rather suggests that she rejects the notion of a generalized language deficit among disadvantaged children. Still, however, such children are seen as being in need of remedial attention.

A well-known American project for disadvantaged children was that of Klaus and Gray (1968; see also Gray and Klaus 1970). Framed within the environmental-deficit approach, the programme was aimed at black children in Tennessee whose home life was characterized as noisy, disorganized and generally less than ideal for the 'proper' development of cognitive skills. A debt to Bernstein is acknowledged; Klaus and Gray provide their definition of the lower-class restricted code thus:

> A restricted code is one in which most of the meaning must be carried by other aspects of the total situation: facial expression, intonation rather than words spoken, the circumstances. The child, thus, does not learn to use language effectively. (1968, 8)[22]

---

[22] The essence of this quotation is traceable to Bernstein's earliest paper (1958).

Like Bereiter and Engelmann, these authors feel that the language of disadvantaged children is 'conspicuously retarded' and, therefore, their educational programme placed considerable stress upon teaching such children how to speak. A similar programme is that of Weikart and Lambie (1968; see also Lambie and Weikart 1970)—they too emphasize the need for the disadvantaged child's language to be attended to in a formalized, structured manner. They show somewhat more sophistication, however, in their realization of the linguistic heterogeneity found among disadvantaged children, and thus stress an individualized approach.[23]

Overall, a usual characteristic of early (pre-1970) programmes of compensatory education is an acceptance of the linguistic deficit theory, and this acceptance is often based upon some acquaintance with Bernstein's early work. This is true not only for those individual programmes mentioned here but also for the massive American *Head Start* project—designed to give poor children preschool experience which would allow them to enter the regular school itself on a more equal footing with others. Springing from President Johnson's 'war on poverty' in 1965, and fuelled by Coleman's report on equality of educational opportunity (1966), *Head Start* was soon dealing with hundreds of thousands of children (Kellaghan 1977, Klaus and Gray 1968).

In recent years, however, the concept of compensatory education has soured somewhat. In part this is because the hoped-for gains in children's academic performance were either nonexistent or ephemeral (see Edwards, in press). Also important, however, was the growing support for the difference position on disadvantage which, while not necessarily ruling out some forms of intervention (Kellaghan 1977), made the term 'compensatory education' seem quite inappropriate and undercut the philosophical stance of most of those involved in it. The difference position was, in turn, most directly animated by linguistically-sophisticated investigations of the language of disadvantaged children (see chapter 3).

More recent programmes of intervention have approached the difficulties of disadvantaged children in a somewhat more enlightened manner. In Britain, for example, the Plowden Report (Great Britain: Department of Education and Science 1967) focused attention upon the problems of children in urban areas and recommended the identification of 'educational priority areas' on the basis of a number of visible criteria including large family size, receipt of state benefits and poor housing.[24] The result is thus a geographical approach to disadvantage not unlike that employed by earlier American efforts. Nevertheless, perhaps because of the smaller scale of operations, the reports of educational priority projects do give considerable information about children and their communities which tends to look somewhat beyond the more obvious criteria of material disadvantage. There have in fact been five such projects—in London, Birmingham, Liverpool,

---

[23] A relatively early paper attesting to the linguistic diversity among disadvantaged children is that of Sigel and Perry (1968).

[24] Useful comments on the British educational priority programmes may be found in Chazan 1973, Halsey 1972, Little and Mabey 1971 and Robinson 1976. The approach has also received attention in Ireland—both north and south (see Breathnach 1976, Wilson and Trew 1975).

Dundee and the West Riding (see Barnes 1975, Midwinter 1972, Morrison 1974, Payne 1974, Smith 1975).

Although these British projects have, like the American programmes, attempted remediation of children's language, they have generally tried to pay more attention to the individual child and are less inclined, perhaps, to see things from the traditional view.[25] Thus, for example, Lady Plowden (1970) noted that

> we are in danger of thinking that overnight we must make the whole population think the same way as we do ourselves ... education for the deprived child [should be] *complementary* to his home ... rather than *compensatory* which really means that the home has no merit.   (12)

This view may not be firmly within the *difference* line on disadvantage, but it is surely some way removed from the hard-line deficit approach typified elsewhere.[26]

To bring the discussion fully back to language I should mention, finally, the language remediation project described by Gahagan and Gahagan (1970). Based directly upon Bernstein's notion of language codes, the programme was devised to instruct working-class London children in the elaborated code. The form, like that of other programmes, consisted largely of structured activities and language drills.

2.3.1   Criticisms of compensatory education and verbal deprivation

As I stated at the beginning of this chapter, conclusions regarding the deficit view of language, and its manifestations in programmes of compensatory education, are closely related to the more general criticisms of the environmentalist approach to disadvantage which were made in chapter 1. The major point with regard to language is that any deficit view is saturated with a middle-class bias. Now, prejudices against certain speech styles are common and perhaps universal (see chapters 4 and 5); when, however, the bias is not expressed merely in terms of personal preference for a given form, but also in terms of assumed correctness or logic, then we can see the beginnings of *verbal deprivation*—the linguistic counterpart to sociocultural deprivation.

The whole structure of compensatory education seems to be built on sand. If the language of disadvantaged children is not deficient, then there is nothing to compensate for. We may, for practical purposes, wish to increase or broaden a child's linguistic repertoire, but this is another matter; any attempt to do so is not likely to succeed if it is founded on a basic ignorance or misunderstanding of a child's (any child's) linguistic capabilities. Because I believe that most inter-

[25] One of the most recent developments in the individualized approach has been the work of a Schools Council project. The aim has been to identify children 'at risk' of educational disadvantage, from the time of first school entry, through the use of a battery of psychological screening devices (see Edwards, in press, Evans 1973, 1975, 1976, Schools Council 1972). Further and more general information can be found in Wedell and Raybould 1976; for an American example of a similar approach, see Holliday and Olswang 1974 and, for some initial Irish data, J. R. Edwards 1974.

[26] For an example of an intervention programme whose administrators adopted a more eclectic view of disadvantage, see Kellaghan 1977.

vention programmes have suffered from such a lack of linguistic awareness, I have not gone into much detail concerning their actual language remediation procedures; in fact, these are for the most part highly-structured language drills in specific aspects of 'correct' English, and most appear curiously old-fashioned. Instead I have merely sought to give some impression of their philosophy, especially insofar as this can be related to the work of Bernstein.

The ignorance of the importance of cultural relativism, and the blind imposition of middle-class standards to which this ignorance leads, are the major issues in any discussion of compensatory education and verbal deprivation (Sroufe 1970, Tulkin 1972). Of specific importance here is the use of middle-class testers or interviewers, using middle-class instruments, in middle-class settings, to investigate lower-class behaviour. Such an approach has yielded large amounts of data, all of which are suspect on the grounds that they derive from contexts unfamiliar and possibly upsetting to lower-class respondents. This is not to say, of course, that psychological or linguistic investigations are necessarily without value; it is just that extreme caution is needed. For example, we have seen that Hess and Shipman, on the basis of their investigations, point to the need for 'resocializing' the disadvantaged child. This is a direct imputation of lower-class family inadequacy and is a view shared, to a greater or lesser extent, by most involved in compensatory education. Surely one would want firmer and more unassailable evidence than is currently available concerning the difficulties of disadvantaged children before interfering with family structures in such a manner.

Sroufe (1970) summarizes the misgivings of many, as follows:

> Do we have the right to impose middle-class standards on lower-class and black families? ... Are we confident that the middle-class value system, including the current school system, is an appropriate standard of health? If middle-class behavior patterns are to provide the outcome criteria, is it not necessary to seek and explore shortcomings in *these* patterns? (143)

Sroufe's point is a good one; however, the argument against compensatory education and language deficit is still incomplete. Besides criticizing the deficit viewpoint itself, as I have tried to do in this chapter, it is also necessary to consider the evidence of those who claim that disadvantaged language is *different* language. For this reason I shall defer further attention to the matter until some additional information has been presented and discussed.

3

Different language: current views of disadvantaged speech

'When *I* use a word,' Humpty Dumpty said in a rather scornful tone, 'it means just what I choose it to mean—neither more nor less.'   Lewis Carroll

'No one has succeeded in finding a primitive language.... No one has convincingly demonstrated that there is some thought or idea, expressible in some language, that cannot be expressed in another.'   Gleitman and Gleitman (1970)

In this chapter I wish to discuss the work of those who, through linguistic and psychological study, have attempted to show that the language of disadvantaged children is not deficient but different with respect to that of the middle class. The work is doubly important; not only does it represent a useful extension of language investigation *per se*, it also successfully attacks the myth of verbal deprivation. In fact this latter function has taken on, in recent years, a crusading tone—mainly because linguists, some psychologists and others were appalled at the costly and ill-informed programmes of compensatory education, which they saw as proceeding from false premises. The exposure of these is thus seen not only as an academic duty, but also as part of a larger duty towards society which carries the cost of such programmes (see, e.g., Labov 1973a).

3.1   Cultural relativism and the logic of language

We have already seen, in the previous chapter, that the 'strong' form of the Whorfian hypothesis—that language determines thought—is generally rejected. What is accepted is the influence of language upon our habitual ways of considering the world. Similarly, the environment has some formative influence upon the way a language develops. The point to be made here is that languages tend to be suited to the immediate needs of their speakers. Therefore, any consideration of language and linguistic behaviour must also involve some larger view of culture. It is certainly the case that languages differ widely in grammar and vocabulary, but it is *not* the case that languages can be shown to be better or worse than others.

No-one would claim that French is better than English, or that English is better than German; and, as the quote at the opening of this chapter indicates, no linguistic evidence has demonstrated that such value judgements can be made about *any* language—regardless of the degree of development of its culture. Lenneberg poses, and answers, the same question as follows:

> Could it be that some languages require 'less mature cognition' than others, perhaps because they are still more primitive? In recent years this notion has been thoroughly discredited by virtually all students of language.   (1967, 364)[1]

Thus, when we compare two languages, we are not entitled to use such terms as 'better' or 'worse'. Another way of looking at the matter is to consider the logic of language(s). It is clear that any use of the term *logic* must be restricted to apply to only one language at a time, and in fact it is equivalent to the term 'grammar'.[2] That is, it is logical (grammatical) in French to use two elements to express negation (*ne . . . pas*); in Standard English, a double negative is not grammatical. Is French less logical than English? Of course it is not, since it can easily be seen that what is termed grammatical is not an absolute, but a result of convention only.

It is of course true that, although languages cannot be branded as illogical, or worse than other languages, they are not all equal in their complexity (Hymes 1974). Keenan (1974) notes that languages are not exactly equivalent in their expressive power, although this does not mean that some are more expressive than others. Rather, languages reflect different varieties of the human condition and, hence, differ themselves. There are no 'poor', 'illogical', 'deficient' or 'primitive' languages (Langacker 1972, Stubbs 1976, Trudgill 1974a).

The realization that languages simply differ from one another has, thanks to anthropological and linguistic evidence, been with us for some time. What is interesting is that it is only relatively recently that acknowledgement has been made of the same relationship existing between varieties of the *same* language. Naturally, this realization of equality between language varieties is not new to linguistics; however, due to popular prejudices and the influence of middle-class standards (see Cole and Bruner 1972), language varieties which differ from these standards have often been downgraded (see chapter 4). Here, it should be borne in mind that

> just as there is no linguistic reason for arguing that Gaelic is superior to Chinese, so no English dialect can be claimed to be linguistically superior or inferior to any other.... There is no linguistic evidence whatsoever for suggesting that one dialect is more 'expressive' or 'logical' than any other, or for postulating that there are any 'primitive', 'inadequate' or 'debased' English dialects.   (Trudgill 1975, 26).

Nevertheless, linguistic evidence does not necessarily alter popular stereotypes and, I suppose, few linguists are naïve enough to think that dissemination of their views will quickly change social perspectives on black English, Cockney or *Joual*. What has brought linguists into the area of disadvantaged speech, however, is the way in which some academics—especially those concerned to 'correct' the speech of disadvantaged children—have assumed that some types of language or speech

---

[1] It is interesting to note that, at the time Lenneberg wrote this, the deficit viewpoint on disadvantaged language was at its peak.

[2] I am not, of course, considering here the attempts by Chomsky and others to elucidate an underlying deep 'logic' common across languages.

are better or more logical than others (see previous chapter). Quite simply, as Labov (1973a) has stated, linguists over the past few years have had an important job to do: to combat the theory of deficient language varieties.

3.2   The work of Labov and other American linguists

Among the best-known of those supporting the *difference* view of disadvantaged language is William Labov, an American linguist. His studies have been directed at dispelling the myth of verbal deficiency which animated so much of the educational intervention movement. In one sense, therefore, Labov may be seen as the counterpart to Bernstein (or rather, to the early Bernstein; or perhaps, to Bernstein misinterpreted). As Stubbs (1976) has noted, there are difficulties in comparing the work of Bernstein and Labov and, indeed, the two have not had a great deal to say to each other; Bernstein, for example, refers briefly to Labov in his 1973a paper. Nevertheless, it may be a useful starting-point to consider some of Labov's views of Bernstein's work.

One of Labov's general criticisms of Bernstein, and one which stands regardless of whether or not Bernstein is (or has been) misinterpreted, is the influence his work has had upon programmes of compensatory education. Labov traces this influence through to the work of, for example, Bereiter and Engelmann (see previous chapter). Labov also refers to some of the grammatical analyses made by Bernstein and his colleagues:

> One does not uncover the logical complexity of a body of speech by counting the number of subordinate clauses. The cognitive style of a speaker has no fixed relation to the number of unusual adjectives or conjunctions that he uses.   (1977b, 258)

Further, Labov (1973b) expands upon Bernstein's theory of elaborated and restricted code, as well as upon the work of Lawton (1969), when noting that elaborated code is not always desirable (see also below). Labov points out that, although the elaborated code can be very useful, much is eliminated by the most skilled users of language (storytellers, narrators, etc.), and the most desirable language is often the simplest. Thus, at the same time as he denies the validity of equating the elaborated code with 'better' language, Labov also implies that lower-class speech may often be more direct and powerful than the hesitant and pause-filled conversations of the middle class which, he notes, may well be seen as 'turgid, redundant, and empty' (1973a, 34).

Labov's most publicized assault on the concept of verbal deprivation comes in his paper on the logic of black English (1973a). Widely reprinted, it documents the rule-governed nature of the black English vernacular (hereafter, BEV) and demonstrates that it is *not* an inadequate or substandard variety of the language. Labov begins by giving an example of the sort of interview upon which much of the verbal deprivation myth is based, a situation which shows the black child in less than ideal circumstances. A small black boy is questioned by a large, white, middle-class interviewer in an attempt to elicit speech; in such a threatening (or, at least, unusual) context, the child says little, reporting only in what Labov terms 'defensive, monosyllabic behaviour' (27). Thus, considering the context, the child's behaviour is unsurprising; Labov's point, of course, is that very often

> such interviews are used as evidence of the child's total verbal capacity, or more simply his verbality. It is argued that this lack of verbality explains his poor performance in school. (27)

The bulk of Labov's article is an attempt to show that such an argument is totally invalid, based as it is upon spurious findings. When, for example, an eight-year-old child is 'interviewed' in a more relaxed situation, his increase in verbality is amazing. With the addition of another eight-year-old, a supply of potato chips, the introduction of 'taboo' words and an interviewer who literally drops to the child's level by sitting on the floor, the child's volume of speech is vastly larger than that obtained in the formal interview.

By this simple demonstration, Labov shows that the young black child is not 'nonverbal'[3] and, in addition, that formal tests involving speech production (as occur, for example, in school) will likely put him in an unfavourable light. The point is clearly to make teachers and others aware of this, so that unfair categorizing of a child's ability can be avoided. Referring directly to the deficit theorists, Labov notes that

> the view of the Negro speech community which we obtain from our work in the ghetto area is precisely the opposite from that reported by Deutsch, Engelmann and Bereiter. We see a child bathed in verbal stimulation from morning to night. (1973a, 33)

Labov next turns his attention to the popular connection between the elaborated speech of the middle class and the greater flexibility and subtlety which it is supposed to entail (see above). Here he wishes to show that it is possible to see lower-class speech as more forceful, less redundant and more direct than that of the middle class.[4] To do so he contrasts the speech of a lower-class black 15-year-old with that of an upper-middle-class black adult. In response to a question asking why God (if he exists) would be white, the adolescent replies

> Why? I'll tell you why. 'Cause the average whitey out here got everything, you dig? And the nigger ain't got shit, y'know? Y'understan'? So—um—for—in order for *that* to happen, you know it ain't no black God that's doin' that bullshit. (1973a, 38)

Labov notes the skill and complexity of this response; it is not Standard English (hereafter, SE) but the message is unequivocal. One also feels the willingness of the speaker to commit himself to a position, and to relate this directly to the questioner. This is quite different from the approach of the second speaker—an adult, college-educated man—in discussing witchcraft. He says, in part:

> I do believe that there is such a thing that a person can put himself in a state of *mind*

---

[3] Shuy (1971) has commented that no 'nonverbal' child that he has encountered has remained so in a non-intimidating context. Bernstein (1973a) also rejects the idea of the 'nonverbal' child.

[4] The reader will recall here discussions of how easy it would be to see middle-class behaviour as deficient and lower-class as more appropriate, once one has escaped from the assumption of the correctness of middle-class norms (see chapter 1).

(Mhm), or that—er—something could be given them to intoxicate them in a certain—to a certain frame of mind—that—that could actually be considered witchcraft.   (39–40)

Here we see that the speaker is less willing to commit himself to a position, wishing no doubt to avoid overstatement, and making it plain that the subject is one which admits of subtle shades of opinion. Analysing the full passage from which this excerpt is taken, Labov feels that impressions of the speaker as an educated and informed person are merely reflections of our 'long-conditioned reaction to middle-class verbosity' (41).

Labov's comparison of the two speakers is an attempt to show that when one looks at what is actually said, having suspended the usual middle-class norms by which we identify the cues of 'good' speech or speakers, it is by no means clear that the second respondent is any more rational or intelligent than the former.[5] In fact, Labov obviously feels that the redundancy and verbosity of middle-class speech often means that the basic idea to be communicated, if clearly thought out at all, is lost in a welter of qualifications and hesitations (see also Labov, 1976g).

Another important aspect of Labov's (1973a) article bears upon the distinction between the comprehension of a statement and the reproduction of it.[6] Here a simple test is employed in which a child hears a statement and is asked to repeat it. Thus:

I asked Alvin if he knows how to play basketball

may be repeated by the black child as

I ax Alvin do he know how to play basketball

or

I axt Alvin does he know how to play basketball

A teacher hearing such a sentence might be inclined to think the child's grammar, pronunciation or even cognitive ability less than adequate. However, the grammar and pronunciation evidenced in such repetitions are regularities of the child's dialect, and are not substandard attempts to imitate SE patterns.[7] With regard to the child's thinking, and his grasp of the *meaning* of the original statement, it is clear that there is no deficiency. He has comprehended the meaning and has simply reproduced it verbally in the form most familiar to him. Labov acknowledges that it may prove useful to the child (especially at school) to consider more carefully the explicit structure of SE and, in short, to better recognize the value, in some contexts, of paying closer attention to surface detail. The danger to which Labov points, however, is the false equation that may be made between the child's use

[5] I shall refer to this point again, when discussing some criticisms of Labov (see below).

[6] This comparison will be further discussed, with regard to its implication for reading (see chapter 5).

[7] A *dialect* being a variety of a given language which differs from another in certain aspects of grammar, pronunciation and vocabulary (see chapter 4); Labov's work on BEV grammar is mentioned below.

of a nonstandard English (hereafter, NSE) form and some putative deficiency in cognitive ability; thus Labov reiterates that 'there is nothing in the vernacular which will interfere with development of logical thought' (1973a, 52).

Overall, it is not difficult to understand why Labov's paper (1973a) has been so influential. He has suggested that the 'nonverbality' of the black child is an artefact of the situation, that there is at least some doubt that middle-class speech is more desirable than that of the lower class, and that it is difficult to infer cognitive ability from verbal style. It is no overstatement to say that this article is the single most powerful assault upon the environmentalist position on disadvantage in general, and upon verbal deprivation in particular.

Much of Labov's more technical investigation has concerned itself with specific aspects of BEV grammar, attempting to show that, like any other language system, BEV conforms to rules which its speakers have internalized. Here I shall briefly mention some of the more notable aspects of the work.[8]

Consider, for example, the use in BEV of the copula verb. Labov (1976b) presents some instances of the *absence* of this element, as follows:

She the first one started us off
I know, but he wild, though
We on tape

In these sentences, the SE 'is' or 'are' is not present. Does this mean that speakers of BEV are unaware of this verb form? Consider further these statements which, like the ones above, derive from Labov's interviews with blacks:

I was small
She was likin' me

Here the past tense of the verb 'to be' appears. How is it that the verb appears here but not in the former sentences? Labov's studies reveal a regularity governing this linguistic behaviour: in contexts in which SE can *contract* (e.g. *They are going* can become *They're going*), BEV can *delete* (e.g. *They are going* can become *They going*). We have, therefore, a rule—different from the one obtaining in SE but no less logical.

The regularity is further evidenced by the fact that where SE *cannot* contract, BEV *cannot* delete. Thus, a sentence like

He's as nice as he says he's

is, according to the rules of SE, incorrect; contraction is not permissible in the final position. Labov notes that it is, likewise, incorrect to say in BEV

He's as nice as he says he

Just as SE cannot contract in this case, so BEV cannot delete the copula. One can see, then, that a view which treats BEV (at least in this situation) as illogical or deficient is suffering from an inadequate grasp of the relevant linguistic evidence.

[8] The interested reader can consult Labov's works for fuller accounts; here I am omitting many details.

Another interesting and informative element in the copula system of BEV is illustrated by Labov (1976a) with the following sorts of sentences:

She be standin' with her hand in her pocket
He be always fooling around

Here the 'be' indicates habitual behaviour; if these statements did *not* include 'be', the BEV speaker would, instead, be referring to a present action only (see also Menyuk 1970). Again, the weight of Labov's evidence is to show the rule-governed nature of BEV.

One feature of BEV is its use of the double negative, or negative concord (Labov 1973a, 1976c). Thus, the SE sentence

He knows something

becomes, in the negative

He doesn't know anything

In BEV, the positive

He know something

becomes

He don't know nothing

Thus BEV, like certain world languages, customarily employs the double negative so frowned upon by teachers of English (thus: if you say 'You don't know nothing' you are *really* saying that you know something). In fact, of course, speakers of SE *do* use double-negative constructions; the clue to the fact that they are not deemed ungrammatical lies in the stress employed. Thus it is perfectly appropriate to say

He does *not* know *nothing*

meaning that he does, in fact, know something. The difference between this double negative and the use viewed so poorly by teachers is that here, by stressing each of the two negative elements, it is clear that the double negative is *intended*. Exactly the same sort of stress will be employed by the speaker of BEV who says

He *don't* know *nothing*

Overall, when a double negative is intended both BEV and SE speakers will use stress to indicate this. The real difference between them lies in the use, among BEV speakers, of the *unstressed* double negative in contexts in which SE speakers use only the single negative.

Yet another regular feature of the BEV is the omission of the possessive 's' (see Labov 1976d, Torrey 1973), giving rise to sentences like

We at Jane house
That's Peter doggie

Note again that there is no ambiguity here, and the sentences are perfectly under-standable. Ambiguity stemming from deletion of the possessive 's' *is* possible, how-ever, in some cases, although it seems not to be a formidable obstacle to the BEV speaker's ability to understand. Torrey (1973), working with second-grade children

> asked them to choose between two pictures representing *The man teacher* (a man standing before a class) and *The man's teacher* (a woman teaching with a man in the class). Many could select the latter picture for *The man's teacher* and name the two pictures correctly in standard English even though they themselves did not spontaneously use the possessive 's' in conversation.   (70)

So, as for the repetition task mentioned previously, it seems that the BEV speaker can understand SE forms even when he does not ordinarily employ them himself. In BEV itself, presumably, possible ambiguity is avoided by stress and contextual cues.

A similar BEV grammatical difference is the absence of the 's' in the third per-son singular of present tense verbs. Thus:

It look like you don' brush your teeth

As Torrey (1973) notes, there are few sentences in which misunderstanding will result because of the absence of this 's'—' "The deer runs" would be a case, since only the "s" of "runs" tells how many deer' (69).

A general consideration of these and other grammatical differences between BEV and SE leads to the conclusion that each variety has a rule-governed language system. The confusion and ambiguity which one might expect if BEV were, as is sometimes supposed, a substandard variety, do not occur. Pronunciation dif-ferences also exist, of course, between the two varieties but these are of minor importance with regard to arguments about the relationship between language and cognitive skills, or logic. Some of the more common pronunciation variations found in BEV include:

> 'th' becoming 'd' (*they* and *that* becoming *dey* and *dat)*
> 'th' becoming 'f' (*with* and *both* becoming *wif* and *bof*)
> 'th' becoming 't' (*something* becoming *someting*)
> omission of some final consonants (*most of* becoming *mos' of*)

These forms are not, of course, unique to BEV; other varieties of English make use of them as well ('th' becoming 'd' or 't', for example, is common in Dublin working-class English). As with grammatical features, it is the regularity with which these pronunciation variants occur which is most telling here (Hunt 1974, Labov 1976d, Trudgill 1974a).

What conclusions can one draw from these investigations of BEV? First it is a valid *dialect* of English; therefore we must reject any notions of substandardness (although we may term it a *nonstandard* variety). Second, although dialect studies often focus upon differences between language varieties, it should not be forgotten that dialects usually have more shared than unique features; Labov (1976a) notes that 'the great majority of the rules of BEV are the same as the rules of other English dialects' (37). And, when discussing dialect differences, it should be borne in mind that dialect speakers generally comprehend standard forms, even if they do not habitually use them. The 'gears and axles of English grammatical machinery are available to speakers of all dialects' (Labov 1976a, 64). A final point, therefore, is that BEV is best characterized as a valid variety of English, closely associated in most respects with other varieties, but also differing in certain regular ways. It has, Labov (1973a) notes, the capacity to express the same cognitive content as SE. The educational implications, therefore, are clear; BEV is *not* substandard, black children are not verbally deficient and, therefore, the aims and approaches of the bulk of the intervention programmes are misguided (see also Dillard 1973).

Although it is probably fair to say that Labov's work has received the most attention, other American linguists have also considered the difference-deficit language issue, especially in connection with BEV. Shuy (1968, 1970), for example, has investigated the BEV of Detroit to determine its identifying characteristics and, incidentally, to study the best way of conducting such sociolinguistic surveys. As with the work of Labov, it was found that the black dialect is rule-governed and regular in the ways in which it differs from SE (see also Shuy *et al.* 1967, Wolfram 1969).

Wolfram, a colleague of Shuy, has also reported on sociolinguistic investigations among Puerto Ricans in New York City (1973). He was particularly interested in the ways in which the Puerto Ricans, similar in social status to the blacks, reflect their proximity to the latter in their language styles. For example, two features of BEV noted above are the use of 'f' for 'th' (e.g. *wif* for *with*) and the use of 'be' as a marker of habitual action (e.g. *She be standin'*). Wolfram demonstrates that on these and other linguistic features there is a relationship between the degree of Puerto Rican-black contact and their use. This regularly-observed consequence of language contact would appear to imply the rule-governed nature of BEV itself.

Finally, it is worth mentioning the work of Stewart (1970, 1972a) and Dillard (1973, 1977) who, through their studies of the history and origins of present-day BEV, reinforce even further its rightful place as a valid English dialect. A recent article on the subject by Traugott (1976) discusses the historical development of BEV which, 'though largely assimilated into the various English vernaculars, still has features which clearly distinguishes [sic] it from them' (93). This, of course, is similar to the point of view adopted by Labov (see above). Traugott also reminds us that there is more than one variety of BEV, although the term usually refers to the urban speech of Detroit, New York and Washington.

For the most part, the work of Labov and the others investigating BEV has been accepted without much criticism. There have however been a few points raised which should be mentioned here. Bernstein (1973a) is critical, not of Labov's work *per se*, but of the interpretation of *his* work by Labov (see above). Bernstein thus notes that, apparently, Labov has considered only his early work, which (as we have seen) he now admits himself to have been less than completely clear. Bernstein reiterates his rejection of the verbal deficit theory, and generally aligns himself with the *difference* approach to language variation.

Robinson (1972) also comments on Labov's rejection of Bernstein's work, especially on his remarks concerning the inappropriateness of counting a speaker's clausal constructions as a measure of logical complexity (see Labov's quote at the beginning of this section, p. 52). Although Robinson agrees that one cannot argue from quantitative differences (such as the proportion of clauses used) back to any qualitative distinction, he does feel that Labov's approach tends to close off questions about the significance of these quantitative differences themselves. As we have seen before (chapter 2), Robinson is concerned with the possible *functional* differences in language, and language use, which may exist between groups; these, presumably, could be reflected in language structures (see also Robinson 1975).[9]

Another point concerns Labov's description of a sample of black middle-class speech as verbose and redundant (see above). Although Labov was critical of the middle-class speaker's unwillingness to commit himself to a position (as compared with the directness of the lower-class black adolescent), it may be that his interpretation is less than complete. Differences observed in style may have been due, in part, to the age difference between the two speakers; thus, the directness of the adolescent may reflect a certain brashness of youth. A related, and more important, point is that, although the middle-class sample was vaguer and less direct, these qualities may be appropriate when discussing such issues as witchcraft or the existence of God. The longstanding historical interest attaching to such issues presumably attests to the fact that they do not admit of easy resolution. Thus, it may well be that the directness of lower-class speech is not as appropriate in this context as it might be in others; perhaps Labov's range of topics should have been broader.

However, these comments notwithstanding, there is no doubt that Labov and his colleagues have scotched the idea of verbal deficiency among black speakers in the United States. The import of their work is simply that BEV is not the substandard variant it has long been considered to be by teachers, administrators of compensatory education programmes, academics and others.

3.3   Further work on 'different' language

As one might expect, the initial linguistic studies of Labov and others have prompted many investigators to look more closely at what were once assumed to be substandard language variants. The preponderance of all this work has been carried out in the United States; because of the close connection between disadvantage and race the language-deficit view, and its refutation, have constituted a more highly-charged issue there than elsewhere.[10] Stubbs (1976) has questioned the applicability of much of this work, therefore, in other contexts, although he goes on to note that some preliminary studies in Britain have suggested that parallels can reasonably be drawn.[11] The important thing here, however, is not whether

[9] The reader might recall here the brief discussion in chapter 2 of the work of Halliday. To my mind, the possibility of functional language differences between groups remains an open question.

[10] It is also true, too, that greater resources have been available in the United States for sociolinguistic research.

[11] Trudgill (1974b), for example, conducted a study of class differences in Norwich, a work which

similar linguistic variations will be found in the speech of disadvantaged populations in different parts of the world; it is the demonstration that, in general, the deficit view of nonstandard speech is invalid. In this connection, BEV makes, in many ways, a useful test-case since it diverges more than do other English dialects from SE, and because it was for so long considered to be substandard and illogical English. Thus, the demonstration that BEV is a valid dialect, coupled with the general evidence concerning the intrinsic sufficiency of all languages (section 3.1) makes, in my view, a very strong case against linguistic deficiency theories in general. And, it is precisely this generality which one wishes to establish as the starting-point for any study of language varieties. it is in this sense of having cleared the air, as it were, that the American linguistic studies are so important.

Following these studies, psychologists and educators have conducted empirical investigations to establish further the validity of BEV and other nonstandard dialects. Marwit and his colleagues, for example, report a series of studies demonstrating the predictability of BEV productions in certain tasks; this predictability, of course, argues for a regular rule-governed system rather than some substandard approximation to SE.

Thus, Marwit *et al.* (1972) gave black and white second-grade children a task in which they were required to supply the present, possessive, plural and time-extension forms of nonsense syllables. For example, shown a picture of a reclining stick figure, the children were told, 'This is a man who knows how to *pid*. What is he doing now?' They then had to supply the appropriate response to complete the answer, 'Now he ____.' Examples of the other three grammatical forms studied are as follows (each was accompanied by appropriate pictures):

(a)　Plural: 'This is a *lun*. Now there is another one. There are two of them. There are two ____.'
(b)　Possessive: 'This is a cup that belongs to the *lun*. Whose cup is it? It is the ____.'
(c)　Time-extension: 'This is a man who knows how to *mork*. He does this *all the time. All the time*, he ____.'

Nonsense syllables are employed in such tasks so that one may test the child's general grasp of rules rather than his knowledge of vocabulary.[12] Marwit *et al.* hoped that the results of the experiment would show that white children would give SE forms of the syllables, and that black children's responses would be of a regular, but nonstandard, variety. Thus (based upon some of the BEV forms we have already discussed) it was expected that whereas white children would make the response 'He *pids*' or 'He *is pidding*', black youngsters would say 'He *pid*'. Similarly, for the other three forms, it was expected that white children would say 'There are two *luns*', 'It is the *lun's*' and 'All the time, he *is morking*' (or '*morks*'); black

---

draws upon similar investigations in New York City by Labov (1966). In these studies the difference viewpoint is taken for granted; they are thus not directly applicable in the present context.

[12] This technique is an adaptation of that first used by Berko (1958) to study the development of children's morphological inflections.

children, it was hypothesized, would tend to respond with 'There are two *lun*', 'It is the *lun*' and 'All the time, he *be morking*' (or '*mork*').[13]

In fact, the hypothesis was largely borne out; black children consistently used more BEV forms of the nonsense syllables. Marwit *et al.* argue that such consistency is hardly compatible with a deficit view of black speech, but instead corroborates the work of Labov and others. In further work, variations on this experimental theme are presented. Thus Marwit and Marwit (1973) replicated the study but, this time, half of the group of black and white children were presented the task, and the task instructions, in BEV. Also, both black and white examiners were employed. The results were as before, and were obtained regardless of the manner of task presentation. Again, the authors feel that this demonstrates that one is dealing, with BEV, with a regular linguistic variety which is relatively unaffected by what they term the 'presentation mode'.[14] Marwit and Marwit also note that the race of the examiner had *some* differential effect upon children's responses and, while this did not alter the main thrust of the findings, they call for further investigation into the matter. We have already noted, in this regard, the dramatic examiner effects demonstrated by Labov.

In a further study, Marwit and Marwit (1976) readministered their test to fourth-grade children who had participated two years previously in the Marwit *et al.* (1972) investigation. The black children once more provided more BEV responses, and the white children more SE. The interesting point here is that both black and white children showed an increasing use of SE from the earlier (second grade) to the later (fourth grade) sessions. Marwit (1977) found, further, that this process extended to children in seventh grade (about 12 years of age). Both Marwit (1977) and Marwit and Marwit (1976) are less than clear in their discussions of these trends, and in the absolute amounts of BEV and SE used by the children; nevertheless, the general direction is clear enough. Black children, who use more nonstandard forms than white children, tend to decrease their use of these forms with age (see also Bountress 1977, 1978).

Will BEV therefore disappear altogether? It seems unlikely since, although its use may decrease in *these* situations, it may have *increasing* peer-group value outside the school as the child moves into adolescence. Ramer and Rees (1973), in investigations similar to those of Marwit and his co-workers, have also observed the decreasing use of BEV with age, but note that it is never completely abandoned. Once again, the reader should bear in mind that BEV and SE are more alike than different and, therefore, that it is not surprising that the black child's familiarity with, and use of, SE will increase as he progresses through school.

---

[13] It is not to be expected that black children would *always* use BEV forms. They often use SE and, indeed, as Labov has noted, there is a large degree of overlap between the two dialects. Further to the point, Williams *et al.* (1977) note that a speaker may use BEV and SE within the same sentence: 'I took it off my des' and lai it on his desk.' Here the simplification of a consonant ending is employed in the first, but not in the second occurrence of the word 'desk' (see also Seymour and Seymour 1977). The point of Marwit's study is simply to show that when a nonstandard form *is* used, it adheres to a rule system and its structure can therefore be predicted.

[14] One is reminded here of the sentence-repetition tasks mentioned previously in which black children repeat a statement in BEV even when it is presented to them in SE.

Baratz (1969) conducted a study involving sentence repetition in which both black and white children participated, and in which both standard and nonstandard English sentences were used as stimuli. The results once again support a 'difference' view of BEV. Black children were better than white children in repeating nonstandard sentences while the opposite held when standard sentences were presented. In addition, errors (i.e incorrect repetitions) made by children were systematic. Thus, 97 per cent of the black children, when asked to repeat

I asked Tom if he wanted to go the picture

responded with

I aks Tom did he wanna go ...

Conversely, 68 per cent of the white children who were asked to repeat

Do Deborah like to play wif the girl that sit next to her at school?

replied

Does Deborah like to play with the girl that sits next to her at school?

For most children, black or white, statements tended to be repeated in a manner most familiar to the child; the high percentages of children employing the *same* alteration of the stimulus indicate a uniformity of language. Baratz summarizes her study:

> Using standard English as criterion for tests that ask, 'How well has standard English been developed in this child?' is excellent; however, using standard English as criterion for tests that ask, 'How well has this child developed language?' is absurd if the primary language that the child is developing is not standard English.   (1969, 899)

One is not denying that children using language forms that deviate from SE may experience difficulties; the point here is simply that these difficulties do not derive from linguistic deficit.

Foreit and Donaldson (1971) have criticized Baratz's study on some technical points of analysis and, more importantly, have taken her to task for stating that 'black children are generally not bidialectal' (Baratz 1969, 899). As we have seen in the work of Marwit and colleagues, black children *do* seem to have considerable facility in both comprehension and use of SE and, indeed, Baratz's own findings appear to support this (i.e. the children showed ability in translating from SE to BEV in the repetition task). This point, though important, does not alter the general import of Baratz's results, which can be taken as further support of the linguistic validity of BEV. Her findings were confirmed in a later study by Seitz (1975), who also made two further points of relevance. First, not all black children show equal familiarity with BEV, children from higher socioeconomic status levels being more adept in SE.[15] Second, low SES black children attending integrated

---

[15] Muehl and Muehl (1976) also demonstrate that, among black college students, there are differences in BEV competence. This is a useful note, since it reminds us that black speakers do not all have equal facility in the vernacular.

schools were better on SE and poorer on BEV than their counterparts in segregated (black only) schools. Some further refinements are added by Gay and Tweney (1976); they found that although black children's *production* of BEV forms decreased with age, their *comprehension* of the forms increased. This again emphasizes the bidialectal abilities of black children, at least by the middle years of school (Gay and Tweney's subjects were in the sixth grade), in the sense that they seem increasingly able to use SE if the context appears to call for it.[16] The authors note that

> on several occasions when a white adult mistakenly entered a testing room [the experimenter was black], black subjects immediately switched from black English responses to standard English responses when presented with black English stimuli. (266)

In Britain, V. Edwards (1976a, 1976b) has described features of West Indian English which set it apart from the standard, and which may cause difficulties for both speaker and listener. I shall take up the latter point in chapter 6; here I wish only to note that, with West Indian English as with BEV, one is dealing with a dialect *different* from SE. Although in its broadest forms, West Indian English is sufficiently divergent from SE that some have argued for its definition as a separate language (Bailey 1966), it has several similarities with the less discrepant BEV. For example, one observes the deletion of the 's' in third person singular verbs, thus:

The boy come
My brother go to work

Also, there is omission of the possessive 's':

The man car
John hat

In addition, copula deletion is evident, as in BEV:

The story good
Winston coming

These, and other regular features, mark West Indian English as a distinct dialect with rules of its own, just as we have seen such features delineate between BEV and SE in the United States.

Other British studies, not dealing with black or immigrant speech, have interpreted speech differences more or less within a different-language framework. They are, in fact, closely related to what one might term the 'new' Bernstein approach (see chapter 2) in which the possibility of linguistic deprivation among disadvantaged children is apparently rejected.

Francis (1974) engaged disadvantaged and non-disadvantaged children in a

---

[16] Further information regarding the comprehension of SE by black children will be found in Copple and Suci 1974, Feldman *et al.* 1977, Hall and Turner 1974, Hall *et al.* 1973 and Marwit and Neumann 1974.

story-retelling task (i.e. the child listens to a story and then tells it to the investigator). This technique has enough of a play element in it to hold the child's interest and, while allowing considerable freedom of speech, does provide some common basis of comparison for all subjects. The stories of the children were taperecorded, transcribed and analysed for amount of speech and clausal complexity. Since the children were each tested at four ages (every six months from 5 years 3 months to 7 years 3 months) Francis was also able to comment on developmental trends. All children told longer stories as they grew older; the amount of speech produced was similar in both groups of children, although the disadvantaged children tended to use less grammatically 'complex' sentences. However, the *within* group difference in this regard was greater than that obtaining *between* groups. Also, it was not the case that the disadvantaged children never used certain constructions, but rather that they used somewhat fewer of them than their non-disadvantaged counterparts. We might perhaps think of these children, like BEV speakers in the United States, as having knowledge of speech forms which they do not habitually use very much. But they do have an understanding of them, which presumably can be drawn upon if necessary; indeed, just as we have seen the increasing use of SE among BEV-speaking children in America, so the disadvantaged children in Francis's study showed increasing use of clausal constructions with age. Once again, therefore, it appears as if we are observing differences in customary language usage, along class lines, which are not very large and which, in fact, may decrease over time (at least in relatively formal contexts).

Similar results have been obtained with Dublin disadvantaged children (Edwards 1977b), employing the story-telling technique used by Francis. Analyses of the children's speech revealed that the disadvantaged children used fewer complex sentence structures that did middle-class children—but, they used some. It was made clear in the study that

> one should not generalize from these results, obtained in a school setting, to speech in other situations. However, it is school performance that is the primary concern here. Length and complexity of sentences ... are aspects of communicative ability which schools generally aim to improve. On such measures, the [lower-class] children ... are at a disadvantage.   (69)

The disadvantageous aspects of certain speech forms are clear, and will be discussed further in chapter 5. What should be noted here is the emphasis upon language difference rather than linguistic deprivation of deficit. The educational problem (such as it is) is not one of children who do not know how to use subordinate clauses but of children who customarily make *less* use of them than do others.[17] It is worth mentioning again, too, that even were it found that disadvantaged children did not use a single clausal construction, we could still not infer that they were unaware of their existence, or of how to use them.

A study by A. Edwards (1976) demonstrates further the difficulties in simply ascertaining that differences in sentence complexity regularly occur across classes.

[17] The reader will recall here the work of Robinson (1965), cited in the previous chapter, showing the use of elaborated code by working-class children.

Using standard measures of clausal and verbal complexity, the author found that although a range of children, from middle- to lower-working-class, were examined, 'large and consistent speech differences did not appear' (108) among 11-year-olds. Edwards notes that the experimental situation (in his study, undirected linguistic interviews) may have affected the samples obtained (a common dilemma) but, insofar as the formality of the context probably resembled the school setting more than anything else, the results hardly argue for much discontinuity between lower-class children and the school.

There is a most interesting point here. Consider, first, that many of those who argued against Bernstein felt that his data were obtained in formal contexts which were inappropriate for eliciting lower-class speech samples. Second, Bernstein responded by saying that his experimental settings were similar to the formal context of the school, and that therefore one was entitled to generalize from the results of such studies to school performance (see Trudgill 1975).[18] Third, the results of A. Edwards's study, summarized in the previous paragraph, suggest that even in formal situations, disadvantaged children do not necessarily seem to be at a loss. Although, as we shall see in the following chapters, there is ample evidence that disadvantaged speech is downgraded by teachers and others, these last findings demonstrate that one must be careful in deciding exactly what such negative evaluations are based upon. For Edwards's results suggest that one cannot always look for such bases in vocabulary and syntax variations since these, quite simply, may not be present.[19]

Overall, the information presented in this section, and the preceding one, suggests very strongly that disadvantaged speech is different speech. If the nonstandard variety in question differs widely from SE (as in the case of some forms of West Indian English), then it approaches the status of a separate language; here there is little difficulty in viewing the system as merely different. If, on the other hand, the dialectal variation is not great (as, for example, with BEV and other social class dialects) then, of course, the implication is that the majority of such speech is, in fact, SE. And, as we have seen, those differences that *do* occur (copula deletion, omission of the possessive 's' and the like) conform to regular rules of usage. So again one is dealing with difference rather than deficit.

We have established, I think, a firm *linguistic* basis from which we can proceed to consider the essentially *social* factors of importance in the perception and use of disadvantaged or nonstandard speech and language. Before turning to such considerations, however, there are one or two further matters which can be dealt with appropriately here.

[18] This is the point which I made in the previous quotation (Edwards 1977b).

[19] Edwards *did* find class differences in terms of the context-dependence/independence variable (i.e. the extent to which the child was able to describe an event without using 'illegitimate' references to people or objects which assume the listener shares some background knowledge). On this measure, the lower-class children were more 'context-bound'; see Hawkins 1969 and Schatzman and Strauss 1955, discussed in the previous chapter.

3.4   The elicitation and interpretation of speech samples

We have seen, in the first two chapters, criticisms of the environmental-deficit approach which were based upon the inadequacy of the testing procedures often used (see also Cleary *et al.* 1975). The imposition of middle-class norms upon children for whom they were obviously inappropriate illuminated the difficulty caused by ignorance of cultural relativism and 'culture-fair' testing. Nowhere, perhaps, is this problem more acute than in the obtaining and interpretation of speech samples. Labov (1973a) demonstrated, for example, how easy it was to elicit speech from a lower-class black child if the context were made non-intimidating and, in so doing, criticized Bereiter and Engelmann and others who had erected the verbal deprivation theory upon speech data obtained in incredibly naïve and heavyhanded ways (see also Wolfram 1976). There seems little doubt that a small black child faced with a large white examiner will not produce his best in a structured interview situation. There remain, however, problems involved with speech sampling even when one has recognized and disposed of the more obviously inappropriate approaches.

As a general introduction, we can note that Cazden (1970) and Goffman (1972) have both discussed what they refer to as the 'neglected situation'. That is, until investigators give due weight to the context in which speech is obtained, the interpretation of obtained speech will be less than ideal. This goes beyond the basic inadequacy of the formal interview situation *per se*, and addresses the issue of the *type* of speech that different contexts will evoke from the same informant. As Joos (1967) and others have pointed out, we all have access to different speech styles which we employ on different occasions. Delivering a formal lecture, chatting with friends in the pub, and talking with one's spouse are all likely to call forth variations in style. What Cazden, Goffman and others discuss is that, having recognized this rather obvious linguistic fact of life, those who are engaged in eliciting speech for analysis must consider more closely what the contextual demands are, as perceived by the speaker. For if generalizations about linguistic behaviour are desired it is surely necessary to understand what constraints were operating at the same time the data were acquired. Linguistic methodology in this connection has been discussed at some length by Labov (1972, 1977a, 1977b), and it is to his work that I turn now.

The object of the exercise, very often, is to observe, record and interpret *natural* speech—speech customarily used by the respondent with friends, at home and at work. As Labov (1972) states

> Either our theories are about the language that ordinary people use on the street,
> arguing with friends, or at home blaming their children, or they are about very little
> indeed.   (109)

The obtaining of such natural speech is, however, a difficult exercise, and Labov (1972, 1977b) outlines some of the relevant factors in this process. Some of these we have already touched upon.

First, Labov notes that there are no 'single-style' speakers; any given context will elicit a style which forms but one aspect of the speaker's repertoire. And, as has been noted, style shifting can occur *within* the same context (e.g. the use of BEV *and* SE by the same speaker in one situation).

Second, the speech style in which one is most often interested is the speaker's vernacular, 'in which the minimum attention is paid to speech' (Labov 1972, 112). That is, there exists a negative relationship between the 'naturalness' of speech and the degree to which attention is focused upon it; as one pays greater attention to speech, so the style will tend to shift. Thus, for example, a lecturer will, having planned his delivery beforehand, move away from a casual style to a more formal style (Joos 1967). This style shifting can occur whether attention is being given to speech by the speaker himself (as above), or if the attention comes from someone else. If, for example, a person is asked direct questions about language, 'their answers will shift in an irregular manner toward (or away from) the superordinate dialect' (Labov 1972, 111). That is, an interviewee may shift to a more standard style, or indeed may move farther from it, thus accentuating his own nonstandard-ness. The difficulty for the observer, obviously, arises inasmuch as the direction of this process may be hard to predict.[20]

Overall, Labov feels that these factors leave the linguistic investigator with an *observer's paradox:*

> To obtain the data most important for linguistic theory, we have to observe how people speak when they are not being observed. (1972, 113)

This problem obviously cannot be directly overcome, but Labov has outlined some ways to reduce the influence of the observer's presence and, therefore, to facilitate the speaker's use of his vernacular.

The first of these involves choosing suitable topics for the speaker to discuss. Labov has found three topics to be most useful in this regard. They are:

> death, and the danger of death
> sex (i.e. male–female relations in general)
> moral indignation (over perceived unjust punishment, for example)

Such topics often involve the speaker to such an extent that the more formal aspects of the situation (for example the presence of an interviewer with a taperecorder) are overridden; that is, the influence of attention upon speech is reduced.

Another way to facilitate the production of the vernacular is to allow the speaker long digressions from the topic under discussion. Labov (1977c) points out that, in many cases, interviewers cut speakers short if they feel that they are rambling; he, however, advocates giving speakers their head. Thus: 'whenever a subject showed signs of wanting to talk, no obstacle was interposed: the longer he digressed, the better chance we had of studying his natural speech pattern' (91).

A related device is the investigator's attention to 'outside' influences. Thus, in talking with the interviewer, a speaker may break off to answer the telephone,

---

[20] Giles (1973a) and Giles and Powesland (1975) have discussed a related issue—accent convergence/divergence—and have attempted to account for the occurrence of one or the other by analysis of contextual factors.

scold a child or talk to some third person. If such occurrences can be noted or recorded by the investigator, they are often found to provide excellent samples of more casual speech.

A final manner of reducing the influence of the observer's paradox is exemplified by an aspect of Labov's investigations of English in New York City (1966). Interested to study social class differences in the pronunciation of 'r' in words like *car* and *four*, Labov asked people in stores where a particular sales department was located knowing, in fact, that it was on the fourth floor. After getting the response 'fourth floor', he would then lean forward and say 'Excuse me?', whereupon the respondent usually repeated 'fourth floor', this time more carefully and emphatically. By this simple expedient, Labov obtained four examples of 'r'—two from the casual 'fourth floor' and two more from the emphatic repetition—from respondents completely unaware of the purpose of the exercise.

The advantages of such methods of investigation, Labov feels, go some way towards reducing the problems summarized by the term 'observer's paradox'. He does not of course rule out information which may be gained in other, more formal ways; the use of sentence repetition tasks among BEV speakers, for example, has been most valuable. Labov simply cautions against reliance upon such methods alone for the investigation of a speaker's usual patterns of speech (see also Harrison 1976).

It is also possible, of course, to record people who are unaware of the procedure. Such methods naturally require subjects' subsequent permission for use of the data so acquired. A related device is to equip speakers with radio microphones. This method, often used with children, relies upon the speaker forgetting about the presence of the microphone and, therefore, producing natural speech (see, e.g., Wootton 1974).

A useful technique for eliciting speech from younger children is the story-repetition method (see above; and Edwards 1977b, Francis 1974) in which the child retells to the investigator a story just heard. This is actually a simplified version of a procedure used by Piaget (1952) and Houston (1973) in which, to study information transmission among small children, the experimenter tells a story to child A, who tells it to child B, who then tells it back to the experimenter. As mentioned in the previous section, this method at once allows some comparison across children and offers considerable freedom of speech to the individual child.

One can, of course, argue that such a technique is less than ideal since it does not tap truly spontaneous speech and, in fact, is most often used in a formal setting (often at school). Here, however, one can realize that obtaining samples of speech of the sort used at school can be quite useful. That is, many investigations take for granted the adequacy of the child's vernacular and, in short, accept the *difference* viewpoint of nonstandard speech; they may simply be interested in the more formal 'school language'. So long as it is realized that such studies may say little or nothing about the child's language at home or at play, they may be valuable for considering speech in this one rather important context (see Edwards 1977b, 1979b, Yoder 1970; see also section 3.5 below). In fact, some such studies are carried out precisely in order to demonstrate the need for greater linguistic awareness on the part of teachers and schools who are often inclined to view the school language of disadvantaged children as deficient (see chapter 5).

One can also take steps, in eliciting speech samples at school, to reduce the influence of the formality of the setting. This is clearly more difficult than when one is studying speech in the field, but much can be done. A. Edwards (1976) notes, for example, that the experimenter in his study spent considerable time with the children in class before beginning the investigation proper. Familiarization of this sort can be quite useful since children often get used to an outsider fairly soon (see e.g., Wright 1960). This procedure obviously involves more time than many investigators are used to investing. Still, it should be stressed; too many studies in schools are quick affairs whose results suffer because of the strangeness of the whole exercise to the children, the ignorance of important contextual factors by the investigator, or both.[21]

In addition, children can be assured, directly or indirectly, that their co-opera-tion is appreciated, that their participation is valuable and that the investigator is really interested in what they are saying. Rather than trying to make the tapere-corder inconspicuous (an attempt which is rarely successful), the machine can be left in full view, and the child can be told that he will be able to hear himself after-wards. One generally wishes to reduce the formality of the situation while, at the same time, making it clear that, together, speaker and listener are engaged in a useful exercise in which communication is valued. To this end, it is better to give the child some simplified (but true) account of the purpose of the study, rather than to ask him to 'play a little game'.

Cutting across all these suggestions, however, is the important and intangible factor of the personality of the investigator. Can he or she get along easily with children? Labov (1972) has noted that there are 'personality differences among linguists which will inevitably lead to specialization' (111). For some, observing and recording speech samples (with children or adults) will always be difficult or strained, and may be better left to others.

3.5   Disadvantaged speech: therapists' and clinicians' views

So far I have said nothing directly about the role and interests of the speech clinician with regard to the disadvantaged child. As one might expect, views among remedial specialists have changed as the broader psychological and linguistic understanding of disadvantaged speech has grown. Of course, the compensatory education pro-grammes for disadvantaged children were very direct attempts at remediation. However, the children were rarely treated individually in these; more often, since the presumed language deficit was seen to be symptomatic of classes of children, relatively large-scale intervention was considered to be more appropriate.

---

[21] Several years ago I spent some months studying a bilingual education programme, coming to know virtually all of the children on a first-name basis. The value of the data obtained was significantly enhanced by the consequent increase in my understanding of the children and of the school context generally. While not proposing quite so long a period of involvement in all cases, I think that the more time spent with one's subjects the better.

Speech clinicians have, of course, been aware of the work of Bereiter and Engelman, Cazden, Blank, Labov and others, but as Shriner (1971) notes:

> The language handicaps of the disadvantaged child were not originally of primary concern for speech pathology and audiology, in part, because we (the profession) were told that other professional groups were adequately serving the needs of these children, and in part, because the problem of language among the economically disadvantaged is only now receiving full recognition. (1143)

The problem for the clinician, as for all those concerned with disadvantaged speech and language, has been to come to some conclusions regarding the so-called difference-deficit controversy. The same general trend which we have already observed in psychology and linguistics is, not surprisingly, reflected in the writings of speech clinicians. That is, there has been a gradual but steady move away from the view that disadvantaged speech is substandard and an increasing recognition that it is a valid, if nonstandard, speech variety.

Some of the standard works have not considered socioeconomically-related speech variation as a topic of unique concern. Morley (1957), for example, does not deal with the area.[22] Dickson (1974) only briefly notes the influence of 'environmental deprivation' upon language deficit. Anderson and Newby (1973), in a revision of a book first published in 1953, give minimal attention to the issue of disadvantaged speech, and where they do it is a rather curious mixture. They are aware of the work of Labov, and of the difference-deficit debate, and, perhaps not wishing to become embroiled in linguistic battles, state that it is 'unwise ... to offer any authoritative recommendations' (232). Elsewhere, however, they seem firmly within the environmental-deficit camp:

> Children from the upper strata of society are exposed to an environment that provides opportunities for richer and more varied experiences, both verbal and non-verbal, than are available to the children whose lives are more circumscribed, monotonous, or barren because of social and economic limitations. (74–75)

These authors also cite, without comment, work testifying to the greater occurrence of language and speech deficiencies among disadvantaged children than among other segments of society. Again, while seeming to acknowledge that different social backgrounds may produce different, but adequate, speech patterns, Anderson and Newby can state that 'culturally deprived' children may speak a 'degraded form of English that must be called simply substandard ... habits of long standing will need to be eradicated or severely modified' (214).

This volume is of interest, I think, because it demonstrates the existence of some sort of half-way position between deficit and difference views of disadvantaged speech. In this, the authors are not alone. Shriner (1971), for example, is also aware of the difference-deficit debate, yet still employs the term 'substandard speech', and notes that 'restricted language development may limit [a child's] intellectual potential' (1145). Even in later works, although the difference position is either directly or implicitly accepted, there is little information for the speech

---

[22] Nor is it treated in the second edition of the book (1967).

clinician on the issue in general (see, e.g., Bloom and Lahey 1978, Byrne and Sher-vanian 1977, Eisenson and Ogilvie 1977).

This may reflect, of course, the realization that, in terms of language disorders, there should be no reason to assume any greater frequency among disadvantaged children than among any other group. That is, once clinicians are aware that the appropriate norms of 'correctness' are not those of the middle class, but rather of the child's own speech community, then disadvantaged speech *per se* becomes somewhat of a non-issue for them (see, e.g., Yoder 1970). Thus the modern speech therapist might be inclined to agree with Dillard (1973) who states that

> the speech pathologist-correctionist, in the raw state, has singularly little to contribute to the problems of the 'disadvantaged'.   (268)

The danger, however, with current texts on speech disorders which do not deal explicitly with disadvantaged, nonstandard language, is that, in the absence of specific information to the contrary, the remedial specialist may well tend to see disadvantaged speech as deficient rather than different simply because, like everyone else, he or she may find it difficult to shake off the comfortable influence of middle-class norms. Also, Dillard (above) speaks of the clinician in the 'raw state' (whatever that may be) as having little to contribute to the disadvantaged speaker; could it be that, in some other state, the clinician *does* have a role to play? Many think so and, for that reason, relevant linguistic information should be provided to the profession. It may be worthwhile, therefore, to review briefly here the debate over disadvantaged speech in the remediation profession.

Some of the earliest views were those expressed by Raph (1965, 1967) and Grotberg (1965); the clinician is advised of the deficient nature of the speech of the disadvantaged child and, in fact, a stance similar to that of Bereiter and Engelmann (1966; see chapter 2) is adopted. Thus, Raph (1967) describes the child's speech as retarded, resembling the language of 'privileged' children of a younger age. The link between language and intellectual functioning is also asserted; Raph refers to the disadvantaged as lacking the 'language facility required to do independent thinking and problem-solving' (1967, 212).

These views were not to stand unchallenged for long, however, since linguistically-oriented clinicians were quick to reply (e.g. Baratz 1968a, Weber 1968); in fact, from the end of the 1960s it becomes increasingly difficult to find clinicians advocating a deficit viewpoint. This presumably reflects the gradual dissemination and acceptance of the work done by linguists espousing the difference view (see 3.2 and 3.3). In addition, however, experimental studies conducted specifically by or for remediation specialists reinforced the acceptance of the dialectal validity of disadvantaged language (e.g. the work on morphology by Ramer and Rees 1973, Shriner and Miner 1968).

Accompanying this revised viewpoint came the realization that clinical work with disadvantaged speakers could hardly be equated with that dealing with speech disorders in the rest of the population. Before any remedial action is taken, it is clear that the clinician must be able to sort out dialect differences from real speech and language defects (see Seymour and Seymour 1977). This in turn requires that

the therapist be familiar with the nonstandard forms used by disadvantaged children and with the appropriate models with regard to which any therapy should
be conducted (see also Cazden 1971, Monsees and Berman 1968). Adler (1971),
for example, sees the task of the speech therapist in these terms; in addition he
feels that, apart from working on speech defects that truly *are* defects (given the
norms of the nonstandard speech community), the role of the clinician also includes
that of teacher. Thus, while acknowledging the validity of the difference position,
there is also a need to instruct children, for practical purposes, in SE (see also
Baratz 1968b, Yoder 1970). Overall, the clinician must be familiar with the given
nonstandard dialect so as to sort out dialect variations from true defects; then
the latter can be treated and the former expanded upon.

Many clinicians who accept the difference viewpoint thus see a need for training
in SE beginning at a preschool level. This type of intervention is not, however,
universally accepted. Some, for example, feel that SE additions to the child's repertoire should be the almost incidental result of the regular school programme, once
informed and well-trained teachers are procured. Any conspicuous intervention,
preschool or otherwise, is considered at least inappropriate and at worst potentially
damaging to the child. Nevertheless, a number of clinicians advocate formal SE
instruction for the disadvantaged child (see, e.g., Adler 1971, Cazden, 1968b, Grady
1973). Here we may simply recognize that a concern for the expansion of children's
linguistic repertoires is valid and appropriate; I shall reserve until later any discussion as to the best ways of achieving this end (see chapter 5).

Yoder (1970) has provided a useful overview of the clinical approach to disadvantaged speech. He notes, for example, that there is no evidence that speech
or hearing difficulties are any more pronounced in disadvantaged populations than
elsewhere. In fact, for one speech disability—stuttering—there is some suggestion
that children of higher socioeconomic status actually suffer *more*. Here Yoder cites
the work of Morgenstern (1956) who found, in Scotland, that children of semi-
skilled parents stuttered more than those of unskilled labourers. This was related
to greater parental aspirations for children in the former group, which results in
more pressure on the children to do well at school which, in turn, is seen to lead
to greater frequency of stuttering.

Yoder also feels that much of the clinician's work with the disadvantaged lies
in instruction rather than remediation. In this connection, he advocates the recruit-
ment, as speech specialists, of minority group members who would, of course,
be familiar with given nonstandard dialects and hence be more sensitive to the
distinctions between dialect difference and speech defect. Finally, Yoder comments
on the unfair use of tests, standardized on the middle class, to assess the performance of disadvantaged children (see chapters 1 and 2 above). Nevertheless, he
points out that such biased tests can be useful in comparing disadvantaged speech
on some desired feature with that of middle-class norms (see section 3.4 above).
Such tests

could be used at various stages of instruction as an index of progress in developing the
additional language or dialect system. Ironically, the more culturally biased such tests

are, the more benefit they will be in this case, so long as they are used as a basis for describing differences instead of deficits.   (411–12)

Further, a paper by Seymour and Seymour (1977) has presented for clinicians a review of dialects in general, and BEV in particular, from a linguistic difference point of view. Upon this basis the authors erect a 'therapeutic model for communicative disorders' which requires the differentiation of dialect difference from 'pathological deviation'. Since the disadvantaged child (in this case, the BEV speaker) is seen to possess considerable facility in both BEV *and* SE (see section 3.3), Seymour and Seymour feel that the use of nonstandard dialect is under the influence of social and educational factors, and is not a clinical concern. They acknowledge that nonstandard speech may involve *social* penalties, but this issue is a longstanding one, unlikely to be changed rapidly and, in any event, a nonclinical matter. Thus, this very recent article completes the picture, as it were, of clinicians' views of disadvantaged speech. From an initial deficit position, the profession is now more likely to see such speech as a matter not of linguistic concern but, rather, of social or sociolinguistic interest. It is at this point I shall take up the discussion again in chapter 4.

3.6   Disadvantaged speech: an overview and a starting-point

It is appropriate, before proceeding further, to review briefly what has been discussed with regard to disadvantaged language and speech. Very generally, the position is that any deficit view of linguistic behaviour is incorrect—no language, or language variety, has been shown to be more accurate, logical or capable of expression than another. Rather, it should be realized that different language communities develop speech patterns that differ in their modes of expression, vocabulary and pronunciation. There is also the possibility that different groups assign different functions to language; this is what Bernstein apparently feels to be the import of his work, and it is an issue studied by Halliday.

It is quite illegitimate, however, to claim that any such differences somehow alter or constrain basic intellectual or cognitive functioning. It is true that disadvantaged speech may prove a social liability—a matter to which I turn in the next chapter—but it is evidently not a cognitive disability, nor a linguistic problem *per se*. Thus one should have no hesitation in condemning the notion of 'substandard' speech, although, given the power of middle-class norms, we may refer to social or regional varieties as 'nonstandard'. This latter adjective should not be seen as pejorative; it simply acknowledges certain power and status relationships which we all know to exist in society.

For a concise summary of some of the important issues surrounding disadvantaged speech, a paper by Houston (1970) is helpful. She outlines five major contentions about such speech and, drawing upon work which has been discussed above, effectively refutes them. They are:

the language of the disadvantaged child is deficient;
the disadvantaged child does not use words properly;

the language of the disadvantaged child does not provide him with an adequate basis for thinking;

to the disadvantaged child, language is dispensable; such children prefer to communicate nonverbally;

the language of the disadvantaged child, since it represents his culture and environment, should be left alone and not changed in any way.

The first four of these are clearly points within the general deficit view of disadvantaged speech; from evidence reviewed here we can, as does Houston, reject them. The last one, however, is the extreme pole of the other, different-language, side of the argument, and it constitutes one of the major issues to be faced by difference theorists.

This is the reason behind the title of this brief section; having rejected a deficit interpretation, one is still left with the question of what, if anything, is to be done about disadvantaged speech. Linguistic validity is one thing, social or educational approval quite another. Thus, having reviewed linguistic evidence bearing upon disadvantaged speech, we may now consider the issue implied in the opening paragraph of the preface to this book—the social or sociolinguistic nature of the difficulties attendant upon the use of nonstandard speech varieties. In fact, the cynical reader might suggest that all the material covered up to now has been a preamble and, in a sense, this is quite correct. But preambles sometimes require extended treatment; and in this case I feel that it would have been most undesirable to have neglected consideration of certain views of disadvantage and disadvantaged speech, even if they were presented so as to be rejected.

The social and educational problems of nonstandard speakers and, especially, the role of the school in any attempted alteration or expansion of their linguistic repertoire are now the issues to which we must turn. To end here, we can consider the following statements by Gumperz and Hernandez-Chavez (1972) who note both the *linguistic* validity of different speech varieties, and the *nonlinguistic* problems often associated with them. Thus:

> There is overwhelming evidence to show that when both middle-class and non-middle-class children, no matter what their native language, dialect or ethnic background, come to school at the age of five or six, they have control of a fully formed grammatical system.   (84)[23]

But also:

> Our data suggest that urban language differences ... do have a significant influence on a teacher's expectation, and hence on the learning environment.   (105)

[23] Perhaps 'a well-formed grammatical system' would be a more accurate statement here.

4

Nonstandard speech: a social issue

'One grievous failing of Elizabeth's was her occasional pretty and picturesque use of dialect words—those terrible marks of the beast to the truly genteel.'   Thomas Hardy

'It is impossible for an Englishman to open his mouth, without making some other Englishman despise him.'   G. B. Shaw

The working assumption from here on is that disadvantaged speech is not deficient speech. Nevertheless, arrival at this position hardly eradicates the difficulties encountered by disadvantaged speakers. Rather, we can now clearly view such difficulties as social in nature instead of reflections of intrinsic linguistic flaws. As I pointed out in the preface to this book, social problems are perhaps more tenacious than others, since they involve attitudes and values and may be quite resistant to change, even in the face of strong opposing evidence. We should not expect, for example, that the linguistic data bearing on disadvantaged speech will rapidly alter social attitudes towards it.

It is necessary, therefore, to consider at this point some aspects of language varieties and attitudes and values connected with them. To understand the difficulties faced by disadvantaged speakers, we should have some awareness of the more general sociolinguistic themes which are important; this will be the emphasis of this chapter. Later I shall turn specifically to the educational implications of disadvantaged speech.

4.1   Dialect, accent and style

As has been briefly noted before, the term 'dialect' refers to a language variety[1] which differs from others in certain aspects of vocabulary, grammar and pronunciation. Dialects (of a given language) are often distinguished from separate languages on the basis that they are, unlike the latter, mutually intelligible. This criterion is not without its difficulties (cf. Giles and Powesland 1975, Trudgill 1974a) and, indeed, many people have difficulty comprehending certain dialects of their own language. The distinction between language and dialect, however, does not pose much of a problem in the present context.

[1] Following Trudgill (1975), I shall use 'variety' from here on to refer to language differences in circumstances in which the more specific terms—'dialect', 'accent' or 'style'—are not appropriate.

Given the linguistic and psychological evidence already discussed, we can see that the disadvantaged speech once rejected as illogical and substandard is, simply, an example of dialect variation. Such speech is now often referred to as 'nonstandard' dialect. This term does not (or should not) carry any derogatory linguistic implications, but it does indicate that there is some dialect which is seen as 'standard'. What *is* Standard English (SE) and who uses it?

SE may be simply considered as that dialect most often spoken by educated members of society; it is the form usually employed in writing, and is generally used by the media (indeed, in the United States, the term 'Network English' is commonly used; cf. Ferguson 1974, Giles and Powesland 1975). Most importantly for disadvantaged children, SE is the form of the language used and promoted in schools. Linguistically, there is nothing which accords SE special status; nevertheless, because of its widespread social acceptance it is, in relation to other dialects, *primus inter pares*.

The power of a standard variety derives from historical accident and convention. Parisian French, for example, is usually taken as the standard dialect of that language yet, if history had decreed that some other centre were to be the capital of France, then presumably *its* linguistic variety would now be the accepted standard. Similarly, if York rather than London had been the centre for the royal court, then the BBC newsreaders of today might sound quite different. Dittmar (1976) rather pedantically puts it as follows:

> The *Standard* is that speech variety of a language community which is legitimized as the obligatory norm for social intercourse on the strength of the interests of dominant forces in that society.   (8)

While it is not exactly true that SE is obligatory for all people at all times, the association between power, or status, or education, and a standard dialect is unquestionable.[2] The relationship between some accepted form of social status and the dialect spoken by those holding such status is thus the principal determining factor involved in the creation of a standard. Once a standard exists, or while it is in the process of forming, zealous efforts are often made to guard it from outside influence and 'impurity'. Although, linguistically, these efforts are wrong-headed and rather ludicrous, inasmuch as they treat language as a static rather than a dynamic entity, they are hardly surprising. France, Italy, Spain and other countries have, or had, prestigious academies for the protection of language (cf. Bowen 1970, McDavid 1970).

As we have already seen, it is an all-too-easy step to equate high social status with high linguistic status. From such an equation flow the notions of linguistic deficit and substandard speech which linguists have had to work hard to counter. It is worth pointing out, again, that a standard variety is simply one dialect among others.

'Accent' is a term more restricted than dialect, inasmuch as it denotes

---

[2] Not all languages have standard forms. For a discussion of some aspects of the processes by which standard varieties emerge, see Fishman (1972).

pronunciation variation only. Speakers sharing the same dialect may differ markedly in their pronunciation without employing different lexical or grammatical forms. In practice of course, dialect and accent variations are often both present in the repertoire of any given speaker. The reader will recall here the discussion of BEV speakers in the United States who are, as they grow older, increasingly able to switch to SE. Just as we speak of persons being bilingual, so we should be aware that many are bidialectal. Also, it is not difficult to see that a speaker of some regional dialect of English may also frequently use SE, in which case only accent difference will point to his geographical origins; this phenomenon is commonplace in Britain (see Trudgill 1975). There is, in addition, the use by some of a *non*-regional accent, RP (received pronunciation)—i.e. 'BBC English' or 'the Queen's English'. RP-accented speakers thus use SE without betraying their regional origins, and such usage is common among broadcasters, public school pupils and the aristocracy (to mention only some of the more obvious examples). Trudgill (1975) summarizes some aspects of the social status associations attaching to dialect and accent variation in Britain, thus:

> At the 'bottom' of the social scale we can find a wide range of geographical dialects and accents. ... At the other end of the scale we find standard English, with its small regional variations, together with either RP ... or moderately regional accents, depending on how near the 'top' the speaker is. (21)

In this confusion of speech varieties which lead to the assignment of differing amounts of social prestige, it is not difficult to see where the disadvantaged speaker falls.

A further element of language variation is that of *style*. This term (in the sociolinguistic context) refers to variations, within a dialect, which reflect the social context within which speech occurs. Most often, styles alter in terms of the formality or informality of the situation, which may govern the choice of lexical items. For example, a speaker of SE might, on one occasion, say

I am extremely tired

In another setting, the same speaker might phrase the same thought as

I'm bloody knackered

These variations reflect perceptions of what is appropriate in different situations, although both are SE. Even small changes in style can alter quite remarkably the tone of a statement. Replace 'tired' with 'fatigued' in the first example above, and the sentence takes on a rather pedantic air (see Trudgill 1975).

One of the best-known treatments of style in English usage is that of Joos (1967). He postulated five styles which range from the extremely informal (intimate) to the highly formal (frozen). Between these lie casual, consultative and formal styles. Joos discusses the attributes of each and the contexts in which each tends to be elicited. For present purposes it is sufficient to note that most, if not all, speakers have a variety of linguistic possibilities open to them. Whether speakers select from their repertoire in ways which seem appropriate to others is, of course, another matter.

It has been suggested that Bernstein's elaborated and restricted codes may be simply style differences (cf. Trudgill 1975). The codes are certainly not connected directly with dialect or accent, as some have supposed; Bernstein himself is quite explicit on this point (1973a). We have already noted some evidence (e.g. Robinson 1965) for the use of elaborated code in working-class speech, evidence which suggests the inaccuracy of equating restricted code with nonstandard dialect. Kochman (1969) also points out that the elaborated code can occur in nonstandard dialects, just as the restricted code may be employed in the standard (see also Muehl and Muehl 1976). Trudgill (1975) again summarizes the matter rather neatly, with two apposite examples; he notes that a sentence like

The blokes what was crossing the road got knocked down by a car

is nonstandard and in an informal style, but nevertheless is 'elaborated' inasmuch as it contains a subordinate clause and a passive verb. On the other hand, a sentence such as

The gentlemen were crossing the road and a car knocked them down

is standard dialect with more formal vocabulary yet, lacking the grammatical complexity of the first statement, is not an example of 'elaborated' code.

The common confusion between restricted code and nonstandard dialect has doubtless created difficulties for disadvantaged children; as we have noted before, much of this confusion can be attributed to Bernstein's own early and ambiguous writing. It is now clear however that code differences, whether they are examples of style variation or whether they represent some additional theoretical refinement, are not dialect differences. If one substitutes the term 'styles' for 'registers', the following quotation from Delahunty (1977) seems useful:

> The relationship between registers and codes is somewhat problematical and there would seem to be some redundancy in the concepts if they are taken together. In general it is likely that registers are a set within the elaborated codes of a language or dialect. (140)

Delahunty, apparently, would place code between dialect and style in the language-variety hierarchy. Houston (1970), who also discusses the term 'register' (she broadens it somewhat to include a range of styles) has noted what she terms the 'school register' as comprising, for disadvantaged children, many of the grammatical features suggested by Bernstein's restricted code. Viewed in this way, the problems faced by disadvantaged children may not require the introduction of codes into the discussion at all; they may, rather, be difficulties in the selection of context-appropriate styles or, indeed, difficulties arising from the simple fact that the language styles of one group may not correspond to those of another. There is no doubt, however, that whether dialect, accent or style is under discussion, the forms used by certain groups are viewed unfavourably, and it is this negative social evaluation which causes the greatest problems.

4.2 Attitudes towards language varieties

As the two quotations at the head of this chapter indicate, social prejudices directed towards language varieties are longstanding. Linguistic data notwithstanding, there is little reason to suppose that such prejudices will rapidly disappear, since views of language often correspond to views of the social status of language users; in this sense, the language, dialect or accent employed provides a simple label which evokes a social stereotype which goes far beyond language itself.

We can begin here by observing that even dictionary definitions of dialect and accent help to sustain the view that nonstandard language is less correct language. The Oxford English Dictionary, for example, notes that dialect may be considered as

> one of the subordinate forms or varieties of a language arising from local peculiarities of vocabulary, pronunciation, and idiom.

This definition is implicitly held by those for whom the term 'dialect' conjures up an image of some rustic, regional speech pattern; for such people, SE is not a dialect at all, but the correct form from which all others diverge. On 'accent', the OED is not much better; it is, we find, a mode of utterance which

> consists mainly in a prevailing quality of tone, or in a peculiar alteration of pitch, but may include mispronunciation of vowels or consonants, misplacing of stress, and misinflection of a sentence.

Again, this does not correspond well with the value-free judgements of linguists. It does, however, reflect many popular conceptions of what an accent is, and who has one. It is still not difficult to find people who deny that they speak with any accent at all.[3]

In Britain, the popular prestige of the RP accent continues unabated. Wyld (1934) had noted that any unbiased listener would view it as the most pleasant variety, and the one best suited for public discourse. Atkinson (1975) demonstrates the prestige of RP outside Britain—citing a German student of English who apologized for speaking with an American accent. And, in a recent article in *The Sunday Times*, we find that Professor Higgins lives on in the form of a speech instructor dedicated to helping people eradicate unwanted (i.e. non-prestigious) accents (Emerson 1978). The prestige of RP is simply the complement to the lack of prestige in which other, nonstandard accents and dialects are held. Although having no particular *linguistic* superiority, could the high-prestige RP constitute a speech form which is somehow more *aesthetically* pleasing? Giles *et al.* (1975) and Giles *et al.* (1974) provide some evidence that such aesthetic judgements do *not* provide the basis for the high status and prestige accorded to accents such as RP.

---

[3] Reference to the OED definitions cited here was prompted by Delahunty (1977).

Their studies begin by formulating two possible hypotheses concerning the supposed aesthetic qualities of accent. The 'inherent value' hypothesis holds that there *is* something intrinsic to certain accents which makes them more pleasant and mellifluous than others. This is apparently the position held by many, and was the view of Wyld (1934; see above). On the other hand, Giles *et al.* (1975) also postulate an 'imposed norm' hypothesis which is more respectable in terms of the linguistic evidence already considered. Here, the high status of certain accents, and their accepted pleasantness are seen merely as reflections of the status of their speakers. Giles and his colleagues tested these hypotheses by having voices listened to by judges who were unfamiliar with the language varieties used. If listeners who were thus unaware of the status connotations of certain varieties still found some to be more pleasant than others, then the 'inherent value' hypothesis would receive some support.

In fact, however, the two studies demonstrated that listeners did *not* make the distinctions between language varieties which would have supported the 'inherent value' postulation. In Giles *et al.* 1975, 35 Welsh adults listened to European French, educated Canadian French and working-class Canadian French voice samples. Asked to rate the pleasantness and prestige of the voices on nine-point scales the judges, who were almost entirely ignorant of French, did not single out any one of the varieties. In Quebec, however, earlier studies had shown a clear preference among French speakers for European French accents in aesthetic terms. The social connotations of certain styles, so apparent to those familiar with the context, were evidently not relevant to the judges in this study. The results suggest that there is nothing inherent in certain accents which makes them more pleasant than others; if one can remove the social stereotypes usually associated with accent (as was done here), aesthetic judgements appear not to discriminate among varieties.

In the second study, Giles *et al.* (1974) asked 46 British undergraduates who knew no Greek to evaluate the aesthetic quality of two Greek dialects, the Athenian and the Cretan. The former is the prestige standard form, while the latter is a nonstandard variant of low status. As in the first investigation, no significant differences between the two dialects were found. In fact the small, non-significant differences which did occur revealed a tendency for the British judges to rate the Cretan variety as more pleasant and prestigious than the Athenian.

These studies suggest that judgements of accent quality and prestige will not discriminate against nonstandard variants if judges are unaware of the social connotations they carry. The validation of the 'imposed norm' hypothesis indicates the essentially arbitrary (but powerful) nature of social evaluations of speech *qua* speech. The value of the investigations for studies of the speech of the disadvantaged is obvious; not only are nonstandard varieties not *linguistically* inferior in any way, but the *social* evaluations of them say nothing of any inherent quality of the speech itself. We are left with the importance of social stereotypes which certain speech styles evoke for those able to associate (erroneously or not) style with speaker status. As Trudgill (1975) notes, it may be unreasonable to suppose that we will stop finding some dialects or accents more pleasant than others, but we should at least realize that our views on the matter are simply ones of taste and convention.

Trudgill (1975) also provides another telling example of the arbitrary nature of accent judgements. In England, speakers of RP do not pronounce the post-vocalic 'r'—as in the words *cart* and *mar*. Thus, the absence of this feature is associated with high accent prestige. In New York, on the other hand, exactly the reverse holds.[4] The higher the social status of the speaker, the more likely he is to *use* postvocalic 'r'. The following (from Trudgill 1975) clearly shows the differing social connotations of pronouncing 'r' in New York and Reading. The figures represent percentages of possible postvocalic 'r' pronunciations actually used by speakers surveyed in the two locales.

| | *Percentage of postvocalic 'r' pronunciation* | |
	New York	Reading
Upper-middle-class speakers	32	0
Lower-middle-class speakers	20	28
Upper-working-class speakers	12	44
Lower-working-class speakers	10	49

Once again, we find confirmation for the view that accents, or features of accents, are associated with different degrees of social status, and it is this latter variable which, when identified through speech cues, leads to favourable or unfavourable reactions to speech. The fact that what is 'high' class in one society is 'low' class in another is but a neat example of the arbitrary nature of the whole evaluative process.

If we accept the power of social convention and social stereotype with regard to accent and dialect evaluation, then it will come as no surprise that, apart from the standard form, there may be considerable variation in the judgements made of other, nonstandard varieties. In considering this aspect of the topic, we shall approach more directly the issue of disadvantaged speech.

While many regional or class dialects are perceived unfavourably by standard dialect speakers, there does seem to exist more than a simple dichotomy between good (standard) and bad (nonstandard). Among the latter, Trudgill (1975) suggests that, in Britain, urban speech patterns (e.g. those of Birmingham, Glasgow and Liverpool) are generally seen as more unpleasant than are rural varieties (e.g. that of Devon). Once again, the explanation offered is in terms of the social connotations of certain accents or dialects; for many people rural areas have a certain charm absent in heavily urbanized, industrialized centres. Thus rural dialects, although not as prestigious as the standard, may be viewed more favourably than urban dialects which are generally tied more closely to class differences as well. Similarly, Wilkinson (1965) proposed a three-part hierarchy for English accent prestige. At the top is RP (and some foreign accents), next come various British regional accents and, at the bottom of the scale, the accents of urbanized areas.

[4] Further information about 'r'-pronunciation in New York will be found in Labov 1966, 1977a.

In these hierarchies, disadvantaged speakers, who employ nonstandard speech patterns, are most frequently found at the lower end of the scale.

4.3   The 'matched-guise' technique and accent/dialect evaluation

Many studies of reactions to accent or dialect have employed the 'matched-guise' technique developed by Lambert and his colleagues in Montreal (cf. Lambert 1967, Lambert *et al*. 1960). In this methodology, judges evaluate a tapered speaker's personality after hearing him read the same passage in each of two or more languages, dialects or accents. The fact that the speaker is, for all 'guises', the same person is not revealed to the judges (who typically do not guess this). Judges' ratings, along various dimensions, are then considered to be reflections of their stereotyped reactions to the language variety concerned, since potentially confounding variables (pitch, tone of voice, etc.) are of course constant across voices.

The matched-guise technique has been criticized, most importantly for its alleged artificiality (cf. Agheyisi and Fishman 1970, Lee 1971, Robinson 1972). That is, judges hear a series of disembodied voices all speaking the same words and are asked to rate the speakers on various personality scales. Do the judges, who generally comply with requests to assess speakers in this way, nevertheless feel that it is a pointless task? How would the judgements stand up in the light of more information about the speakers? Giles and Bourhis (1973) and Giles and Powesland (1975) have attempted to show that, despite these potential difficulties, the technique remains a useful one. If we are aware of its limitations and if overgeneralization of results obtained is resisted then, in fact, the matched-guise technique *does* appear useful. Employed in many different contexts, it seems to provide a modest addition to, rather than a distortion of, our understanding of speaker evaluation through speech.

Finally, it is worth recalling exactly what the matched-guise methodology aims to elicit; it is not the speech *per se* which is being evaluated, but rather the speaker. The speech sample serves as a convenient identifier, facilitating the evoking of a social stereotype. Thus, as Robinson (1972) suggests, speech itself is, in one sense, irrelevant—any status tag would do, including perhaps a simple written description of the speaker.[5] At the very least, however, the force of both popular prejudice and linguistic research indicates that, among cues to personality, speech is of some considerable importance.[6]

4.3.1   British studies

Early work in Britain using the matched-guise technique was conducted by Strongman and Woosley (1967) and Cheyne (1970) who investigated reactions to British regional accents. In the latter study, it was found that both Scottish and English

[5] Giles 1970, discussed below, *did* in fact use such labels as a supplement to the matched-guise procedure itself. The two approaches yielded quite similar sets of results.

[6] Useful overviews of the topic will be found in Giles and Powesland 1975 and, for North American investigations, in Gardner and Lambert 1972.

judges tended to view Scottish speakers as possessing less status than their English counterparts. Although the voices are not particularly well described by Cheyne, it appears as if more standard accents evoked greater prestige judgements than regional varieties. Giles (1970) employed 13 guises to study a variety of accents, including RP, Irish, German and West Indian. The judges, 177 secondary school children, tended to assess the speakers in terms similar to those suggested by Trudgill and Wilkinson (see section 4.2 above). That is, RP was accorded the highest degree of status, aesthetic quality and communicative content (this last variable being a measure of the perceived ease of verbal interaction with the speaker). In the middle ranks were regional accents (South Welsh, Somerset etc.); at or near the bottom of the scale were Cockney, Birmingham and Liverpool accents.

Further studies have revealed that reactions to accent may vary along more than simple status dimensions. Lambert (1967), for example, categorized the dimensions on which judges evaluate speech samples into three groups. Some dimensions (e.g. intelligence, industriousness) are seen to reflect a speaker's *competence*, some (e.g. helpfulness, trustworthiness) reflect *prsonal integrity*, and some (e.g. friendliness, sense of humour) underlie *social attractiveness*.

Investigating RP, South Welsh and Somerset accents along these lines, Giles (1971) found that although RP was evaluated most favourably in terms of *competence*, the other two accents elicited higher ratings on *integrity* and *attractiveness*. These ratings were obtained from judges who were themselves from South Wales or Somerset.[7] In a later study, Giles (1973b) presented taped arguments against capital punishment to a number of groups of South Welsh and Somerset school children. The recordings were in four different 'guises'—RP, South Welsh, Somerset and Birmingham—of decreasing prestige. The children's own views on capital punishment had been elicited earlier. In this study the dependent measures were the children's assessments of the *quality* of the arguments heard and their views on capital punishment after hearing the recordings. On the first measure, the higher the accent status, the more favourable was the quality of the argument perceived to be. In terms of attitude change, however, only the regional accents proved effective. Thus the rather intriguing result of the study is that a message in a high-status accent may be seen to be of higher quality *without* necessarily being more persuasive than one presented in an accent of lower prestige. To employ Lambert's terminology once again, it appears that *competence* need not always lead to greater influence; perhaps the results of Giles's experiment indicate that, for the children, the regionally-accented guise possessed more *integrity* and *attractiveness*, and it was these qualities which figured in persuasion (see also Giles and Powesland 1975).

Overall, these British studies of accent evaluation demonstrate that stereotyped judgements of personality are made on the basis of speech samples and that a hierarchy exists, at the bottom of which fall the urban accents typical of most disadvantaged speakers. As we have seen, although standard accents connote greater prestige, there is also some indication that regional accents may evoke a greater sense

---

[7] Similar distinctions among accent-guises, with regard to Lambert's three broad personality dimensions, were found by Edwards (1977c) in a study of Irish regional accents.

of integity or social attractiveness than the more standard forms (at least when the judges themselves are regionally-accented speakers).[8] A sense of in-group solidarity evoked by hearing lower-prestige accents may thus be an important factor in promoting trust and liking. Perhaps the speech patterns of disadvantaged speakers are seen as quaint, down-to-earth etc. The fact remains, however, that these patterns seem not to elicit an association with speaker competence (reflected by such features as intelligence, ambition and industriousness) which *is* evoked by standard accents or dialects. Since personal competence is a factor of some importance, one might consider that the disadvantaged speaker, with a regional or class speech style, comes out somewhat the worse in the exchange.

4.3.2   Canadian and American studies

In 1960, Lambert *et al.* studied the reactions of French- and English-speaking college students in Montreal towards French and English 'guises'.[9] On most of the 14 dimensions investigated (ambition, intelligence, sense of humour etc.), the English-speaking judges reacted more favourably to the English guises. Of greater interest were the ratings given by the French-speaking judges. Not only did they too evaluate the English guises more positively than the French versions, but they actually gave less favourable responses to the *French* guises than did the English-speaking judges. Lambert *et al.* interpreted these findings as evidence of a 'minority group reaction'. That is, the French-speaking students, perceiving themselves inferior in some ways to the English-speaking population, may have adopted the stereotyped values of this latter group and, in so doing, actually downgraded members of their own group more than did the English-speaking students. The findings are reminiscent of the British examples just discussed, inasmuch as we see that it is not only speakers from the high-status group who react favourably to their own speech patterns; rather, the stereotypes are also accepted by members of groups which are lower in prestige. This phenomenon is, I am sure, one which may easily be observed in many societies, especially perhaps those in which the original inhabitants have been colonized by other, more powerful peoples. But although the phenomenon (downgrading of one's own group and speech patterns) may not be a surprising one, it is still a disturbing one, and I shall return to it in some detail in the next section.

A further investigation of the views of French speakers in Quebec is that of d'Anglejan and Tucker (1973). Here the aim was to study not reactions towards French or English speakers, but rather towards different French dialects. A large sample (N = 243) of French-Canadian students, teachers and factory workers were first asked their opinions of Quebec, European and Parisian French. They were unwilling to accept the view that Quebec French is inferior to the other two, or that Parisian French is the 'best' form of the language. They also indicated that

---

[8] Powesland and Giles (1975) found as well, however, that listeners with standard accents (medical undergraduates) also rated RP speakers less favourably than Bristol-accented speakers in terms of sincerity.

[9] This study was, in fact, the first to use the matched-guise technique.

they felt speech style generally to be less important than other aspects of personality so far as academic or vocational success was concerned. Nevertheless, when presented with the taped voices of upper-class and lower-class French-Canadian speakers, and European French speakers (*not* via the matched-guise technique), subjects downgraded both Canadian styles on such dimensions as ambition, intelligence and degree of education; even in terms of likeability, the European speech style evoked a more favourable response. In this case, then, it seems that judges who speak a nonstandard variety not only demonstrate the (by now) familiar pattern of positive response to a more standard form in terms of *competence*, but also in at least one aspect of *social attractiveness*.

The Canadian studies are of some interest, as I have tried to show briefly above; in the United States, however, investigations of reactions towards accent and dialect variation bring us more directly to the problems of disadvantaged speakers. This is because of the close connection, in the United States, between ethnicity and disadvantage. Thus, studies of Mexican-Americans and blacks are, in effect, studies of disadvantaged speakers, and of prime concern here. It should not be forgotten, however, that it was work first begun in Canada that has inspired much of the American work and, indeed, much of the British as well. The matched-guise technique, even where it is not the actual method of investigation, has stimulated a great many interesting and valuable sociolinguistic enquiries.

In the United States, the Mexican-American population is relatively low in socioeconomic status, and the positive value attaching to ability in English (and, hence, greater opportunity in the surrounding society) indicates that, somewhat like the French Canadians, this American ethnic group may suffer a 'minority group reaction' (see Lambert *et al.* 1960, p. 84 above).[10]

Carranza and Ryan (1975) asked 64 Mexican-American and Anglo-American students (of Spanish) to judge speakers of English and Spanish along a number of personality dimensions. Sixteen speakers were presented on tape talking either about a domestic event (mother making breakfast) or a school event (teacher giving a history lesson), in English or Spanish (i.e. four examples of each of the four combinations of topic and language). In addition, the dimensions used by the judges were either reflections of prestige or status, or of what the authors termed 'solidarity' (i.e. friendliness, kindness, trustworthiness).

The results bear some similarity to findings already discussed from other contexts. Over all judges, English was viewed more favourably when the topic was school-related, Spanish when the topic related to the home. Further, English was reacted to more favourably on status-related traits *and* solidarity traits; in the latter case, however, the differences in judgements made between English and Spanish speakers were much reduced. Thus, again, we note a tendency for a low-prestige language variety to have somewhat more positive connotations in terms of integrity and attractiveness (represented in this study by the solidarity dimension) than on status *per se*, both for members of the low-prestige group *and* for more middle-class speakers. An additional refinement of this study was to demonstrate the importance of the topic of speech employed. In another study, Ryan and Carranza

[10] Further mention of Mexican Americans will be found in chapter 6.

(1975) found similar results when considering the evaluations of SE and Mexican-accented English by Mexican–Americans, blacks and Anglos (i.e. white English speakers). SE speakers were perceived as higher in status than were Mexican-accented speakers. Also, Arthur *et al.* (1974), using the matched-guise technique, studied the reactions of white Californian college students towards guises involving Mexican Americans speaking either SE or another dialect; the so-called 'Chicano' English was negatively stereotyped on a number of personality dimensions.

A further study (Ryan *et al.* 1977) found that the *degree* of accentedness influenced judges' evaluations of speakers. English-speaking college students in the United States, rating Spanish-English bilinguals reading an English passage, indicated that favourability of impressions decreased as degree of accentedness increased. Thus, the negative stereotype associated with this variety, at least, of nonstandard speech appears to strengthen with the amount of nonstandardness.

Turning to studies involving black speakers in the United States, we can consider first the work of Tucker and Lambert (1969). Presenting a number of different American English dialect varieties to three groups of college students—northern white, southern white and southern black—it was found that all groups evaluated the 'Network' speakers most favourably (Network English being roughly the American equivalent of British SE). Other regional dialects were evaluated differently by the judges. A recent study by Irwin (1977) points generally to the greater status accorded white speakers in relation to black speakers. The voices of 25 black and 25 white college students were evaluated by judges, almost all of whom were white. Not only did the judges correctly identify the race of the speakers more than 90 per cent of the time, but also, in terms of voice quality, fluency and apparent confidence, the black speakers were viewed less favourably than their white counterparts.

These studies, and others, confirm what is popularly well known: speech patterns of regional speakers, ethnic group members and lower-class populations (often all one and the same) elicit negative evaluations, at least in terms of status or prestige, from listeners—and this effect seems to apply whether or not the listeners are standard speakers themselves.[11]

Several writers have pointed out the need for repeated investigations, via speech studies, of the stereotypes associated with certain groups of speakers. This is because social stereotypes may well change as groups re-evaluate themselves and the society surrounding them. Thus, ethnic groups who are increasingly proud of their distinctiveness may accentuate differences between themselves and others, may reject aspects of mainstream society which formerly seemed alluring, and may exercise increasing amounts of political and economic sophistication. As a function of all this, reactions to speech may well change too. The reader will recall that the study by d'Anglejan and Tucker (1973), although it confirmed the high perceived status of standard speech, nevertheless did show French Canadians to be unhappy, at one level, with comparative status labels among dialects. In a study

---

[11] The studies on accent and dialect discussed here are but a small selection of the many available; I have naturally chosen those which seemed most appropriate for present purposes. For those interested in the larger topic of speech style and social evaluation *per se*, see Giles and Powesland 1975.

of French speakers in Maine, Lambert *et al.* (1975) found that reactions to a number of French and English dialects revealed generally less downgrading of local speech patterns than might have been expected previously. Thus it may well be that the resurgence of interest in ethnicity and 'roots' in the United States has made its mark in perceptions of speech. In Canada, the recent election of the Parti Québécois has meant much realignment of attitudes by and about French Canadians, and this too will doubtless have its effects in speech evaluation. Blacks in the United States have also, of course, experienced a revitalization of pride which will presumably change, to some degree at least, their perceptions of their own speech patterns. Finally, Bourhis *et al.* (1973) provide some indication that, in Wales, bilingual (Welsh–English) speakers may now, in this age of interest in devolution, be seen more favourably than RP-accented speakers.

The point that language attitudes can and do change in the light of altered social circumstances is interesting, though not particularly surprising. What we should not forget, however, is that such changes may occur for group members vis-à-vis their own dialect without necessarily occurring among members of the larger society—the perceived status of nonstandard dialects may be quite slow to change among standard speakers. Thus, the negative status connotations may, for many important situations, remain unchanged. Also, changes in ethnic-group feeling may only occur for large and (potentially) politically important groups. There may not be such changes in attitude among members of less well-organized or more marginal disadvantaged populations. Thus, for example, Flores and Hopper (1975) found slight preferences for the speech styles of Mexican Americans who referred to themselves as Chicanos; the fact that the judges were Mexican-American themselves, and that the term 'Chicano' is associated with pride in culture and language may indicate, however, that such preferences are fairly restricted in scope (on this topic see also Giles *et al.* 1977, Ryan and Carranza 1977). In short, I think we would be wrong, or at least premature, to assume that changes in the perceived prestige of nonstandard and disadvantaged speech styles are currently lessening to a considerable degree the social difficulties of their speakers, especially in situations of contact with middle-class or standard speakers.

4.4   Nonstandard English speakers' views of their own speech

In what has just been discussed, I have noted the general tendency for nonstandard speakers to accept the larger, and negative, stereotypes of their speech styles. The feeling that one's own speech is not 'good' is a common phenomenon, for the reasons of status and prestige already mentioned. Yet it is a disturbing one, especially when one considers how easily the process may be exacerbated by those who might be expected to know better (teachers, for example: see chapter 5). We might well agree with Halliday (1968) who notes that

> A speaker who is made ashamed of his own language habits suffers a basic injury as a human being; to make anyone, especially a child, feel so ashamed is as indefensible as to make him feel ashamed of the colour of his skin. (165)

Thus, although we are aware that in many societies negative views of certain styles exist and will probably continue to do so, we should try to combat the more damaging aspects of this phenomenon; these are likely to reside in encounters in which the lack of language status is brought home *personally*, especially to an individual at an early age. Again, therefore, we can note the general importance of the home/ school interface, and the need to produce and encourage teachers who will not contribute to the process of negative stereotyping.

In 1976, BBC Television broadcast a very interesting series of six half-hour programmes entitled 'Word of Mouth' (Bragg and Ellis, 1976). The series considered a number of British accents and dialects (those of Glasgow, Edinburgh, London and Liverpool among them) with their historical and social associations. In the course of this, many individual speakers were presented; some of their comments were directly relevant to the issue of perceived prestige.

For example, two Cockney families, resettled in a suburban area of Essex, provided personal views of the Cockney speech style. They noted that many regarded it as 'common' and that it sounded 'funny' to those who speak 'properly'. Reference was also made to the perceived link between language and occupational chances (see section 4.6 below) One speaker remarked of another, 'You won't end up on the Board of Directors with a voice like that.' Overall, it was quite apparent that not only were these speakers aware of the *general* stereotypes associated with Cockney English, but also that they had personal and direct experience of such views.

The reliable theatrical device, for production of a comic effect, of having a duchess speak with a Cockney accent has its more mundane counterparts as well. Indeed, the perceived incongruity which produces comedy in such instances would hardly be effective without an audience for whom the rich social connotations were deeply ingrained. Given that people are aware of negative stereotypes of their own speech styles and, indeed, that they themselves have accepted them in many cases, we might ask why low-status speech varieties continue to exist. After all, it would seem that realization of the potential limitations, in practical terms, of some varieties might lead to their eradication.[12] It can hardly be alleged, either, that nonstandard speakers are without adequate models for language alteration; nowadays, more than ever before, the pervasive influence of the various public media means that virtually all have at least passive access to standard forms. Nevertheless, the levelling of local speech styles predicted by some as the inevitable consequence of the ubiquitous media seems not to have occurred.

I have already mentioned briefly that revitalized pride in one's culture can lead to a new pride in speech styles—aspects of the American black and Chicano movements are examples here. Carranza and Ryan (1975) have referred to the 'solidarity' function of language in this connection: a group's language, though lacking general social prestige, nevertheless may act as a powerful bonding agent which provides a sense of identity. Ryan (1979) elaborates on the theme of the persistence of low-

[12] One often notes this process, of course, at an individual level—the successful film star who adopts a standard accent is a good example. Even here, however, we often find that the original style is not rejected completely, and may be reverted to when the individual returns 'home'.

prestige varieties in a paper devoted to the question. Again, she stresses *solidarity*, drawing examples from earlier work with Mexican Americans. However, as I have noted above, the sort of solidarity discussed by Ryan seems to be a recent and perhaps restricted phenomenon in which earlier self-denigration has now given way to positive admiration and allegiance to the group dialect. Yet we also see a disinclination to alter speech styles on the parts of groups (like the Cockneys mentioned above) which have not experienced any sudden upsurge in group pride, and who continue to adhere to the larger society's unfavourable stereotypes of their speech patterns. Can we put this down to a more generally liberal attitude towards speech variants *per se* on the part of current society? It is true that views are not as rigid as they once were; nevertheless, they still exist with some force, as the studies of the preceding section show. Perhaps there is a bit more to this question.

The solidarity, or group-bonding, function associated with a common language style, even though it be nonstandard, is powerful and general even, I believe, among populations not particularly noted for a highly visible group pride. Group identity is a known quantity, and in that sense is safe; an attempt to alter one's speech style, on the other hand, may be seen as a risky undertaking involving the assumption of some new role. Failure may lead to a sense of marginality—a sense of not being a full member of *any* social group. Thus, nonstandard speakers may be trapped. In addition, there are more concrete hazards related to any attempt to change styles.

A Mexican American who abandons Spanish for the socioeconomic rewards of English may, according to Carranza and Ryan (1975) be seen by his friends as a *vendido*—a 'sell-out', a defector to the other side. These authors also discuss the dilemma of the Mexican American who, not wishing to abandon Spanish, is caught between the desire to maintain the original culture, language and identity, and the practical need to learn English to advance in mainstream American society. This is not quite analogous to the problems faced by the nonstandard English speaker, but there are similarities. A Cockney grandmother, in the BBC series mentioned above, remarked that if her grandchild were to talk with a 'la-di-da' accent, his mates would label him 'a queer' (Bragg and Ellis 1976).[13] A related point was made in another programme of the series—the sense many nonstandard English speakers have that an RP accent may be 'put on'. This association between a 'posh' accent and a speaker who may be a social climber was doubtless an influence upon the findings discussed previously—i.e. that RP speakers were not always seen as favourably as regionally-accented speakers in terms of personal integrity and social attractiveness. And, over and above all these factors, we must of course bear in mind that, just as standard language varieties convey culture and tradition, so too do nonstandard forms. It would be entirely contrary to the arguments of the previous chapter and, indeed, to the tone of the book as a whole, to neglect

[13] One is reminded here of Orwell's observation in his essay 'England your England' (1964; originally 1941) that 'nearly every Englishman of working-class origin considers it effeminate to pronounce foreign words correctly' (74). Possibly there is some analogy between foreign words and SE for nonstandard speakers.

this intangible, yet powerful, value which attaches to all natural languages and language varieties.[14]

Another factor which operates to deter nonstandard English speakers from attempting to alter their speech styles is that, for some groups, it is seen as a rather pointless exercise. Those who are distinct from Standard English speakers on dimensions other than language alone will particularly subscribe to this view. Recalling that speech prestige derives from such sources as political and economic power, Kochman (1976) points to the primary importance of the social views which lie behind reactions to speech *per se*. Thus, insofar as one's reactions to black English are really reflections of attitudes towards blacks themselves, the language is secondary. The implication, of course, is that for a black person, the learning and using of SE may not necessarily alter his life very much. On the other hand, there are many people (mainly white people) in comfortable circumstances who do not speak SE; Kochman (1976) suggests that nonstandard speech is but a handy label to be used when required—for example, as a rationale for refusing a job to someone. As Wiggins (1976) notes, the social difficulties faced by blacks occur largely because they are black, not because they do not use SE (see also Covington 1976, Taylor 1971; see also chapter 6). Similar remarks were made by a black adolescent in the television series of Bragg and Ellis (1976). In short, while not underestimating the importance of speech and language, we should equally not overestimate it. The authors just cited would doubtless agree that, for groups visibly distinguishable from others, nonstandard speech is but one of the cues which can invoke a negative stereotype. If it were to lose this status—if blacks, for example, were regularly to use SE—then some other factor could well take its place.[15]

4.5 Nonstandard English, sex and covert prestige

An interesting phenomenon, which appears to operate both in Britain and in the United States, is the association between working-class and disadvantaged speech and 'toughness' or masculinity. Labov (1966) has commented, for example, that 'masculinity is unconsciously attributed to the unmodified native speech pattern of [New York City]' (501). This speech pattern is largely a nonstandard one; thus, Labov (1977d) notes that 'New York City, as a speech community, may be regarded as a sink of negative prestige' (136). In this connection, the association between nonstandard speech and masculinity is important, since it inhibits widespread abandonment of the low status form (see preceding section).

Labov (1977d) has described, for example, the large degree of 'linguistic insecurity' among the lower middle class of New York. Members of this group are highly sensitive to 'stigmatized' features of their speech patterns, are complimented if told they do not sound like New Yorkers and have strong views about 'correct'

[14] Labov (1966) has also commented on the counterbalancing influence of the cultural values of nonstandard English speakers, which act as a check upon attempts to abandon what he calls 'stigmatized' speech forms, especially among males (see also section 4.5 below).

[15] Some interesting preliminary work on reactions to blacks in Cardiff who are apparently indistinguishable, linguistically, from their white counterparts, will be found in Giles and Bourhis 1975.

speech. Consequently, they exhibit what Labov, in a somewhat extended use of the term, calls 'hypercorrection'—that is, when one analyses speech samples elicited in contexts ranging from informal to formal the speakers, who normally use low-prestige forms, increasingly use higher-status variants. In fact, in the most formal contexts, these respondents' usage of prestige forms actually *surpasses* that of the upper middle class; hence the reference to 'hypercorrection' (see also Labov 1977e). In addition, the lower-middle-class respondents, asked to indicate which variants they customarily used, tended to say that they used high-status forms; of course, this was not an accurate self-perception but it is revealing in terms of their sensitivity to linguistic status.

This apparent downgrading of personal speech styles and the presence of hypercorrection do not, however, lead to wholesale linguistic defection. It is here that the positive associations of masculinity with working-class speech constitute what has been termed 'covert prestige'; the term seems an apt one inasmuch as it describes an apparently powerful yet hidden phenomenon. Covert prestige is not restricted to members of the working class, but is shared to some degree by middle-class speakers as well although they may not admit to it or, indeed, may not be aware of it.[16]

In Britain, the work of Trudgill supplements and confirms that of Labov in the United States. The former (1974a) notes that the masculinity of working-class speech may derive from the tough or rugged nature of working-class life. Earlier, Trudgill (1972) presented some evidence in which the theme was developed. He asked respondents in Norwich to indicate the pronunciations they usually gave to words commonly having more than one pronunciation (e.g. the word *tune* may be pronounced either [tjʉ:n] or [tʉ:n]).

Although Norwich speakers, like their counterparts in New York City, tended overtly to downgrade their own speech patterns, Trudgill's findings were somewhat unlike those of Labov. The latter found that respondents tended to over-report the use of high-status pronunciations; Trudgill's results indicated that *males*, both working-class and middle-class, claimed to use *nonstandard* forms even when they did not customarily do so.[17] It seems clear that working-class, nonstandard forms have an attraction which cuts across class boundaries; it is this attraction which provides the covert prestige held by such forms.

If covert prestige is based upon associations between nonstandard speech and masculinity, then it appears to be a phenomenon of influence for males rather than females. Indeed, Labov (1966) notes that the positive masculine connotations of nonstandard speech, for men, do not seem to be balanced by similar positive values for women. Again, the work of Trudgill (1972) bears this out; female respondents

[16] A personal anecdote concerns an apparent manifestation of covert prestige. A middle-aged, upper-middle-class American university professor (male), being pressed by colleagues (also male) on an academic matter, exclaimed, 'Ain't no way I can do it!' It seemed as if, in this use of nonstandard forms, the usually SE-speaking professor wished to create an impression of directness and firmness, while at the same time keeping things at an informal, all-pals-together level.

[17] This variation in results from America and Britain may be due to a lesser degree of assimilation of middle-class speech norms among the British working class, or to Trudgill's revealing subanalyses of sex differences; probably both are important.

in Norwich, unlike their male counterparts, tended to claim more *standard* usage than they actually employed.

Generally, women are found to be more disposed towards standard, middle-class styles (Fischer 1958, Thorne and Henley 1975, Trudgill 1972, 1974a). Thus, they have been seen by some to produce 'politer' and more 'correct' speech than their male counterparts. The reasons for this lie, apparently, in the greater linguistic insecurity of women (see Labov 1966) which itself may reflect a greater degree of status-consciousness coupled with a greater lack of social definition for women (as opposed to men, who have their occupational definition to sustain them; see Trudgill 1972, 1974a).

A recent Dublin study by Edwards (1979a) attempted to consolidate and test some of the implications discussed above in a context involving prepubertal children. Although in young children physiological sex differences relating to speech production are not very marked, judges typically can guess their sex (on the basis of taperecorded speech samples) with a high degree of accuracy—usually of the order of 75–80 per cent (see Meditch 1975, Sachs 1975, Sachs *et al*. 1973, Weinberg and Bennett 1971).

It would seem that children's early appreciation of, and adherence to, social norms concerning men's and women's speech allows such accuracy in sex-identification. The purpose of my study was simply to see whether, bearing in mind what has already been discussed, differential accuracy in sex-identification would occur for disadvantaged and non-disadvantaged children. Voice samples of 20 working-class and 20 middle-class 10-year-old children were presented to 14 adult judges who were asked to identify the sex of each speaker. In addition, 5 other judges were asked to rate all the voices on four dimensions related to masculinity/ femininity.

To consider the latter point first, it was indeed the case that, over both sexes, the voices of working-class children were perceived as rougher and more masculine than those of their middle-class counterparts. Thus, the association between masculinity and working-class speech noted by Labov and Trudgill was confirmed. We could also note here that the study of European and French–Canadian speech by d'Anglejan and Tucker (1973), discussed earlier, revealed that the latter voices, although seen as generally low in prestige, were rated as tougher sounding.

The major finding of this study (Edwards 1979a), however, and one which further supports the notion of covert prestige, was that, although there was, as in previous work, a high overall degree of accuracy in sex-identification (about 84 per cent), the errors made were not randomly distributed. In fact, as the figure below shows, there was a significant interaction, in terms of errors made, between social class and the sex of the child. Among the working-class children, few boys were mistaken as girls, but errors made about girls were considerably greater. For middle-class children, the pattern is reversed; more errors are made with the boys than with the girls.

The explanation provided for these results (Edwards 1979a) may be given in brief form here. It appears as if the general masculinity of working-class speech caused girls to be misidentified as boys (by the middle-class judges). Middle-class

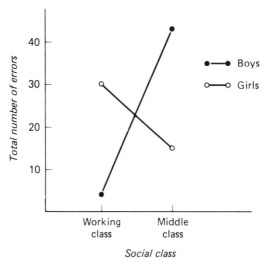

Social class

Interaction between social class and sex of child in terms of errors of sex identification

speech, relatively more feminine, allowed the operation of what we might term the 'boys sound like girls' principle—a notion which reflects the fact that, at puberty, it is the boys' speech which changes most markedly in assuming adult characteristics.[18] It appears, in general, that different social conventions operate for working-class and middle-class speech, that young children are aware of these, and that the children reflect this awareness, in their own speech patterns, by adherence to the appropriate norms. Differential accuracy in the identification of children's sex is thus seen, in this study, as a reflection of these social processes.

Overall, the relationship among nonstandard speech, covert prestige and masculinity seems an interesting and informative one. It partially explains the lack of a general abandonment of low-prestige varieties in circumstances where this might be possible, and it provides a useful approach to the larger (and increasingly studied) topic of sex differences in speech (cf. Thorne and Henley 1975). The informative value of covert prestige for an understanding of the social aspects of disadvantaged, nonstandard speech is fairly obvious; however, the topic also demonstrates how important the study of nonstandard speech can be for the wider issues of sociolinguistics.

4.6   Nonstandard English in the job market

In section 4.4, it was noted that speakers of nonstandard speech varieties may feel that they are at a disadvantage in terms of occupational choice and/or success. Here, I want to consider very briefly whether this is, in fact, a reasonable assessment. Moulton (1974) claims that it is: 'The lower-class speaker who, for whatever reason, is unable to learn middle-class English will generally be barred forever from holding a middle-class job' (4). Moulton goes on to note, aptly

---

[18] Further comments on the 'femininity' of middle-class speech will be found in Trudgill 1974a; see also chapter 5 below.

enough, that most of us would not wish to be the client of a doctor or lawyer who said, 'I seen him when he done it.' This is not, of course, simply to cast us all as unredeemed stereotypers since, after all, such a doctor or lawyer is a pretty hypothetical being. Nevertheless, the statement stands as merely an extreme example of the potential importance of the relationship between speech and occupation. The Cockney speakers already mentioned (Bragg and Ellis 1976) who felt that their speech would prevent them from reaching some board of directors also had more practical and immediate concerns in this area. One, for example, wished to become a telephonist but felt her speech a barrier to this. This same girl had been told, by a headmaster, that although she might be able to join the Army, a career in the Women's Royal Naval Service would not be likely. Apart from this intriguing comment on inter-service status, the remarks generally reflect the importance of speech style for aspirants to certain careers.

Hopper and Williams (1973) investigated the reactions to different speakers of professional job interviewers who screen candidates for positions. On the basis of taperecordings of simulated interviews with black, Mexican-American, southern white and SE speakers, the judgements indicated that standard speech was seen as more important with regard to executive positions, and of little importance in connection with labouring jobs. Thus, other things being equal, the nonstandard English-speaking candidate is likely to be stereotyped as more suitable for a lower and more menial occupation. Other things, of course, may well *not* be equal—i.e., the nonstandard speaker may have other, more salient qualifications for a higher position. But this study suggests that a well-qualified nonstandard speaker may not have a chance to display his skills since his speech, at the initial job-interview, may effectively bar him from doing so.

A related study by Hopper (1977) attempted to extend this line of research, in particular trying to disentangle race (black v. white) from speech (SE v. nonstandard). The method was similar to that used in the Hopper and Williams (1973) study; four speakers were employed, one representing each of the possible race and dialect combinations. Unfortunately, the results were unable to show whether race *or* dialect was more important in this context, since the interaction between them overshadowed their separate effects. Interestingly enough, the black SE speaker was viewed most favourably of all; nevertheless, the judges were aware of the race of the speaker and, presumably, of the social desirability attaching to equality of hiring opportunity in the United States. Consequently, as Hopper notes, the research reports only what employers *say* they would do. Certainly, several writers feel that what employers *actually* do is discriminate against blacks (e.g. Kochman 1976, Wiggins 1976).

In a recent Canadian study, Kalin and Rayko (1978) asked 203 college students to imagine themselves personnel consultants seeking to fill four jobs of varying status. They rated 10 'candidates' on the basis of some limited biographical information and brief voice samples. The 10 speakers comprised five English-speaking Canadians and five speakers with foreign accents (Italian, Greek, Portuguese, West African and Slovak). Judgements made were analogous to those reported by Hopper and Williams (1973) inasmuch as the Canadians were rated more highly for higher-status jobs. Unlike the Hopper and Williams study, however, it was *not* the case that speech characteristics were unimportant with regard to low-status positions; rather, they proved instrumental in relegating the foreign-accented speakers to these jobs. That is, the five foreign speakers were actually rated *more* favourably than the English Canadians for the low-status occupations. So, again, it appears that deviations from standard speech may have implications in the job market.

It must be borne in mind that studies of the relationship between speech characteristics and occupational chances are few in number and tend to suffer from artificiality of one sort or another. Nevertheless, the authors have tried to document more precisely what is commonly accepted—the detrimental effects of certain styles upon job success. It is worth noting, perhaps, that, given the current state of society, the lack of consideration given to certain nonstandard speakers for high-status jobs is not entirely unjustified. That is, with the relationship usually obtaining between lower-class urban speech styles and relative lack of education, a prospective employer might reasonably consider that a speaker with such a style would not be qualified. Indeed, as with the example of the nonstandard-speaking doctor cited by Moulton (above), the situation may be almost entirely hypothetical. This is one of the possibly artificial aspects of the studies discussed in this section.

However, the rejection of foreign-accented candidates (demonstrated in the Kalin and Rayko study) seems more possible and, thus, more disturbing. Overall, we might conclude that whether seeking employment, or looking for promotion, the nonstandard speaker is likely to be at a disadvantage, perhaps unfairly so. In the case of promotion, the disadvantage may continue even after he has had the opportunity to demonstrate his skills; social views of speech, and what they reflect of social stereotypes, may keep him in the back rather than allowing him into the shop front.

4.7 Variety in nonstandard English

I mentioned in section 4.4 that nonstandard speech varieties, like their standard counterparts, carry cultural and traditional values. Naturally enough, just as the speech styles themselves differ, so too do the reflections of such values in speech. Since it has been necessary in this chapter to outline many negative connotations of nonstandard speech, it may be of some use here to illustrate, very briefly, the fact that nonstandard speech has its own richness and flexibility. Since the topic is somewhat peripheral, for present purposes, being largely the domain of dialectologists and anthropologists, I shall only give one or two rather extreme examples of what is a fascinating area of study in its own right. The interested reader can easily follow the matter further.

Consider first London thieves' jargon which is related to, but not precisely identical with, Cockney dialect. A detective superintendent (interviewed in Bragg and Ellis 1976) provides two illustrations:

  (a)   He was at the whisper down the Wick and he got a carpet
  (b)   Someone's been on the trumpet and now I'm a dot on the card

In example (a), a petty thief is under discussion; he was working a confidence trick ('the whisper') in Hackney Wick, for which he was arrested ('got a carpet'). The 'whisper', incidentally, relates to a racing swindle in which an individual tips the six entries in the race to six different people. One, of course, has to win and after the race the tipster goes to the person to whom he whispered the winning number, and asks for some (monetary) appreciation of his information. A good game since, as the policeman giving the example pointed out, 'You're on an earner, every race'. In example (b), a criminal confronted by a policeman is saying that someone has informed on him by ringing the police ('been on the trumpet'), and now he's likely to be convicted for an offence ('a dot on the card': from racing terminology, in which the favourite entry is marked on one's racing card).

Examples of occupation-related terminology were also presented in the series of Bragg and Ellis (1976). One interesting case concerns the dialect of fishermen in the northeast of England. Some of these, working out of Scarborough and off Flamborough Head, are known as 'cobble' fishermen. Now, 'cobble' is thought to derive from a Celtic language and simply means *boat*. But, by a creative twist, fishermen have seized upon the similarity of the term to 'cobbler' and have constructed a 'cobbler's compass' in which points of the compass are given names related to shoemaking. Thus, north is *nail*, south is *sole*, east is *heel* (or *'eel*) and west is *welt*. Boxing the compass, using these terms, is thus a unique and colourful exercise.

Since it is one of the best-researched nonstandard dialects, it is not surprising that Black English Vernacular in the United States has been described as well in terms of its verbal richness. We have already seen that Labov (1973; see chapter 3 above) praised BEV, in comparison with SE, for its directness and vigour. He has gone on to consider elsewhere the verbal skills which users of BEV employ; in particular, he describes the speech event known variously as 'sounding', 'signifying' or 'the dozens' (Labov 1976e). Basically, this is a verbal game in which ritual insults about the players and their families (especially mothers, sisters and wives) are traded.[19] Much of the game is of a scatological or sexual nature, and insults progressively become more and more extreme. A very mild example of the sort of exchange involved is taken from Labov (1976e); four different speakers each pass a comment relating to someone's mother, thus:

(a)   There go Willie mother right there
(b)   Your mother *is* a lizard
(c)   Your mother smell like a roach
(d)   Your mother name is Benedict Arnold

'Sounding' is a game with rules; the exchanges comprise ritual insults and are not to be taken as personal remarks. The goal is clearly to have the last word, to express a sentiment that no one else can 'improve' upon. Thus, some speakers have a reputation for being excellent players, others do not, and still others may not participate at all. The successful player is one whose repertoire of insults is large and who

[19] A brief footnote in Goffman 1961 provides several early references to 'the dozens'; the origin of the name is unclear (Dillard 1977, Labov 1976e).

can immediately summon the apt phrase. The command of language, and the use of metaphor and allusion, clearly show that BEV speakers, far from being verbally deprived, are talented language users and innovators (see also Abrahams 1976, Dillard 1973, 1977, Kochman 1972, Labov 1976g).[20]

In general, one should realize that nonstandard speakers, like all others, have many unique and innovative devices which colour their speech patterns. Indeed, these devices are often important facets of the nonstandardness itself. It is possible no doubt to view them as quaint, exotic or even repellent; but without the diversity they represent, the larger language would be the poorer.

4.8 Summary

In this chapter I have introduced some fairly basic sociolinguistic concepts in an attempt to look in some detail at social perceptions of disadvantaged, nonstandard speech and language. Apart from being necessary, this procedure has served I hope to make it clear that the issue of nonstandard speech is part of the larger topic of the social evaluation of *all* forms of speech, and of sociolinguistics in general. I have not, in fact, used the term 'disadvantage' very much in this chapter; it can be understood, however, that disadvantaged speech is nonstandard speech and that, in many cases, the reverse also holds. Any form of nonstandard language is liable to prove disadvantageous in some contexts, for reasons which I hope are by now fairly obvious.

The most important factor in what has been discussed is that, although eliciting some degree of positive evaluation, disadvantaged speech is generally viewed as low in prestige and status. This perception is not only that of the SE speaker, but has also been largely internalized by speakers of what Labov might call 'stigmatized' varieties themselves. Yet it was also pointed out that there are powerful attractions intrinsic to disadvantaged, nonstandard speech and that, like the negative-status connotations it evokes, its 'covert prestige' is perceived by more than its own speakers. This covert prestige, and the uncertainty attaching to attempts to alter linguistic style, are strong inhibiting forces which act to lessen the likelihood of widespread abandonment of low-prestige varieties. In fact, in some cases at least, nonstandard language users are experiencing a new (or renewed) pride in their speech forms and, far from wishing to approach the standard, desire to accentuate these differences.

Nevertheless, for most disadvantaged persons, speech is a potential handicap which is difficult to overcome. I discussed briefly some of the studies investigating the relationship between nonstandard speech and occupational chances. Despite their artificiality, they tend to confirm what most suspect—nonstandard speakers may well be at a disadvantage in the job market. This observation brings us back to a point mentioned very early on; it is at the point of contact between nonstandard and standard language varieties that disadvantage really finds its definition.

If the nonstandard English speaker lived, like some isolated tribe, away from

[20] As implied above, not all blacks are equally adept at these linguistic exercises. For an interesting account of the behaviour of 'lames'—those on the outside looking in, as it were—see Labov 1976f.

mainstream society, disadvantage would hardly be an issue. But because he does not live like this, and because he constantly comes into contact with the larger society—indeed, is forced to do so—he inevitably comes up against the power of social evaluation in which his speech is compared to that of others, and generally comes out second best. At this point, the speaker can fairly be said to be at a disadvantage. And all of this, one should remember, occurs without any tangible linguistic or aesthetic evidence which might legitimately cast one language variety in an inferior position to another. In considering sociolinguistic convention, we are confronting a formidable and pervasive influence which rests simply on the pillars of political, social and economic power. In the chapter to follow, I turn to one of the single most important channels of that influence—the school.

5

Nonstandard speech at school

'The concept of cultural relativity, upon which ... linguistic relativity must ultimately depend, is a very old one now. Why is it that it still seems shockingly new to almost the entire world of teachers?' Dillard (1973)

'Children should be helped to as wide as possible a range of language uses so that they can speak appropriately in different situations and use standard forms when they are needed.'   Bullock Report (1975)

In this chapter I wish to discuss some further aspects of the social evaluation of disadvantaged speech—those which occur in the educational setting. I shall not deal here with so-called 'compensatory education' (see chapter 2), nor with education for non-English-speaking children (see chapter 6). Rather, the aim here is to look in some detail at the nonstandard English speaker at school. As I have mentioned before, the school is perhaps the single most important point of contact between SE and NSE speakers; this is so for several reasons. First, the school is a powerful and visible SE institution; second, school is generally a child's first 'break' from the home; third, the school receives, and begins to work with, the child at a young and impressionable age; fourth, the school's influence extends over a decade or more for most children.

It is a truism, therefore, that the school will have considerable influence over the child. For NSE speakers this generally involves long contact with SE speakers. This in itself is not a bad thing. After all, given the exigencies of life, many NSE speakers will *wish* to come to grips with SE-speaking society in order to obtain greater monetary and status advancement. Thus, I should hardly propose the total abandonment, by the school, of the connection with middle-class, SE-speaking society. Rather, I want to examine here some of the ways in which school treats NSE speakers, and some of the implications this may have for academic success or failure.

By way of summary to what has gone before and introduction to what is to follow, we might consider briefly the nature of early child/school contacts. For many children, school is a rather natural continuation and extension of home life; the same sort of behaviour (including linguistic behaviour) is supported and encouraged in both. Disadvantaged children, on the other hand, often experience a rather sharp discontinuity between home and school (indeed, the fact of this discontinuity is an integral part of the very definition of disadvantage). Brandis and Bernstein (1974), for example, note the home/school discontinuity obtaining for working-class children; they go on to claim that, therefore, such children's earliest experiences at school must include a necessary process of socialization in the ways of the school. Only when the children have thus been brought into line, as it were, will their behaviour be seen as appropriate by teachers (see section 5.2.1. below).

Those who have viewed the disadvantaged as forming a separate subculture have gone so far as to say that the early home/school discontinuity may be akin to 'culture shock'—that phenomenon we have all experienced on finding ourselves in a foreign and unfamiliar context. If we accept that some degree of discontinuity may exist for disadvantaged children at school, then this chapter may be seen as a comment on it. What does disadvantage *mean* at school—how do children, parents and teachers perceive it, and react to it? This large and important issue forms the basis for what follows.

5.1 Traditional aspects of the school

It may be useful to begin here with a note or two on some relevant aspects of what one might term school 'atmosphere'. Perhaps the first thing of importance is the realization that teachers, like all other members of society, hold perceptions concerning different language varieties. They are not immune from the attributions of prestige (or the lack of it) made of certain language variants. In addition, teachers are probably more concerned with language *per se* than are others; this, of course, is because language in all its forms is of central and continuing importance in school. Highet (1950) has noted, for example, the basic nature of communication; speaking of the teacher, he states:

> Let him be good at communication, and even if he is a mediocre scholar, he can be an excellent teacher. ... Communication is an essential function of civilization. Teaching is only one of the many occupations that depend upon it, and depend upon it absolutely. (87)

And, just as the effective teacher must be a good communicator, so this talent is nurtured and encouraged in pupils—with good reason, for it is surely the case that the acquisition of knowledge alone is not the sole purpose of education. We must be able to transmit and use what we know; at the very least, we must be able to communicate with ourselves, in the sense of ordering and categorizing material. Here, language is indispensable.

Besides this valuable stress on written and spoken language, however, the teacher has typically held rather firm views as to what is appropriate or correct, and what is not. It is not enough to communicate, it is also necessary to communicate properly. It is here that we can begin to understand the difficulties which teachers may impose upon disadvantaged children who employ nonstandard language varieties. The task of the teacher is clear; the children must be instructed in the correct manner of speaking (i.e. using the standard forms). Accompanying this process has been the almost inevitable downgrading of the children's habitual speech patterns. Again, the teacher doubtless feels that he or she is acting in the best long-term interests of the child in effecting a replacement of 'poor' English with 'proper' English. The child, however, may feel somewhat differently about the process; it does not take much imagination to realize that the downgrading of one's speech style may be psychologically damaging.

Nevertheless, we might acquiesce in the process if it were seen to be based upon firm ground, just as we are prepared to give children bitter medicine for the good of their health. But, as we have already seen, the evidence available leads to the conclusion that, linguistically, NSE speakers do not require such medicine. Therefore, to enforce a policy in which their speech styles are seen as less than adequate, and to be replaced as soon and as thoroughly as possible, seems not only harsh but unnecessary. It is another question whether a policy of *addition*—expansion of children's linguistic repertoires—is appropriate. After considering in some greater detail the dynamics of language usage and attitude at school, I shall have more to say on that point.

Another introductory note, also of some importance to the NSE speaker, is whether the school may be seen as essentially a *feminine* institution. This is clearly related to the connection between NSE and masculinity noted in the previous chapter, where it was pointed out that if NSE is perceived as relatively more masculine in tone than SE, then the latter must be relatively more feminine. If this is so, then schools may not only be more attractive and rewarding to girls than to boys (see, e.g., Brophy and Good 1974) but, in addition, may be differently perceived by SE and NSE speakers. Trudgill (1974a) reports differences in the use of SE and NSE by boys and girls who were native English Creole speakers. After six months learning of SE, the girls used only 7.5 per cent NSE verb phrases; the boys, however, still used 29 per cent. Furthermore, it seemed clear that the boys associated SE with femininity, and would amuse themselves by using standard forms in 'girlish' voices. Possibly such reactions may be due to the fact that, in many countries, women teachers predominate, especially in the earliest school years, and may thus reinforce the association among school, SE and femininity.

Labov (1976e; see also Dittmar 1976) has noted the subtle interactions between NSE speakers and school in the United States. Generally, the reaction of many BEV-speaking children towards school is one of indifference or antagonism. This is of course an issue which goes beyond linguistic attitudes alone, but it is nevertheless one in which language plays a part. Labov notes, for example, that 'lames'— those who are in some sense isolated from the major social and cultural aspects of the black lifestyle—cannot compete with other children in the BEV verbal games which were noted previously (section 4.7). In fact, for various reasons,[1] they are more inclined to accept the influence of mainstream society, and to accommodate to SE. Thus their peripheral relation to the nonstandard culture opens the way (or perhaps impels them) to greater success in school. Lacking the toughness and street-wisdom of others, and having little facility in verbal behaviour associated

---

[1] These include such factors as separation from the peer group due to parental pressure, physical or mental weakness, or a child's perception of the advantages of mainstream society (Labov 1976f).

with these qualities, the 'lames' tend to adapt better to school. Thus, the 'lames' create for many BEV speakers an association between weakness and unacceptability, and the school; also, more indirectly perhaps, between lack of facility in the 'tough' BEV and the SE taught and used at school.

Overall, therefore, it appears that school may well create and sustain negative connotations of SE for NSE speakers. As with the phenomenon of 'covert prestige' (section 4.5), these connotations will presumably exert their strongest influence upon young, male NSE speakers. However, to the extent to which the toughness of NSE exists for *both* sexes, then girls too may find SE at school unpalatable. In fact, Trudgill (1972), whose findings of covert prestige in Norwich were discussed in the previous chapter, noted that although this prestige was largely a male phenomenon, it did also appear to influence young females. This finding is suggestive only, in the sense that it is not clear whether it represents a permanent change from the more traditional perceptions of females (i.e. of the higher prestige of SE), or whether it reflects a transient, youth-related phenomenon repeated by each generation. Even if only the latter explanation is, in fact, the reason for Trudgill's results, it nevertheless illuminates the power of NSE at the early years with which we are most concerned here.

The two major points made in this section—the traditional emphasis upon 'correctness' by teachers, and the negative connotations of 'school' English for NSE speakers—will serve, I hope, as a useful introduction to the discussion to follow. In a sense they provide a background from which one may better understand the views of teachers, children and parents to which I now turn.

5.2   Teachers' views of disadvantaged children

5.2.1   General expectations[2]

In chapter 1, I briefly touched upon the work of Rosenthal and Jacobson (1968) and criticisms of it; it will be recalled that this area of investigation purported to demonstrate that teachers, given false information about children in their classes, formed different expectations for what they believed to be groups of bright and not-so-bright children. Further, it was alleged that these expectations had an effect upon children's subsequent school progress. Although there are some misgivings about these sorts of findings—that teachers accept and use incorrect information, and that this hinders pupils' progress—there is little doubt that teachers *do* form and hold expectations about their students. That is, it seems quite reasonable that teachers make judgements which include estimations of likely future development. Furthermore, it may well be the case that, in most instances, such judgements constitute an effective and accurate shorthand device for teachers. With increasing experience in class, and many hours' contact with children, teachers doubtless become skilled and sensitive in this regard. What we must concern ourselves with here, however, are cases in which teachers' expectations may be *inaccurate*. The

[2] A useful and comprehensive discussion of many aspects of teacher expectations will be found in Brophy and Good 1974.

material already presented indicates that one should look most directly at situations in which teacher and pupil backgrounds are not the same and in which, therefore, the accuracy of teachers' expectations may be lessened through unfamiliarity. I am not so concerned here, then, with expectations which are manipulated (as was the attempt in the Rosenthal and Jacobson study) as with expectations which can be seen as essentially natural to teachers but which may have harmful consequences for disadvantaged children.

Rist (1970) has sketched out in general terms how teacher expectations may affect lower-class children; he outlines a circular, self-fulfilling prophecy in which teachers who feel that such children are inherently less able than others communicate this in various ways to the children. Sensitive to this, the children in time respond to what is expected of them, do less well than others, and thus confirm the initial expectations. Rist notes that the early categorization of children by teachers is essential to this process, and implies that once such categorization has occurred it is difficult for children to 'break out'.[3] Naturally, the reason for concern is that the whole process may be built upon shaky foundations—impressions which are initially subjective *and* inaccurate.

Fuchs (1973) considers further the topic of how teachers can 'learn to help children fail'. She stresses that the middle-class values of the school community are imparted to every new teacher, such that notions of environmental deficit and disadvantage are carried on and sustained. Almost before the teacher has had a chance to come to know the children, information about their backgrounds and lifestyles has resolved itself into clear conceptions of the inadequacy of the families in general, and the children in particular. Fuchs notes that the teacher,

> unarmed with the strength that understanding the social processes involved might have given her ... [is] socialized by the attitudes of those around her ... she has learned to behave and think in a way that perpetuates a process by which disadvantaged children continue to be disadvantaged.   (85)

We can hardly be surprised by this process since the school, like other social institutions, acts to perpetuate itself. However, although the process may be understandable, it presents some difficulties for disadvantaged children.

Turning to somewhat more specific considerations, one finds that studies of teachers' expectations of disadvantaged children tend to confirm the general points noted above. In Brandis and Bernstein's (1974) investigation, for example, it was found that teachers in working-class and middle-class areas employed quite different modes of 'selection and control'. Thus, teachers of working-class infant-school children emphasized control over their charges; the child must be socialized into school life before he can fully participate in it.[4] This control, of course, is not so necessary for the middle-class children who, by virtue of their home background, already share much in common with school and teacher.

[3] Specifically, it appeared to Rist in his classroom observations that ability in Standard American English was an important aspect of the categorization process.

[4] 'Socialized' here may be a somewhat euphemistic description of a process by which children are pushed towards the school's concept of appropriateness.

Brandis and Bernstein further suggest that measured IQ is more important for a working-class child's success than for that of his middle-class schoolmate. This is because the working-class child, generally in need of socialization, will not offer much 'appropriate' behaviour, especially in the earliest months at school. Consequently, there is not much to judge these children on, other than the formal test. Middle-class children, on the other hand, can be judged in a number of ways by teachers with whom they have much in common. Brandis and Bernstein put it thus:

> All our evidence ... points to the more appropriate preparation by the middle-class family of the child for school. Thus the majority of middle-class children offer behaviour which the teacher regards as appropriate. As a result appropriateness of these children's behaviour is *less* associated with their measured ability ... more less 'bright' (as measured by tests) children in the middle class have a relatively better chance of becoming successful pupils.   (114–15)

It would appear that the working-class child with a low measured IQ (and recall here all the difficulties associated with the IQ test—see chapters 1 and 2), even at the infant-school level, is already on the road to academic failure. In fact, discussing general patterns of teachers' ratings of children, the authors note that they are very similar to IQ test scores—they are 'substitutable, not just as measures of whatever it is they are measuring, but as potential selective devices in the educational system' (70).

In sum, these findings suggest that negative evaluations of disadvantaged children are almost inevitable because such children are not 'socialized' into appropriate school behaviour. They are thus not likely to do well on IQ tests; this is doubly unfortunate, since teachers have apparently little else to go on (at least in the Brandis and Bernstein study). In any event, teachers' ratings of children closely approximate the results of IQ tests.

The working-class child may elicit teacher expectations which go beyond estimates of his likely school success. Adams and Cohen (1976) found that expectations, based primarily upon information about the child's home background (i.e. 'deprived' or 'affluent'), also included evaluations of the child's home life and general social adequacy. It seems clear that teachers' ratings, for better or worse, derive largely from stereotyped views concerning class differences. Just as an accent or dialect may evoke a sterotyped perception of the speaker (see chapter 4), so an awareness of certain home backgrounds may elicit general and pervasive expectations (on the 'halo' effect of such judgements, see Freijo and Jaeger 1976, Jaeger and Freijo 1975). Of course, in the latter case, language again may well be the trigger in the initial perception of disadvantage.

Thus, teachers' expectations of working-class and disadvantaged children stem from teachers' views of what is, and what is not, appropriate behaviour. The power of social stereotypes acts to ensure that teachers have little difficulty in deciding that, for school life at least, the home backgrounds of disadvantaged children make inappropriate behaviour virtually inevitable. These stereotypes are, in turn, accounted for by the strong and pervasive middle-class norms which schools and teachers accept and promulgate. It is an easy, indeed natural, step, once the rightness of these norms is conceded, to accept that those who do not conform to such standards will perforce do more poorly in school. From this standpoint, the fact that expectations of disadvantaged children's school performance are found to be low is unsurprising.

5.2.2   Teachers' attitudes towards nonstandard English speakers

In this section I wish to expand upon the points made in the last; that is, having briefly noted the generally lower expectations held by teachers for disadvantaged children, we can now consider more specifically linguistic attitudes. There are two interrelated aspects of this topic. First, there are teachers' attitudes towards nonstandard speech *per se*; second, there are attitudes towards, and expectations of, disadvantaged children which are evoked by nonstandard speech. Since these factors are closely connected, and since both usually figure in studies of reactions towards nonstandard speech, I shall not treat them separately.

To begin with, we can consider the following statement by Gumperz and Hernandez-Chavez (1972):

> Regardless of overtly expressed attitudes ... teachers are quite likely to be influenced by what they perceive as deviant speech ... thus potentially inhibiting the students' desire to learn.   (105)

This, once again, is a useful reminder that teachers have attitudes towards accent and dialect variation, like other members of society. With regard to the brief notes given in the preceding section, we can understand that, on the whole, teachers are likely to downgrade NSE and, by extension, the capabilities of its speakers. Trudgill (1975) notes that observation confirms that teachers are not averse to telling their NSE-speaking pupils that their speech is 'wrong', 'bad', 'careless', 'sloppy', 'slovenly', 'vulgar' or 'gibberish' (63).

In this connection, the views of Bernstein (see chapter 2) have all too frequently been misunderstood by teachers to mean that NSE is equivalent to a restricted code and, in essence, inferior. We have already discussed the incorrectness of such views but, as with other social phenomena, what people *perceive* to be correct is often more important than what *is* (on the best available evidence) correct. To avoid repeating what has by now been adequately stressed, little more need be said here. We might just note, however, that the influence of Bernstein has not been restricted to teachers in Britain and the United States. Shafer and Shafer (1975) report, for example, that West German teachers have rather uncritically adopted the equation of low social status with deficient language; in Australia, Thomson (1977) notes similar perceptions. Overall, Trudgill (1975) feels that the influence of Bernstein has been particularly unfortunate since

> at a time when many people in education are beginning to recognize that non-standard dialects are in no way inferior, others have simply had their prejudices about nonstandard speech reinforced.   ·(93)

In fact, however, it seems likely that even if Bernstein had *not* written about re-stricted and elaborated codes, many teachers would still hold what we now begin to see as wrong views of disadvantaged speech.

In an Irish study of teachers' perceptions of the salient characteristics of dis-advantage, Edwards (1974) asked teachers of disadvantaged Dublin children to provide information about their pupils (by way of a questionnaire). In addition, the teachers were individually interviewed, and discussed their conceptions of dis-advantage. Thirdly, each teacher, presented with ten traits commonly associated with disadvantaged children in the literature, was asked to rank these in order of importance as useful and accurate descriptions of disadvantage.

On the ranking task, 'poor language ability' was ranked second in impor-tance—only 'poor living conditions' was perceived to be of greater salience in con-sidering the problems of the disadvantaged child. During the interview, many teachers mentioned language difficulties of various kinds as an important aspect of their view of disadvantage. Finally, the questionnaire data revealed that, overall, teachers reported 28 per cent of the pupils (total $N = 310$) as having difficulties associated with language; of these, 77 per cent were of the 'poor vocabulary' or 'poor self-expression' type. I do not wish to overemphasize the value of these data; after all, the study did not investigate *actual* language usage, nor was there a com-parison group of nondisadvantaged children. Rather, the purpose of the study was simply to consider the characteristics of disadvantaged children in Dublin inner-city schools, as these were viewed by the children's teachers. [5]

Before proceeding further, it is as well to consider what these generalities suggest. They indicate that teachers are naturally concerned about children's speech and language and, not isolated from larger social views, tend to see the speech of disadvantaged children as inaccurate, sloppy and likely to reflect lowered achievement potential—in a word, poor. It would be wrong, however, to assume that such views never change, that teachers' expectations cannot be revised. Clearly, speech is an important aspect of a child's personality, but it is not the only one. Teachers are constantly interacting with children, come to have access to a variety of information about them, and can therefore increasingly place speech in the context of other variables (cf. Edwards 1979b, Fleming and Anttonen 1971). In a study to be considered in greater detail below, Edwards (1979b, 41) found that teachers evaluating children on the basis of speech samples

> quite rightly ... had reservations about how well impressions would stand up with the provision of further information and/or actual interaction with the children themselves.

As we turn to some more specific studies of teachers' views of disadvantaged children, and their speech, we should therefore bear in mind that we are dealing with a small (though important) sample of children's behaviour; and, further, that this is presented most often in a disembodied and somewhat artificial form (i.e. via taperecordings). Nevertheless, the weight of evidence from many sources suggests the great importance of speech generally, as well as the implications it has for other, related issues. To put it another way, there can be no denying that

---

[5] The study had other related purposes which are not relevant here.

the way people *sound* is of some relevance, even when one has additional information about them (see, e.g., Seligman *et al.* 1972, p. 108 below). On this cautionary
note, let us review some empirical investigations of teachers' reactions towards
disadvantaged speech.[6]

5.2.2.1   Empirical studies of teachers' attitudes

A useful study to begin with (although it does not involve teachers' ratings at all)
is that of Frender *et al.* (1970). Two groups of third-grade French-Canadian boys,
who were similar in terms of social class and measured nonverbal intelligence, were
compared on verbal intelligence and certain speech characteristics. One group was
of average school achievement and the other somewhat below-average. The sample
used to judge the speech of the pupils was a short reading passage which was analysed by a linguist unaware of the nature of the study.

On both variables—verbal intelligence (measured by a standardized test) and
speech characteristics—the better achievers were assessed more highly than those
below average in school performance. Aware of the possibility that higher verbal
intelligence might account for more favourable ratings of speech characteristics,
the authors performed a covariance analysis to eliminate statistically any such influence. The contrast in speech characteristics between higher and lower achievers
remained. Thus, the better students spoke more quickly, made more appropriate
use of intonation and sounded more self-confident and assured. The authors concluded that

> a lower-class youngster's style of speech may mark or caricature him and thus adversely
> affect his opportunities to better himself in various situations, including the school
> environment.   (305)

Indeed it seems as if, with other (important) aspects of personality held constant,
the way a child sounds may be correlated with school success.[7]

In a further study, Frender and Lambert (1972) expanded upon these findings.
In a more involved experimental design, there was again found a relationship
between speaker fluency and intonation and school grades for lower-class primary-
school boys in Montreal. However, the interpretation of results is complicated
by the fact that differences in this regard occurred between ratings of a short reading passage and those of a simple recitation of numbers and colour-names (all
children provided both types of sample). The authors, in trying to sort out their
results, also point to the desirability of using, in future research, samples of spontaneous speech; this method, too, has its drawbacks, however, chief among which
is the lack of control over content.

The last study of Lambert and his colleagues in Montreal to be discussed here

---

[6] Elsewhere (Edwards, 1978) I have suggested greater eclecticism in experimental investigations
as a useful, if relatively minor, corrective strategy for decreasing the artificiality often associated with
small-scale studies of large-scale social phenomena.

[7] Other explanations of the findings are possible; Robinson (1972), for example, points to the fact
that speech was assessed via a reading passage on which low achievers might well be expected to perform
more poorly. As we shall see, however, negative reactions towards speech can be demonstrated when
more spontaneous speech samples are used as well.

is that of Seligman *et al.* (1972). Of major interest here is that, in addition to considering reactions to voice alone (again elicited by a reading passage), the judges were also provided with other information—photographs of the children, drawings by them, and written compositions. On the basis of pre-test investigation, the authors selected and combined such information (collected from third-grade Montreal boys) so that the work of eight 'hypothetical' children could be presented to the student teachers who were to act as raters in the study. All possible combinations of 'good' and 'poor' voices, photographs and drawings/compositions were represented in these eight composites.

The findings revealed that all types of information influenced the ratings: boys who had better voices, who looked intelligent and who had produced good compositions and drawings were all judged to be more intelligent, better students, etc. When considering the *interaction* among the types of information, it was found that speech style

> was an important cue to the teachers in their evaluations of students. Even when combined with other cues, its effect did not diminish.   (141)

The study thus supports the contention that, even in the presence of other information (which, in this case, could be manipulated as desired), speech remains a cue of some importance in assessing children. The authors express concern that teachers may make serious judgements based upon information which may be irrelevant to considerations of a child's ability and general school potential.

There seems little doubt, in viewing these three studies as a whole, that speech cues are evaluated and presumably have some part to play in impression formation. To return for a moment to the cautionary note at the end of the previous section, however, we must be careful in interpreting such results (or, indeed, in over-interpreting them). Robinson (1972), in a book which critically reviews many sociolinguistic studies, points out that speech may not always be an irrelevant or erroneous clue to a child's ability:

> If the self-fulfilling prophecy is fulfilled, then paradoxically the argument that certain language behaviours are associated with educational attainments has a reasonable (even if unnecessary) foundation.   (116)

This is a useful point, although it does not detract from the value of the studies reported here. For there are really two related issues in contention here. One is the demonstration that speech style can influence teacher ratings; the other is the manner in which the attitudes behind such ratings may affect children's school progress. The latter is bound to be a more speculative aspect than the former, since it is so difficult to tease out, in natural settings, the influence of one variable among many. And, as Robinson suggests, there is always the possibility that, because of pressure and prejudice, relationships found between speech and school success may have social validity. I trust that the evidence presented in this chapter (and throughout the book generally) will be seen to hang together well enough so that, while not ruling out other possibilities, we may nevertheless consider, with some confidence, that the speech of disadvantaged children is an unfair and often unnecessary handicap to their progress at school.

Further evidence of a relationship between teacher ratings and speech style is provided in a study by Choy and Dodd (1976). Teachers, asked to evaluate SE and NSE (in this case, Hawaiian English) speakers, consistently favoured the SE subjects (fifth-grade pupils). They were perceived, for example, as more confident, better at school, less 'disruptive' in class and likely to achieve greater academic and social success. Apart from the general downgrading of the nonstandard speech variety, the results indicate how wide-ranging these perceptions are; they deal not only with school-related matters, but also with general social capability (which included, in this study, judgements of how happy the children's marriages would likely be).[8]

Similar results are found in a recent investigation by Granger et al. (1977) of the speech styles of black children in the United States. Considering the findings of previous studies, these authors attempted to elicit from children speech samples which would not, as they put it, confound 'task performance' with the actual speech patterns. That is, earlier studies were not able to ascertain precisely whether ratings were primarily influenced by a child's fluency (or nonfluency) of speech, or by the nonstandard aspects of the speech—this is because many investigations elicited samples of speech in rather formal conditions. I have already noted the difficulties associated with using, say, a reading passage; it is a procedure which doubtless favours certain children. However, completely spontaneous speech will also favour certain children and, in addition, removes comparability across speakers. Granger et al. therefore attempted to steer a middle course; children were asked to describe certain features of a picture. In this way, the authors hoped to retain some comparability across children while, at the same time, allowing children to choose their own manner of description. The results are described as follows:

> When the speech productions of black and white middle and lower SES children are carefully controlled for fluency and adequacy of task performance, teachers' ratings and rankings show a distinct social class and racial bias. The class bias appears strongest.
> . . . The findings suggest that the teachers were attending less to *what* a child said than to *how* he said it   (795)

A similar study is that of Piché et al. (1977). As in the Granger et al. study, these authors elicited speech samples by asking fourth-grade schoolboys to tell a story based upon a series of cartoons. And, as in the Seligman et al. (1972) investigation, Piché et al. presented to the raters eight 'hypothetical' children who represented each possible combination of dialect ethnicity (BEV or SE), quality of written composition (previously judged either good or poor) and social class (high or low). The judges for this study were 32 female student teachers who rated these 'hypothetical' children on a number of personality dimensions (e.g. intelligence, enthusiasm, self-confidence). On dimensions related to school achievement, it was found that dialect alone was not a major factor, although social class was. Most of the interpretation of the results rested upon explanations of some rather complicated interactions among dialect, social status and written composition. The main

---

[8] Some remarks on the apparent willingness of raters to make such far-reaching judgements will be found in Edwards (1979b; see below, pp. 113–15).

aspect of interest for present purposes is that, unlike the results of the Seligman *et al.* study, Piché and his colleagues found a more involved pattern emerging in terms of teacher evaluations. In the presence of other information about children, it appeared that the effects of dialect variation (and, in this case, ethnic-group membership) were modified.[9]

So far I have attempted to describe the essential elements of some investigations which have all addressed the same general issue—the evaluation of nonstandard speech by teachers. All have demonstrated that such speech tends to elicit less favourable reactions than do standard forms, although other information may interact with speech in important ways. This should simply remind us, of course, that to pay undue attention to any one aspect of an information 'package' in isolation is liable to lead us astray. Nevertheless, it seems that speech is a factor of importance, either alone or in combination with other material, and regardless of the method used to elicit it or to present it to judges.

Having made these points, it is appropriate now to consider a series of related studies which represents one of the most comprehensive and sustained investigations of disadvantaged speech in the American context. For the last decade or so, Williams and his colleagues have attempted systematically to explore the linguistic attitudes of teacher, and it is to a consideration of this work that we now turn.[10]

Williams (1970a) provides some of the theoretical background to his work, most of which revolves around the (by now) familiar observation that speech evaluations depend upon stereotypes elicited by the label which the speech itself provides. Whereas previous work had demonstrated, on the one hand, the operation of the evaluation process *per se* (e.g. the work of Lambert and his colleagues, discussed on pp. 107–8 and section 4.3.2 above) or, on the other, had attempted to isolate those features or characteristics of speech most important in this regard (e.g. Labov's work on status markers in New York City speech—see chapter 3), Williams is concerned to study both aspects.

This concern received empirical investigation in a study by Williams (1970b). Two groups of fifth- and sixth-grade children (20 children in each), one of higher and one of lower SES, each comprising equal numbers of blacks and whites and boys and girls, were taperecorded while talking freely about two preselected topics. There were thus 80 speech samples. Chicago teachers, 21 white and 12 black, acted as judges in the study, and rated the children on a number of semantic-differential scales; the dimensions included fluency, complexity of sentences, reticence and pronunciation. In addition, scales were included which required the teacher to judge the socioeconomic status of the child's family, his degree of disadvantage, his standardness or nonstandardness of speech, and whether or not he sounded white or black.

---

[9] The study of Piché *et al.* is also the first one discussed here in which videotapes, rather than audio taperecordings, were used to present children to raters. While more natural in some respects, this technique has its own difficulties, some of which the authors discuss.

[10] The overall programme of research referred to here is summarized in Williams 1976; see also Williams 1973, Williams *et al.* 1977).

Factor analysis of the ratings suggested that two dimensions of importance were operating. One of these, labelled by Williams 'confidence/eagerness', reflected such things as the child's perceived confidence and perceptions of social status. The second dimension, which was also associated with social status judgements, related to perceptions of ethnicity and nonstandardness/standardness of speech, and was so labelled—'ethnicity/nonstandardness'. Williams thus felt that, overall, the teachers were evaluating the speech samples (and the children) along two broad factors; one of these appears to relate to ethnicity and ethnic, nonstandard speech patterns, while the second reflects relatively personal attributes of the child himself.

Turning to the question of the specific speech cues which may elicit these reactions, Williams next identified a number of types of cues present in the samples which appeared most importantly related to the ratings. Among these were frequency of pausing (negatively related to confidence ratings) and nonstandard grammatical variants (related to the ethnicity/nonstandardness dimension).[11] This part of the research is obviously one requiring a great deal of work and fine grained investigation, but it would be interesting, to say the least, to refine our knowledge in this area. It must be remembered however that, even if we could isolate the most important speech cues, it is unclear what immediate use this would have. Attempting to alter specific speech characteristics, for example, would be difficult and, for black and other highly visibly disadvantaged groups, of little likely benefit (see chapter 4). On the other hand, a general policy of addition to or expansion of a child's linguistic repertoire, for practical purposes (see below), would render such detailed information almost unnecessary.

A further study (Williams *et al.* 1972) expanded upon the earlier findings. Teachers were asked to provide:

evaluations on semantic-differential scales of three ethnic groups (presented via a simple written label)—these ratings presumably reflecting teachers' overall stereotypes

evaluations of six video-taped samples of children's speech—elicited in a semi-formal manner by asking children initially to respond to two preselected questions

estimations of each child's class achievement level

The subjects themselves comprised low- and middle-status black, white and Mexican-American children living in Texas; there were 125 white and 50 black teacher-evaluators, with varying amounts of teaching experience.

The first result of importance was the confirmation of the previously established two-factor model of teachers' judgements. As in the Williams (1970b) study, the rated dimensions clustered into 'confidence/eagerness' and 'ethnicity/nonstandardness' factors. Second, relationships were found between teacher ratings and child status and ethnicity. Overall, low-status children were seen less favourably on the confidence/eagerness dimension and also as being more ethnic/nonstandard. *Within* this low-status group, the white children were seen more positively, and

---

[11] For examples of some common BEV variants, see chapter 3. On the apparently varying degree of status associated with pausing, see chapter 2.

as less ethnic/nonstandard than the black and Mexican-American children. This last result also obtained when the middle-status children's ratings were considered on the factor of ethnicity/nonstandardness; on the confidence/eagerness dimension, however, black middle-class children were rated slightly *more* favourably than were white children (although both blacks and whites were seen more positively than were the Mexican-American children).

A third finding was that the teachers' general stereotyped reactions to the three ethnic groups studied correlated moderately well with their evaluations of the actual children representing each group. Thus, the author suggests that, in rating the individual child, teachers may be fulfilling their own, more general expectations. Finally, the predictions of children's class achievement were found to be related to the speech sample ratings. With regard to three broad school subject areas, this relation was strongest for areas more directly related to language and language arts. Within this relationship, ratings along the ethnicity/nonstandardness dimension were rather more important than those of confidence/eagerness.

Again, therefore, Williams and his colleagues provide some detailed information about teachers' ratings based upon samples of children's speech. Here, in addition, these ratings have been related to teachers' more general stereotypes, as well as to expectations of children's academic success. We should also note here that black and white teachers' perceptions in this study were remarkably alike; this suggests that speech evaluations may generalize across ethnic (and class) boundaries and may represent the internalization of mainstream social values by members of the relatively poorly perceived groups themselves (see also chapter 4).

In the last study by Williams to be discussed here, the author reviews some of the earlier work, and discusses an important aspect of the methodology of the studies (1974). This revolves around what he terms the 'latitude of attitude acceptance' (see also Williams 1976). Not a new concept in the larger domain of social psychology, this simply acknowledges that raters' evaluations may not be entirely adequately expressed by checking a single point on some semantic-differential scale. For language studies in particular, Williams considers that determining the range of acceptance of judges might be a useful addition to a single mark on a rating scale. The technique to investigate this simply requires the judge, in addition to noting the usual single rating mark on any given scale for any given child, to indicate also those other rating possibilities which would be generally acceptable to him; likewise, those alternatives which the judge would definitely reject can also be indicated. An example might be:

This child seems: Passive $+:\oplus:+:\quad:-:-:-$ Active

Here the judge has indicated that his 'latitude of acceptance' covers the three rating possibilities at the 'passive' end of the scale; his single best estimate is second from the left (circled). The blank in the middle denotes lack of decision or neutrality, while the three minus-signs indicate possibilities definitely rejected. In general, the mean of the latitude of acceptance is likely to represent the one 'best' estimate; thus, the only real addition to knowledge is the deviation about this mean which is generally acceptable to the rater. With further development, the concept may allow us to consider interesting overlaps between judgements of different children (or groups of children) which the methodologies of most current studies do not permit.

So far in this section, I have considered studies performed in the North American context. To introduced some balance and, by so doing, to demonstrate that the American findings seem, *mutatis mutandis*, to apply in other areas, I shall now briefly discuss two of my own investigations (1977b; 1979b) of the topic, both of which were conducted in Dublin. The second of these provides, in addition, a useful follow-up to Williams's (1974) treatment of the 'latitude of acceptance' in teachers' ratings.

In the first study (Edwards 1977b), 20 disadvantaged (working-class) and 20 middle-class Dublin boys comprised the subjects; in each group there were 10 second primary class pupils, and 10 from fifth class. All the boys were, on the information of their teachers, average students. Speech samples were elicited by telling the children a story and having each tell it back to the investigator, in his own words. Five adult middle-class judges were then asked to evaluate the children's intelligence, fluency, vocabulary, general voice quality (e.g. pronunciation and intonation) and communicative ability. On all measures, the disadvantaged children were viewed less favourably than their middle-class counterparts. In interpreting the results, I considered that the lower ratings received by the working-class boys on fluency and communication might well reflect 'poorer' performance, if the norms of the middle-class judges were taken into account.[12] On the other measures, however, especially that of voice quality, we are presumably seeing more subjective impressions which reflect what we can, by now, understand to be pervasive social stereotypes which have nothing to do with intrinsic voice elements.

This introductory study was followed by a larger and more detailed investigation (Edwards 1979b). Here, in addition to testing the generality of the previous findings with regard to speech evaluations, two refinements were introduced. The first was the measurement of any sex-of-rater effects. Previous studies, such as those by Seligman *et al.* (1972) and Williams (1970b), dealt mainly with female teacher-raters—quite reasonably, since in North America most primary school teachers are female. In the Irish context, however, the large numbers of male primary teachers prompted consideration of the judges' sex as a possibly important variable.

The second variant was to attempt to measure the judges' *confidence* in their ratings. The reasoning behind this was, simply, that in rating tasks subjects almost always comply with requests to fill in all the scales provided, even though they may feel that some are less appropriate than others (indeed, during, or at the conclusion of, many experiments subjects often express such doubts). Judges' confidence, or the lack of it, may therefore be of some importance in the overall interpretation of results. Williams (1974) has noted that respondents are willing to make

---

[12] Grammatical analyses and speech-rate measures of the children's stories were also made (see chapter 3), with which the judges' rating could be compared. Ratings of fluency, for example, showed a correlation of ·88 with rate of speech.

judgements after only brief exposure to a stimulus and, as we have seen, these judgements may be quite wide-ranging. The notion of the 'latitude of attitude' that judges were prepared to accept was seen by Williams to extend somewhat the investigator's understanding of the rating procedure; in similar fashion, the assessment of judges' confidence in their ratings, in the present study, may be seen as an expression of how wide their implicit latitude of acceptance might be, if in fact it exists at all.

In the study (Edwards 1979b), two groups of 20 10-year-old Dublin children (10 of each sex in each group) provided the speech samples. One group comprised disadvantaged, lower-class children; the other was a middle-class sample. All children read a short passage selected with the assistance of their teachers and, after a practice trial, were taperecorded.[13] Fourteen teachers-in-training (7 male and 7 female) served as judges in the study.[14] Seventeen semantic-differential scales were used, on which various aspects of the child's personality and background were to be assessed (e.g. fluency, intelligence, enthusiasm, likely school achievement, perceived degree of disadvantage). In addition, accompanying each of these 17 scales was a 7-point scale on which teachers indicated the degree of confidence they felt about the substantive rating just made. Finally, all judges were interviewed at the conclusion of the study on their knowledge and opinions about disadvantage, language and the experiment itself.

The major results were as follows. On every scale, the disadvantaged children received less favourable ratings than the middle-class children; thus, support for earlier work was clear. Factor analysis of the ratings given on all scales showed *all* to be highly interrelated, and only one important factor emerged. Here, we might recall Williams's consistent finding of *two* important factors in teacher ratings—confidence/eagerness and ethnicity/nonstandardness. Since ethnicity is not a factor in the Irish context, it is perhaps not surprising that only one factor—which could simply be termed *disadvantage-nondisadvantage*—was produced here. This result suggests the validity of the idea that teachers' reactions derive from an overall elicited stereotype of disadvantaged children. One would not wish to deny that other scales and other speech situations might evoke other factors; in the school context, however, teachers' judgements of disadvantaged children, on scales relating to language and school ability, may well be rather unidimensional.

With the confidence scales, there was an analogous finding to that obtaining for the substantive ratings; non-disadvantaged children were judged with greater certainty than were the disadvantaged. An interesting difference, however, occurred between the substantive ratings and the confidence ratings, with regard to the sex of the judges. Male raters were found to give higher ratings on the substantive scales than were female judges; for the confidence ratings, however, the

---

[13] For information regarding the relative merits of different types of elicited speech for such studies, see chapter 3; see also the discussion in Edwards 1979b.

[14] Student teachers are often used in these studies, mainly, of course, because they are more accessible than regular teachers. However, arguments can be made for the use of student teachers on more substantive grounds, too (see Cooper *et al.* 1975, Edwards 1979b; see also the discussion teacher training in section 5.5).

reverse was the case. Thus it appeared that, overall, males made more positive ratings, but were less sure of them, while females were more confident about their somewhat less favourable substantive ratings. Apart from indicating that one is not dealing, in rating scales generally, with a simple response tendency for one sex to make higher or lower marks on a scale, there is an intriguing possibility here, which deserves further study (simply because scales are so commonplace in social-psychological and sociolinguistic research): males may somewhat over-commit themselves in their ratings and (in this study) then take the opportunity provided by the confidence scales to 'soften' their judgements, as it were; females, having been more circumspect from the start, may not find this necessary.

Considering the confidence ratings as they relate to each individual substantive scale, it was found that some of the latter tended to be rated with greater certainty than others. Now, we have already noted that all the substantive scales were highly interrelated; in that sense, if a smaller subset were required, it would not make much difference which were chosen. However, considering the differential confidence attached to scales by the judges, some scales can be seen to have greater face validity than others. In general, judges were more confident when asked to rate aspects of personality more or less directly relatable to the speech sample itself (e.g. fluency, reading ability and pronunciation); they were less comfortable, it seems, in dealing with scales relating to such things as the happiness of the child and family socioeconomic status.

In general, this study (Edwards 1979b) confirms, for an Irish sample, the results already discussed which derive from American investigations. Disadvantaged children were rated less favourably than middle-class children on a large number of dimensions, all of which were closely interrelated. In addition, it was found that judges, though willing to fill in all the scales provided, were clearly more comfortable with those that (in their eyes at least) were more directly associated with that sample of behaviour to which they had been exposed. This commendable caution on the part of the raters is something which overenthusiastic researchers would do well to take to heart. Finally, the differences attributable to judges' sex suggest possibilities which may be important to those engaged in rating-scale research.

To end this section, let us consider briefly three studies which point to the complexity of the issue under investigation, and which suggest that all is not completely cut and dried. In two related studies, Crowl and MacGinitie (1974) and Crowl and Nurss (1976) investigated teachers' evaluations of children, based upon taperecordings of 6 black and 6 white boys from the northern United States. In the first study, northern white teachers, listening to the boys give predetermined and identically-worded answers to typical school-related questions, rated the answers of the white boys as being significantly better than those of the black pupils. The second study was essentially a replication of the first, except that southern black and white teachers were the raters; the voices to be judged were the same as before. Interestingly, it was found that the *black* boys' answers were judged most favourably by all teachers. The authors speculate about what may have caused this seemingly anomalous finding; at the least, it should remind us that the topic is not a static one. As Crowl and Nurss put it:

> The relationship between speech characteristics exhibited by speakers of different ethnic groups and listener behavior is more complex than previous work has indicated.   (238)

Taylor (1973) asked a large number of black and white teachers from various regions across the United States to respond to a questionnaire dealing with language attitudes towards black English. This instrument comprised 25 items over four 'content categories'—the structure of BEV, the consequences of its use at school, teachers' feelings about the use and acceptance of BEV, and the cognitive abilities of BEV speakers. The results revealed rather interesting interactions between types of teachers and aspects of BEV. Overall, Taylor notes much *positive* attitude towards BEV and towards language variation in general. He does point out, however, that

> teachers are more likely to agree more strongly with items such as, 'When teachers reject the native language of a student, they do him great harm' than they do with items like 'Teachers should allow black students to use Black English in the classroom.'   (200)

Bearing in mind that responses to a questionnaire may differ in important ways from those to a child himself (or, indeed, to a recorded speech sample), Taylor's data nevertheless serve to demonstrate that language attitudes are subtle and complex.

The implication of all that has been discussed in this section is, however, fairly clear. Teachers, like others, hold stereotyped and often negative views of certain language varieties and their speakers. The importance of this derives from the evidence, presented in previous chapters, that *different* language varieties are not linguistically *deficient*. Thus, in one sense, the data concerning teachers' attitudes are simply another aspect of the more general relationship between certain language varieties and *social* deficit. But teachers' views are rather special, for the reasons given at the beginning of this chapter—their negative evaluations of disadvantaged children may lead to real problems for the child at school.

Before considering what might be done to counteract such problems, it might be useful to turn briefly to a question which has been latent throughout the book so far—can *anyone* speak incorrectly? As concerned with language *difference* as we have been, this seems a reasonable question, and one which has no doubt exercised many interested in the larger issue of language and disadvantage. The justification for mentioning it here, of course, is that it is the most salient in the school context; in addition, it allows us to consider directly, once again, the role of the speech therapist—whether this be a trained clinician or simply the teacher, concerned to correct mistakes.

5.3   Speech therapy at school

In 1976, Trudgill (whose work I have drawn upon considerably) was interviewed in *The Sunday Times* (Pye 1976). The title of the article was the attention-getting

'Bad language ain't wrong', and the gist of it was that the views of NSE now commonly accepted by linguists are not entirely subscribed to by teachers and others. While acknowledging that, in present-day society, children need SE, Trudgill questioned whether they *should* need it. Implicit in this call for increasing 'official recognition' of the validity of nonstandard language varieties is the view that there are few, if any, speech errors committed by children. Does, therefore, the *difference* view of language extend to the point of claiming that no-one speaks incorrectly?

Trudgill (1975) addresses this issue further in a recent book on language and the school. He concedes the existence of mistakes like omissions of words, incorrect spelling and so on in writing; he also discusses slips of the tongue and malapropisms in spoken language. Additionally, there are errors made by foreigners speaking English which derive from interference from their mother tongue.[15] But, apart from these

> we have to say that all normal adult native speakers know and therefore use their own dialect of English perfectly ... native speakers do not make mistakes. (45)

The implication of this for teachers and therapists would seem to be that any errors made by a child can only be seen as such if they represent incorrect or incomplete approximations of the usual adult form. Thus, for example, a child's use of the word 'sheeps' is wrong but understandable in terms of the normal English rules regarding pluralization of nouns. When considering what *is* the 'usual adult form', however, we must always bear in mind the norms for the child's own speech community, and not those of SE alone.

Given that teachers and therapists are often middle-class SE speakers themselves (or, at least, have accepted and use this dialect), their task with the NSE-speaking child is somewhat more involved than it is for his SE-speaking schoolmate. Before any mistakes can be so identified, the teacher or therapist must gain some familiarity with the appropriate norms. That is, if any correction *per se* is to be done, it must be towards the nonstandard model (see also chapter 3). In addition, of course, the therapist will concern herself or himself with what we can term speech *defects*, relatable to physical and/or functional causes. But, apart from working on articulatory disorders and the like, it is not entirely clear that we should do very much at all, even in terms of correcting speech towards the appropriate norm. Studies on general language acquisition and development stress the naturalness of the process for human beings, and the fact that it is not a skill which ordinarily requires direct teaching.[16] The development of language is seen as an activity, which, like learning to walk, simply happens to all normal children. By the time the normal child comes to school, he has a firm grasp of his maternal language and this, of course, applies to speakers of *all* dialects, nonstandard or otherwise.

[13] For example, speakers of French, in which *n'est-ce pas?* is a rather all-purpose phrase, sometimes consider *isn't it?* to be similarly broad in English: thus, *He's a good teacher, isn't it?*

[16] Language development is essentially a psycholinguistic concern which is not relevant in the present discussion. A large literature exists on the topic; for very recent treatments, see Bloom 1978 and Bloom and Lahey 1978.

Thus, much of the language programme at school typically concerns itself with refinements of grammar, composition and spelling, with these often largely directed towards *written* language. It would seem unlikely, therefore, that the therapist well-versed in the intricacies of a nonstandard dialect would find much to correct in a NSE-speaking child's speech. Indeed, as we shall see below, even those difference theorists who acknowledge the utility of SE acquisition for NSE speakers very often feel that any active teaching of SE would be quite inappropriate.

5.4   The educational treatment of nonstandard language

It is now time to consider directly what, if anything, should be done about NSE at school. To summarize the relevant background to the issue, we might note that:

> NSE is not *linguistically* deficient. However, NSE often evokes negative *social* evaluations.
> Although we may hope that the negative connotations of NSE will, with time, decline, there is little evidence that this process will be a rapid one.
> Thus, for practical purposes, success in school and afterwards may well be hindered by the use of NSE.

This brief outline points to a fact which may be unpalatable (given the current state of linguistic awareness) but is nonetheless real: the disadvantaged NSE speaker will benefit from comprehension and use of SE. We have already noted that, for many NSE speakers, SE comprehension presents no real difficulty. The major problem, therefore, is the encouragement of the *use* of SE, at least in contexts in which it is most appropriate. In the following two sections, therefore, we will consider some of the possibilities in this connection.

5.4.1   Standard English instruction: speaking and writing

On the basis of evidence presented so far, the reader will understand that, whatever the method advocated to increase a child's use of SE, the underlying philosophy must be one of *addition* and not of *replacement*. That is, we may desire to expand a child's language repertoire, but we do not want to attempt to eliminate his maternal speech style. I have already discussed the lack of any linguistic reason to try to do so, as well as the (unnecessary) conflict which such a policy would inflict upon the child.

A policy of addition is implied in the so-called *bidialectal* approach to NSE speakers and their problems in SE-speaking contexts. Thus, it is argued that children may find it advantageous to add a second dialect (SE) to their first, nonstandard speech style. But one should bear in mind here that even the most enlightened attempts at encouraging bidialectalism may entail the same problem associated with the older, more implicit school policy of elimination of the nonstandard form. That is, one still runs the risk of stigmatizing the child's original speech patterns in his own eyes. Why, the child might ask himself, is a second dialect stressed after he has been told that his first is perfectly all right? The child may well feel that,

despite the assurances of the teacher, something *must* be wrong with his own manner of speech.

This possibility is the major reason for not emphasizing dialect differences in
any active way in the classroom. Rather, the teacher should speak in a manner
natural to himself, and accept that the children are doing the same. The fact that
the children, over their school career, will have a long exposure to SE surely reduces
the necessity for any active teaching with regard to oral speech production. Thus,
in a paper reviewing the status of the BEV and, in particular, the comprehension
of SE (and, therefore, of the teacher) by black speakers, Hall and Turner (1974)
note that such speakers

> automatically translate the SE into their dialect ... it would serve no useful purpose to
> teach English as a second language to speakers of NNE [Negro Nonstandard English =
> BEV] if the goal is improved comprehension of SE.   (79–80)

Similarly, Trudgill (1975), noting the naturalness of language acquisition,
argues that the teaching of spoken SE is inadvisable on two major grounds: (a)
it is not likely to succeed (unless the child actively desires to speak SE, in which
case formal teaching is unnecessary); (b) there is a possibility that psychological
damage to the child may follow from the linguistic insecurity that such teaching
may produce.

The situation is, however, somewhat different when one considers the writing
of SE. Since this is an area in which *all* children require some instruction, the appropriate approach for NSE speakers is of some importance.

Writing is of course a more formal activity than speaking. It requires more careful forethought and, in addition, allows the opportunity of subsequent alteration.
Trudgill (1975) accepts that some facility in SE writing will prove useful to NSE-
speaking children and advocates, therefore, formal instruction in it. But even here,
he categorizes writing such that not all exercises are seen to require SE usage. Thus
he notes that, for the moment at least, SE will be advantageous in business correspondence and formal out-of-school contexts generally. On the other hand, children should not feel constrained to use SE in creative writing or personal letters
'since no social advantages are likely to result from this' (80). A third category,
academic essays, proves more problematical. Here there may be an advantage in
the use of SE because examiners may not accept NSE; once again, Trudgill's divid-
ing line is drawn between situations in which SE will be of practical benefit to
the child, and those in which it will not. Also, Trudgill clearly hopes that, in time,
even those contexts currently requiring SE will accept NSE. Thus he points out
that

> it is very encouraging to see sentences like *We never done that before* appearing boldly
> in the teacher's handwriting in a child's exercise book.   (83)

One can guess that the frequency of such comments is, however, as yet slight.

Trudgill's remarks on writing are certainly consonant with the tone of this
book. Only where practical considerations demand SE should the child be required
to use it. At the same time, however, I think that it might prove more consistent

for the child if Trudgill's distinctions among *types* of writing were dropped. Even the most creative and imaginative of SE-speaking children has to learn to translate his ideas into writing; surely no great damage to the creative abilities of the NSE-speaking child would ensue if a more or less formal equation of written English with SE was the rule. After all, this would reflect the current state of affairs in written English generally. Additionally, consistency of approach here, from the earliest school years, might make the ability to produce written SE, where it clearly *is* required, more easily acquired.

5.4.2   Standard English instruction: reading

I have left reading out of the discussion so far and, rather strangely perhaps, considered speaking and writing together in the previous section. There are two reasons for this: speaking and writing are both *encoding* aspects of language, while reading is a *decoding* aspect; and a great deal of attention has been given to reading *per se* in the literature. Reading is also worthy of attention on its own because, while writing is the most formal aspect of language and speaking the most informal (thus, forming a sort of contrast), reading falls somewhat between. Although not as active a process as the other two, it does seem to have greater association with SE than does speaking, although possibly (as we shall see) less than does writing. Within a vast general literature on reading, it is not surprising that considerable attention has been directed towards the relationship between reading and disadvantage. For present purposes, reading is of special interest since, within the general *bidialectal* or *addition* approach to the difficulties faced by NSE speakers, several rather clear points of view have emerged.

First of all, we should realize that the process of reading is not one of decoding to sound, but of decoding to meaning (see, e.g., Smith 1973). The examples already provided (see chapter 3) of black children's sentence repetition demonstrate this. Given a sentence to repeat (e.g. *I asked Alvin if he knows how to play basketball*), the child may render it in his own dialect (e.g. *I ax Alvin do he know how to play basketball*), while clearly retaining the *meaning* of the original (see also Trudgill 1975). Further to this, Torrey (1973) has noted:

> The difference in phonology between standard English and black English is not directly relevant to reading. All children who learn to read English have to break a fairly complex code of sound-spelling relationships. The fact that the correspondences are different for speakers of Afro-American does not in itself prove that they are more difficult than for standard speakers.   (68)

Thus, the formalities involved in reading may be different, yet of a similar order of difficulty, for speakers of SE and NSE. Nevertheless, as Harber and Bryen (1976) have noted, one cannot rule out completely the possibility of dialect interference in reading. Thus, especially in the United States, there have been attempts to provide initial reading materials in BEV.

Baratz (1970), for example, has proposed that black children be provided with books written in their own vernacular. The reasoning behind this is that reading competence in one's own dialect is a necessary prerequisite for SE reading ability. Thus, the ultimate goal is SE reading proficiency; Baratz is simply concerned to facilitate the attainment of this end. Her programme, incidentally, calls not only for BEV reading materials, but also for what she refers to as 'transition texts' as a halfway-stop between BEV and SE books (see also Baratz 1972, Johnson 1971, Stewart 1972b).

This point of view has not gone unchallenged. Generally, criticisms centre upon the notion that such an approach may quite simply be unnecessary (cf. Edwards 1977a, Harber and Bryen 1976). This is because we do not know enough about possible dialect interference, and what we do know (for example, the studies demonstrating the BEV speaker's comprehension of SE) suggests that such interference may not, in most cases, be sufficient to cause problems. Trudgill (1975) points out, for instance, that British dialect differences are not likely to be marked enough to create reading difficulties. And, in the American context, Labov (1976h) notes:

> Some writers seem to believe that the major problem causing reading failure is structural interference between these two forms of English [BEV and SE]. Our research points in the opposite direction. ... The number of structures unique to BEV are [*sic*] small, and it seems unlikely that they could be responsible for the disastrous record of reading failure in the inner city schools.   (241)

Similar points are made by Grotberg (1972), Somervill (1974) and Venezky (1970)—the last author notes that, if it could be shown that provision of reading material in NSE would help decrease reading difficulties, then few would object to such provision. Since, however, such evidence is not forthcoming, the time and expense involved in the production of these materials seems inappropriate.[17] Apart from the effort and expense which such production would entail, there would also be all sorts of questions concerning how many varieties of NSE should be catered for, and how and when the transition to SE texts (something which supporters of this approach agree is necessary) would be accomplished.

There is, in addition, some evidence suggesting that whatever the decision taken by psychologists and linguists might be, many parents do not wish to see their nonstandard language variety in school books. These attitudes may be regrettable (in the sense that they may reflect continuing feelings of linguistic inferiority), or they may be practical (parents may see the production of such books as antithetical to their views of the school as an agent of social advancement). One thing is certain, however—parental attitudes should not be ignored. Covington (1976), for example, has pointed out that a sample of black parents

---

[17] A few experimental studies *have* suggested that BEV reading materials might be useful, but the evidence is not strong. A study by Thurmond (1977), for example, introduced a possible Hawthorne effect and, in addition, dealt with high school students rather than the younger children of prime concern here. Similarly, Somervill and Jacobs (1972) reported interesting, yet inconsistent, results for black children's reading and listening comprehension in SE and BEV. In a later article, Somervill (1974) appears to support the view that inadequate comprehension of SE is not likely to be a factor of great importance for many black children (see also Somervill 1975).

in Washington, although wishing to see tolerance of the children's use of BEV in class, was strongly opposed to textbooks written in BEV, and wanted teachers to use SE in instruction (similar opinions are reported by Harber and Bryen 1976, Venezky 1970).

Overall, therefore, the view that reading materials in BEV would be useful is not strongly supported by such evidence as is now available; in addition, there is some indication that, even if it were adopted, it would not sit well with NSE speakers themselves.[18] A variant of the approach, in which points of interference between dialects would be eliminated from reading texts (thus producing a sort of neutral book), can also be criticized on similar grounds. This variant does however suggest, indirectly perhaps, that deletion of certain aspects of school books which are associated with given social groups might be useful. In other words, books might be produced which are more culture-free than at present. For example, stories, roles and occupations might be presented in books so as to reflect more accurately the environments of the children using them; possibly such nonlinguistic alteration might make books in general more relevant for some pupils.

Another major possibility in connection with NSE speakers and reading is to allow such speakers to render the meaning from SE texts in their own dialect (cf. Edwards 1977a, Simons 1974, Trudgill 1975, Venezky 1970). This view is thus closely related to the experimental evidence concerning sentence repetition (see above). Here, no effort would be made to provide materials in NSE since this is seen as unnecessary; rather, the emphasis is upon allowing the reader to express what he reads in the manner most familiar to him. It is expected that the NSE-speaking child at school will develop facility in reading (i.e. in decoding to meaning) SE, just as his SE-speaking counterparts will. When he comes to *encode* what he has read (for example, reading aloud during a lesson), his 'translation' of the information received via the printed page into NSE will be completely acceptable.

It is interesting to note that this approach to reading, perhaps the most widely accepted at the moment, is the most consonant with the *difference* view of disadvantaged, nonstandard speech and language. That is, as we have more and more come to realize the validity and the fullness of NSE, so it appears that there is less and less to 'do' for the disadvantaged child in terms of curriculum alteration. Instead, this approach places reading problems largely in the area of a child's *reproduction* of what he has read, and not in his comprehension. This in turn leads us back to the position stressed throughout this book—i.e. that difficulties encountered by disadvantaged children are likely to be social in nature.[19] In the case of reading, therefore, one would expect that it

---

[18] Production of books written in NSE may be useful for other purposes, however. A booklet written in the style of Ballyfermot, a working-class suburb of Dublin, proved valuable, for example, in the sense that it 'legitimized' the usual speech patterns of the local population (Murphy 1975).

[19] I need hardly point out that disadvantaged children, like any other children, may suffer real reading difficulties; these, however, should be seen to operate independently of class or race *per se*.

is the teacher's attitude towards the way a child reads that will determine if a problem exists or not.

In summary, this approach to reading is, in reality, no approach at all. Just as with speaking NSE in class, so the child is to be allowed to read in NSE. The whole issue thus devolves upon the teacher (see section 5.5) who must conduct the class so that the use of NSE is not stigmatized. Again, as with speaking, it is assumed that the child has the ability to comprehend SE and, in a sense, it is his choice as to whether or not he decides to use it. If he does so decide, then he has an abundance of models (both printed and spoken) to guide him. Of course, the child should not be left entirely on his own in the matter—the teacher should be able gradually to make clear to the child in what contexts SE is most appropriate and where, therefore, its use is likely to be most beneficial. But, as with other important and personal aspects of life, much can be left to the discretion of those most directly involved—the NSE speakers.

A final note here: lest it be thought that such a policy is too *laissez-faire*, we should bear in mind that any more formal or strict approach (even if stemming from the best of motives) is not likely to work and/or may widen a gap which already too frequently exists between the disadvantaged child and the school. In this regard, the Bullock Report on English teaching, in all its aspects, makes the sensible recommendation that the

> teacher's aim should be to indicate to his pupils the value of awareness and flexibility, so that they can make their own decisions and modify these as their views alter.   (Great Britain: Department of Education and Science 1975, 143)

5.5   Teachers and teacher training

So we come to what, more and more, seems the single most crucial factor in the success or failure of the disadvantaged child at school—the attitude of the teachers. Having examined various strands of evidence, we find that they virtually all point to this conclusion. Precisely because of this previous examination, we can be briefer here than might at first seem appropriate. It should be clear enough, for example, that the teacher should allow the use of NSE in the classroom, should not downgrade it and, in attempting to overcome what may be quite natural expectancies, should try and look behind the speech of the children, as it were, before putting then in the familiar academic pigeonholes. We can restrict ourselves here, therefore, to a brief, general consideration of how teachers might be aided and encouraged in these endeavours.

Clearly one of the most important issues is that of teacher training. If we can somehow influence teachers *before* they begin their formal careers, perhaps we can bring about greater change than will be possible once they are set into the system.[20]

[20] This, incidentally, is the major reason for the use of trainee teachers in many studies of reactions to NSE. Information gained *from* beginning teachers allows examination of reactions to disadvantaged speech prior to any large degree of involvement with disadvantaged children; information given *to* beginning teachers may have more positive effects than will the same information given to established teachers. This is not to say, of course, that the current generation of teachers is irredeemable but rather

And, in an area so plagued with set ways of thinking, and firm expectations, perhaps the most important factor to be stressed in teacher training is *flexibility* of outlook. Of course, there are limits in the degree of flexibility that can be taught—if in fact one can formally teach such a thing at all. Perhaps, however, we can hope that flexibility, and a capability to consider the individual rather than operating on the basis of group stereotypes, may derive almost incidentally from the appropriate atmosphere. Just as many things considered important to the full education of children are not taught to them directly, so perhaps teacher awareness and flexibility might become the positive by-products of teacher training.

Since it is my belief that the 'good' teacher cannot be fully analysed, or reduced to constituent parts which may then be duplicated at will in new aspirants to the profession, I have some hesitation in forming specific recommendations as to 'what should be done', and must instead limit myself to what, by now, will be unsurprising generalities. First, of course, all teachers should be made aware of the current trends and findings in psychology, linguistics and, especially, in sociolinguistics. Virtually every study discussed above on the topic of teachers' attitudes and expectations makes this recommendation in some form or other, and clearly it should be attended to. The power of social stereotypes evoked by speech, the validity of nonstandard dialects, the lack of any necessary relationship between speech style and basic cognitive ability—an awareness of all these issues must be transmitted to the teacher, and especially to those who are to teach in disadvantaged areas. One would also hope that teachers would have an awareness of, and a sympathy for, the lifestyles and home background of those children whom they are to teach.

Once in the regular classroom, teachers would benefit from receiving updated information; one can imagine, for example, that it might have been most useful had Labov's (1973a) article on the logic of NSE been speedily disseminated among teachers. In this connection, researchers have a duty to see that they do not spend their professional lives talking only to each other, when issues of some wider relevance are under discussion. Now, for all I know there may already exist for some teachers various avenues for revising and augmenting their information about language and disadvantage. Possibly in-service training courses, professional seminars and conferences do such work effectively. However, from my (limited) experience of such phenomena, I should be much surprised to hear that there is no room for improvement.

Finally, pooling of information among teachers should be encouraged; this is of special importance if we consider for a moment the job we are asking the teachers to do. We are asking them to rethink what may often be longstanding opinions, and to shake off the power of strong social stereotypes. At the same time, we can be sure that society at large will (for some little period at least) *not* do these things. If the teacher is not to feel isolated in attempting to achieve what will thus seem to many a difficult exercise, it is vital that the support of other teachers, researchers and administrators be forthcoming. All should realize that,

that, as for other aspects of social attitude, many (possibly naively) pin their hopes on the young (see section 5.2.2.1; see also Edwards 1979b).

even in the absence of large-scale social change, there are useful things to be done which will help children now. Efforts made by teachers here may, in some way, have an important part to play in the larger social change. Even if this view is seen as hopelessly naïve, it does not invalidate any attempts to reduce the friction between the disadvantaged pupil and the teacher. If, on the other hand, one is more sanguine, then one might agree with Trudgill (1975) that, with regard to changes in the social evaluation of speech, 'school is a good place to start' (70).

6

Immigrants, ethnic minorities and bilingual education

'The most urgent single challenge facing the schools concerned is that of teaching English to immigrant children.'   Great Britain: Department of Education and Science (1971b)

'The key to communication with the society around them must be put into the hands of those immigrant children who lack it.'   Hawkes (1966)

Among disadvantaged groups, one large category with which I have not dealt so far is that of speakers of a foreign language (or of an English dialect considerably removed from SE).[1] Many multicultural societies have sizeable populations of such people, and they present unique problems within the general context of disadvantage. Note here that one is not discussing *all* foreign-language speakers who live or settle in a new country, but rather those who are typically found at the lower end of the socioeconomic spectrum. Here, for example, we refer to the West Indians and Asians in Britain, ethnic groups in countries like Canada, Australia and the United States, as well as the very important migrant worker populations in Europe (the Spaniards, Italians, Turks, Yugoslavs, etc. who come to more prosperous countries: thus, the German *gastarbeiter*).[2] Initially, it was considered that the migrant workers would not stay long in the host country; instead, however, they now constitute permanent blocks in many parts of Europe. In Switzerland, for example, migrant workers make up 20 per cent of the work force, and half a million have been there for more than 10 years. In Germany, they represent 12 per cent of the labour force; 21 per cent have been there for more than 7 years, and 9 per cent for more than 10 (Widgren 1975). Willke (1975b) notes that, in the 'receiving' countries (e.g. Switzerland, Germany, France, Austria) there were, in 1974, 3·2 million children of these 'migrant' workers. Thus the children are now a considerable factor to be reckoned with in the educational systems of several European countries.

It is often because of the common relationship between low socioeconomic

[1] Some of the earlier discussion of Mexican Americans will however be relevant here (see chapter 4).

[2] Little (1978) notes, for example, that in Britain 70 per cent of the black community lives in areas characterized by high degrees of physical disadvantage (see also Great Britain: Department of Education and Science 1967). Also, a recent issue of the *International Review of Education* is entirely devoted to issues in the education of migrant workers' children; see, for example, the introduction by Willke (1975a; see also Verdoodt 1977).

status and ethnic group membership that many minority children are considered disadvantaged. In addition, many immigrants work at low-prestige jobs and live in poor areas. Nevertheless, the ambition and motivation of many immigrant families is high and many, through hard work and effort, create a comfortable lifestyle for themselves in a remarkably short time (see for example the description of the Italians of Montreal, in Boissevain 1971). Thus, other things being equal, we might expect that only a temporary disadvantage would apply to many immigrants. Also, the large and obvious language difficulties of immigrant children at school *could* be only temporary; an intelligent child can, in time, learn the new language and go on to achieve school success, and of course many have done just that.

In this chapter however, I particularly want to consider methods of facilitating this process, as well as factors which operate against it. For, as we have seen, factors connected with social evaluations of speech styles are not likely to be simple; we might expect, therefore, that the hopes for the school success of immigrant children, expressed above, will not always be easily fulfilled. In general, much of what has already been discussed about language and disadvantage can be seen to apply to immigrants and ethnic minority group members. Nevertheless, they present a rather interesting subsection of the larger topic and therefore merit some special attention.

6.1   Prejudice, disadvantage and language

It is clear enough that, traditionally, people have tended to downgrade ethnic groups other than their own, the extent of this depending upon the social distance perceived. Some early social-psychological studies have demonstrated this, and there is little reason to think that ethnocentrism and prejudice have abated much. Of course, given groups can be more or less in favour at certain points in history, but the principle remains. And, for groups who are distinguishable from others in visible ways, a rather high degree of prejudice has been quite constant.

Bogardus (1925) studied the perceived social distance between American raters and a large number of ethnic groups. This distance was found to be greatest for those groups clearly unlike the Americans in obvious ways; thus, the least favoured groups included Mulattos, Koreans, Hindus and blacks. Katz and Braly (1933) investigated self-reported racial stereotypes among Princeton University students and, again, blacks were seen most unfavourably. The Katz and Braly paradigm was followed by Gilbert (1951) and Karlins et al. (1969). In both of these later studies, although some 'fading' of stereotypes was noted, the more or less traditional viewpoints were still in operation. Interestingly enough, the Karlins study found considerably increased favourability towards Blacks; this prompted Sigall and Page (1971) to question whether there really was a decrease in prejudice or whether, given the tenor of the times (the late 1960s), the perceived social desirability of not *appearing* prejudiced had influenced the results. These authors thus devised a rather ingenious experiment in which some subjects were led to believe that their attitudes could be accurately measured by an electronic device. In such a situation, it was felt that when the subject was also asked to give his views orally, his expressed opinions would be closer to his true feelings, and would not reflect the socially desirable response; since the subject believed his attitudes were being monitored accurately anyway, there would appear to be little value in any attempted distortion. Under such conditions, white American students demonstrated the familiar unfavourable views of blacks; other subjects, whose views were measured in a more straightforward way, accorded more favourable status to blacks. It would appear, therefore, that underneath the relatively recent liberal sentiments expressed of blacks, prejudice does indeed remain.

There are, of course, many studies of this topic (for a review, see Brigham 1971); most demonstrate what is popularly well known—that certain racial groups evoke prejudiced attitudes, and that these generally strengthen as a function of the perceived social or psychological distance between the judges and the judged. Those, therefore, who are characterized by skin colours other than white are easy targets of prejudice.

Thus we can understand the first great impediment faced by certain immigrants and ethnic-group members—social prejudice. This is not surprising, of course, and was seen to underlie reactions to the NSE speech of blacks (chapter 4). Here, however, we can expand a bit upon what was mentioned there. The fact that the speech patterns of, say, American blacks, are nonstandard does not imply that use of SE would significantly alter social perceptions of the speakers. In the present context, therefore, it seems apparent that an African or Asian who speaks fluent and highly articulate SE is not thereby exempt from prejudice. In fact, it has been suggested that SE usage might actually *increase* prejudice if this usage was seen as an attempt to come closer to white, SE-speaking society. Once again, I think it worth pointing out that speech *alone* is hardly the key to understanding social or educational disadvantage. Before anything else, then, many immigrants who may or may not be otherwise disadvantaged, are clearly so, given white prejudice directed against them.

Racial attitudes and prejudices are a longstanding and well-known phenomenon in the United States; in Britain, where large-scale immigration of blacks is a post-war phenomenon, the situation is newer, perhaps, but no less evident.[3] A recent newspaper article (Wilby 1978) reported on a highly controversial survey of racist attitudes in British schools (see also Ashworth 1975) and, also recently, there has been much heat generated over proposed policies to curtail immigration. Whether such moves reflect fear, prejudice or good sense can be debated; they indicate, however, the highly visible nature of some groups which, if nothing else, brings them to the attention of the larger society. Ease of identification makes groups easy targets for prejudice, especially in times of economic recession in which scapegoats are often produced. For present purposes, little more need be said, since it is hardly necessary to document further evidence of what is, unfortunately, a common and pervasive social attitude (see, e.g., Great Britain: Department of Education and Science 1971b, Little 1978, Townsend 1971).

[3] Also, of course, Britain's colonial experience strongly reinforced racial prejudice, especially towards blacks (see also Hawkes 1966).

Recipients of prejudice before setting foot in the school, many immigrant children have other difficulties awaiting them. We can recall here that, for disadvantaged children in general, it has been suggested that differences between the values and attitudes of the home, and those of the school, may be severe enough to constitute 'culture shock'. For immigrant and minority group children, such discontinuity is *frequently* severe enough to produce this phenomenon (see Ashworth 1975). Families whose religious, social and political beliefs are alien to those of mainstream society may certainly find the school a strange environment. Attitudes towards authority, discipline and school management may also vary widely. Even culinary habits and varieties of clothing and ornament can be important factors in creating a gap between home and school (see Ashworth 1975, Hawkes 1966, Wolfgang 1975).

The fact that many new immigrants (and ethnic minority members who have lived in the country for some time) tend to live among their own people does not make relationships with the larger society any easier. Although it is an entirely understandable and indeed natural reaction, such 'ghettoization' presents obvious problems. The communities themselves, sometimes formed as protection against inimical forces, and often internally sustained, frequently take some time to disappear. Where existing, they should be viewed sympathetically (see Gans 1962).

Once in school, immigrant and ethnic minority children show the patterns of low school achievement exhibited by indigenous disadvantaged children. In fact, in Britain at least, they appear to do more poorly (see Little 1978, Payne 1974, Willey 1975); elsewhere, too, this seems to be the case (see, e.g., Ashworth 1975, Wolfgang, 1975). A large part of this educational disadvantage is doubtless due to language difficulties, to which I shall shortly turn. Other factors, however, may also operate, analogous to those pertaining to indigenous disadvantaged children. Thus, for example, parents' views of education may vary widely. Ashworth (1975) has reported that, in Canada, it is sometimes found that Chinese parents are extremely concerned to see their children do well at school; East Indians, on the other hand, often wish their children to leave school and go on to work as soon as possible. The heterogeneity within the immigrant community can thus be a real and a complicating factor in the children's education. At the very least, an awareness of this points to the great need for establishing and maintaining a liaison between home and school. This is an issue which has most directly been addressed by those concerned with community relations as a whole, but it clearly is of great importance at the individual level as well.

There seems little doubt that the most obvious and important factor in the disadvantage of immigrant children is that of language. Before considering specifics here, one or two general points of relevance might be noted. First, as we have seen in chapter 4, *some* foreign accents are perceived by SE speakers to be of relatively high status (see, e.g., Giles 1970, Wilkinson 1965); these are not likely to include, however, the English accents of Asian and African speakers. Therefore, facility in English *per se* will not remove the disadvantageous effects accompanying certain speech styles. This is clearly associated, for immigrants, with the age at which they come to their new country. Generally speaking, we can see that the younger the immigrant child is when first entering school, the more likely it is that his English will be close to the local variety. Best of all in this regard are those children born in the country to which their parents have come. This group is sizeable among, for example, the 'migrant' worker population in Europe (see above), and among the Asian and African population in Britain (Willey (1975) notes that about 40 per cent of this group is British-born).

However, those children born in the new country (or living there from a very early age) have another difficulty. I stated in the preceding paragraph that they have the best chance of becoming fluent in the local variety of English; often, however, this local variety is itself a disadvantaged, nonstandard style. As Giles and Bourhis (1975) point out, immigrants who accommodate linguistically to the local style may actually *decrease* their perceived status. Similarly, the BBC television programmes on dialect and accent (Bragg and Ellis 1976), cited in chapter 4, provided several examples of black children speaking with broad Liverpool and Cockney accents. Indeed, this phenomenon is now quite common in British society. The implication for the children is that they may become doubly disadvantaged, on the basis both of skin colour and the use of NSE. Additionally, the fact noted previously that ability to speak SE may not decrease negative social evaluations at all further adds to the difficult situation in which immigrants may find themselves. In general, the disadvantage of such children may be a more subtle and less temporary state than one might first suspect.

However, we can hope that, whatever the situation outside the school may be, the school itself will not exacerbate the difficulties faced by immigrant children and that, in fact, it may work to lessen them. Hawkes (1966) puts it as follows:

> Where language is the only disadvantage, some intensive English teaching is essential to prevent gross injustice to the child, both at the time and for future prospects.... There is no place whatever in a remedial class for children whose only required remedy is in the language.   (50)

Although we may well suspect that language is rarely the only disadvantage, it is, however, an important issue with which the school can attempt to deal (see also chapter 5).

6.2   Non-English-speaking children

It is a generally recognized truism that children learn best when taught through the medium of their mother tongue (Saville and Troike 1971, UNESCO 1953). Therefore it is clear that for non-English speakers in an English school, special provisions must be made. European immigrants to Canada, Pakistani children in Britain, the children of migrant workers in Europe—for all of these the obvious primary necessity is a grasp of the national language.

The actual details of how such a grasp is most facilitated will, of course, vary widely, and hence it is impossible to make hard and fast recommendations here. Nevertheless, some broad aspects can be considered briefly. For example, the number of children concerned, for any given school authority, will dictate to a large extent what can be done. In some cases, if numbers are sufficient, special classes may be created in which children from similar linguistic backgrounds may be given English instruction; this may not, on the other hand, be possible if numbers are small. In the latter case, it is sometimes appropriate to provide peripatetic ESL (English as a Second Language) teachers who will routinely visit the school. There is, in any case, some feeling against separating children from their schoolmates, even where this would allow intensive instruction. The reason is that the social isolation may be more damaging than the instruction is beneficial. Anderson (1973) has recommended that even quite severely handicapped children be accommodated within the regular classroom as much as possible, and this has been seen as a useful procedure for disadvantaged children too (Edwards 1976a, in press). For immigrant children, surely quite a strong argument can be made against undue isolation from other children.[4] Apart from the social dangers attendant upon such isolation, there is a more tangible reason to avoid separation as well—the 'rub-off' effect (Ashworth 1975, Hawkes 1966). That is, children who are placed in regular classrooms will pick up many features of English more naturally and effortlessly than under formal instruction. This is a corollary of a rule which applies to language learning in general—that necessity is the best motivation.

Whatever the methods used to develop in children an understanding of English, the process must be done with care, and with due attention paid to local conditions. Examples of various responses to the needs of non-English-speaking children will be found in Ashworth 1975, Hawkes 1966, Townsend 1971 and Wolfgang 1975; we need only note additionally how important it is that teachers and schools refrain from forming premature expectations of the academic potential of such children. It is clear, for example, that the use of standardized IQ and achievement tests is meaningless for children who do not comprehend what is expected of them. Even, however, where children have apparently begun to grasp the language, great caution must be employed; they may not understand as well as they appear to.

In general terms, therefore, we should try not to treat these children in ways which may create permanent disadvantage where it should only be a transient phenomenon. Once comprehension of English is established, for example, teachers should not show antipathy towards what will be, in many instances, NSE (see chapter 5). Depending upon their age at first school entry, and upon the strength and quality of the home culture, many children will *always* be distinguishable from the indigenous population in terms of speech style. As with local groups, this language difference must not be construed as language deficit.

6.3 West Indian children

Among the larger immigrant population in Britain, West Indian children present a special case. This is because they speak not a foreign language but what we might term an 'extreme' form of NSE. Thus, Trudgill (1975) refers to West Indian NSE as representing a 'semi-foreign' language; indeed, as we have seen in chapter 3,

---

[4] I say 'undue' here because it is obvious that for many children some special attention is vital, and therefore some degree of conspicuousness is unavoidable.

Bailey (1966) has called for the recognition of Jamaican Creole as a separate language. In other words, the distinction between *language* and *dialect* becomes, in this instance, a problem (see also chapter 4). We need not go into the matter here, however, except to note that, whatever the case, West Indian English is extremely difficult for many SE speakers to understand and thus hardly satisfies the criterion of 'mutual intelligibility' which is characteristic of most NSE dialects (see also Stubbs 1976).

The position is further complicated by the fact that West Indian dialect is not itself a homogeneous entity; in fact, the term covers a number of Caribbean speech styles (all of which, however, are related to English). Trudgill (1975) points out that West Indian NSE speakers regard themselves as English speakers, even though their speech may fall at any one of a number of points on a continuum between SE and the broadest creole.[5] Therefore, the situation with regard to West Indian children in British schools is not quite analogous to that of, say, Pakistani children.

Among West Indian children who appear quite competent in English, there may not exist the full comprehension sometimes assumed. V. K. Edwards (whose work on West Indian speech has already been touched upon in chapter 3) has studied some aspects of language comprehension and language attitudes among West Indian children. On the first issue, Edwards's overall conclusion is that the language problems of these children have been underestimated. For example, in a comparison of 40 West Indian and 40 English 11- and 12-year-olds of similar social class and school ability, Edwards (1976a) found that although the groups were about equal in reading ability *per se*, the West Indians' reading *comprehension* was significantly less. This finding is interesting because the equivalence of reading ability might well lead teachers to assume that there also exists equivalence of comprehension of what has been read; this was clearly not so in Edwards's study. This 'semi-comprehension' may thus be more troublesome than the clearer case in which it is obvious that a foreign mother tongue prevents a child comprehending anything (see Trudgill 1975). Also of interest is the fact that more than 75 per cent of the West Indian children participating in the study were either British born or had been in Britain for more than five years; thus, the influence of West Indian English, Edwards suggests, goes beyond an effect relevant only to recent immigrants (see also Little 1978).

Edwards (1976b) comments further upon such findings. The general explanation provided is that West Indian speech is sufficiently distant from SE that dialect interference occurs; in particular, grammar and phonology diverge to such an extent that, unlike other NSE dialects, West Indian speech does create difficulties for its speakers in the British school system which go beyond social or attitudinal factors. Yet the familiar negative social evaluations are also present. Thus, Edwards (1976b) reports that, in evaluating taperecorded speech samples, both teachers and West Indian adolescents viewed West Indian speakers less favourably

---

[5] 'Creole' may be roughly defined as the native language developed and spoken by the children of 'pidgin' speakers. Pidgin, in turn, is a very simplified mixture of a European and an indigenous language which arises through contact between conquerors/settlers and the native population of an area.

than working- and middle-class English children. A West Indian girl who was presented speaking first with a British working-class accent and then in West Indian creole was seen more positively in the former guise. These findings, reminiscent of the work discussed in chapter 4, suggest that attitudinal *and* more substantive factors combine, in regard to West Indian speech, to create problems for its speakers (see also V. K. Edwards 1978).

There may well be, therefore, a need for some individual help for West Indian children, at least for those whose speech style is widely divergent from SE. However, many of the problems encountered could be dealt with by the teacher in the regular classroom. Since we are once again dealing with language difference and not deficit, the problems are not ones requiring speech therapy (Trudgill 1975). And, again, we require teachers who are sensitive to this, so that disadvantage will not be unnecessarily maintained (see also Coard 1971).

Recognition of the special, and sometimes more subtle, difficulties faced by the West Indian speaker has been shown by the production of the BBC radio series *The University of Brixton* (Marriott and Wells). A West Indian author and a linguist have compiled a number of episodes depicting the life of a Jamaican family in London; each programme presents various linguistic points of relevance. Designed for West Indian students of English, the series combines entertainment and education and apparently has met with some success (see also V. K. Edwards 1976b).

6.4   Cultural pluralism and bilingual education

A relatively recent development in the education of ethnic minority-group children has been that of bilingual education. This approach derives largely from the increasing concern for the merits of cultural pluralism, and thus appears to represent a more permanent solution to the education of children with little or no English-speaking ability.

There has of course been interest in Britain in bilingual education, especially with regard to Welsh and Scots Gaelic.[6] And in Ireland, the place of Irish in education is simply State policy (with debatable success, however: see Macnamara 1966, 1971, Ó Cuív 1969). Similarly, in Canada, there has been much recent interest in so-called 'immersion' programmes by which English-speaking children learn French (see Genesee 1976, Lambert and Tucker 1972, Swain 1976, 1978, Tucker 1976). All of these approaches, however, are largely concerned with children, native speakers of the majority or dominant language, learning a second language (or through a second language), and/or children who are members of an indigenous cultural group. Irish in education, for example, represents a foreign language for most Irish children, yet it is obviously of some special interest on traditional and cultural grounds.

[6] For material relevant to Welsh bilingual education, see Betts 1976, Dodson 1962, 1967, Dodson *et al.* 1968, Great Britain: Department of Education and Science 1971a, Jones 1966, Morgan 1973, Price 1978, Stephens 1973 and Thomas 1971. Similar information on the current state of Scots Gaelic in education may be found in MacKinnon 1974, 1977a, 1977b.

Examples of bilingual education for non-English-speaking, non-native children are most recently provided in the United States (see Edwards 1976b, 1977d). Over the last decade or so, a large-scale federally-funded programme of bilingual education has been operating there; several hundred specific projects across the country have been established. Most of these have been directed towards Spanish-speaking Mexican-American children, but they have also catered for French, Portuguese and Chinese speakers, speakers of several American Indian languages, and others. The reason for mentioning these programmes here is that many of the children participating are not only minority group members but are, as well, of low socio-economic status. In fact, the laws regulating these programmes originally stipulated that a 'high concentration' of participants must be from low-income families. Although recent legislation has removed this limitation, the correlation between ethnic group membership in the United States and low family income ensures that the programmes continue to serve mainly poor, disadvantaged groups (see Edwards 1977d).

There is, therefore, an interesting dilemma built into existing bilingual education in the United States. On the one hand, many have seen in it a potential medium for overturning the traditional American 'melting-pot' and for encouraging cultural pluralism and ethnic diversity (e.g. Andersson and Boyer 1970, Fishman 1966, 1970, Fishman and Lovas 1970, Gaarder 1970). Such writers wish to see bilingual education expand to become an integral part of education in general. On the other hand, most bilingual programmes have in fact been of a temporary, bridging nature, in which the primary result has been to facilitate the children's move into an all-English curriculum (Saville and Troike 1971). Gaarder (1970), for example, examined the first bilingual projects and found that the majority operated only at the earliest school levels. Further, Kjolseth (1972) noted that more than 80 per cent of the projects which he investigated were of the 'assimilation' type—far from encouraging cultural pluralism, they operated to increase the ease of assimilation of children into the mainstream linguistic milieu.

Thus, it appears that these American programmes are not so supportive of cultural pluralism as might first seem the case. Those, therefore, who have seen them as servants to the cause of pluralism, and part of a general upsurge in ethnicity, have been somewhat disappointed.

Yet, if the programmes are seen as a type of compensatory education designed to help children of limited English-speaking ability, then they may be counted as more successful. That is, the extra help given in English, and the fact that this is often done in an atmosphere stressing the worth and vitality of the students' *own* culture, may mean that the net effect of the programmes—while not wide-ranging enough for those concerned to promote ethnic identity—may coincide with the needs of the participants rather well. Immigrants and ethnic group members realize the value of English, and the rewards that facility in it may afford their children. For many such people, active outside support for their own language may appear a secondary consideration, and a matter of less urgency than gaining some basic skills in English. In fact, many immigrants made an implicit decision regarding the relative priorities of language and more practical economic considerations when coming to their new country in the first place. All this is not to say, of course, that minority group members will fail to see the value in a child receiving early education in his own language. But, in many cases, this will be appreciated primarily as a manner of making the child's adjustment to the English-speaking system smoother.

Thus, although bilingual education is of debatable importance to the mainten-ance of ethnicity and, therefore, is not primarily a method of encouraging cultural pluralism, it may well be of some considerable use in overcoming the language barrier faced by children who are at once minority group members and disadvan-taged. Viewed in this way, many American bilingual education programmes can be seen as sensitive and useful extensions of a strict English-teaching approach; not only do children receive help in English but they can, at the same time, be instructed in other school subjects through the medium of their own language. If, at the same time, ethnic identity *can* be maintained, so much the better. The important point, in the context of this book, is not so much whether or not the children's heritage and home background can be sustained by the school, but rather that children may be assisted to school success without *downgrading* their back-ground and language. To the extent to which bilingual education programmes, American or otherwise, can promote this service to disadvantaged children of limited English-speaking ability, they are useful and important.[7]

6.5   Teachers and teacher training

Most of the remarks made in the last section of the previous chapter also apply here—teachers of immigrants and ethnic group children must be flexible in their approach, and understanding of the problems faced by their pupils. However, teachers of children with little or no English-speaking ability clearly require special skills. Thus, at a simple level, we need good second-language teachers. The more interesting aspects of the issue, however, are those connected with the teaching of children who *are* English-speaking, though of an extreme NSE dialect (e.g. West Indian children), or who have advanced some way with English ability.

Years ago in Britain, children speaking Welsh, Irish or Scots Gaelic at school were punished for doing so; the language was not to be tolerated. Thus, in Wales there was the 'Welsh Not'—a stick hung round the neck, and used to beat the child found speaking Welsh (Ellis 1974, Jones 1973). In Scotland, a similar device, the *maide-crochaidhe*, was apparently in use as late as the 1930s (MacKinnon 1974). And, in Ireland under the British, a tally-stick, notched to indicate every time a child spoke Irish, was used as a record of misdemeanours (Wall 1969). Similar restrictions on language use have been noted by Stoller (1977) with regard to Span-ish-speaking children in the United States. Stoller also points out that many such children were relegated to classes for the 'educable mentally retarded' because of

---

[7] Whether current bilingual education in the United States is the most economical way to achieve this is however debatable. Generally, the discussion here on bilingual education is only a brief summary of a topic important in its own right.

the equation commonly made between lack of facility in English and lack of cognitive ability.

We have, no doubt, moved on somewhat from such barbarisms, but we must still be on guard against more subtle variants of the process. That is, intelligent pupils must not be ignored by teachers who are frustrated with attempts at communication with them. As Hawkes (1966) has noted, such treatment promotes division between teacher and pupil, and is 'a breeding ground for antagonisms' (50). Clearly, home/school liaison is vital, so that the teacher may become aware of backgrounds which may be quite unfamiliar (see, e.g., Ashworth 1975, Willey 1975).

In many cases the solution lies in more adequate teacher training in which, depending upon the degree of language difference, real specialization may be required. Teachers should be aware not only of language *per se*, but also of language *varieties* spoken by pupils (Edwards 1976b). Thus, the Bullock Report (Great Britain: Department of Education and Science 1975) advocates that teachers of West Indian children have an understanding of Creole, and a positive attitude towards it (see also V. K. Edwards 1976b). In addition, if special teachers are required to work with some children, care must be taken to see that they are well integrated with the rest of the school staff. Just as continuity between home and school lessens the likelihood of difficulty, so too continuity within the school itself is of some concern (see, e.g., Edwards 1976b, Great Britain: Department of Education and Science 1972). Overall, it would appear that much room for improvement exists (Derrick 1973, Great Britain: Department of Education and Science 1971b, Millins 1973, Willke 1975b).

The major concern here, however, is not so much with specifics of teacher training; these can be planned by those directly concerned. Rather, it is with the attitude of teachers. This is because, at every level of the integration of the child into the school system, care must be taken to ensure that disadvantage is not created where it need not exist. Immigrant and ethnic group children have quite enough difficulties as it is. In particular, it should be seen that non-English-speaking children do not suffer from so-called 'language delay'. Of course it will take them time to gain facility in English, but this is hardly analogous to retardation of the developmental patterns of first-language acquisition. Like indigenous children, youngsters of limited English-speaking ability enter school with a well-functioning language system which is, simply, not that of the school.

Thus, the attitude of the teacher and, more broadly, that of education in general, should be that immigrant and ethnic minority children should be helped as much as possible to acquire a grasp of English. During this process, premature judgements concerning children's intellectual abilities should be resisted. With care and attention, we could hope that such children, once fully functional in English, will show the same patterns of success (and failure) as do their local schoolmates. This, at least, is what we should aim for.

7

Summary and conclusions

I hope that the general arrangement of this book has been such that a connecting line of argument can be perceived. If this is so, then the summary required here can be quite brief; thus, I shall simply review some of the more relevant strands of the discussion. Similarly, concluding remarks should be almost redundant if the argument presented has resolved itself in the course of the text. Nevertheless, I do want to take this opportunity to mention one or two things which are suggested by the book as a whole.

7.1 Summary

Overall, the general aim has been to reject the notion that substantive language deficiency is associated with disadvantaged speech, and to propose that any speech-related difficulties encountered by disadvantaged speakers are of a social or socio-linguistic nature. It was considered important, therefore, to show initially that the broader issue of disadvantage itself could most appropriately be viewed in the same way.

Thus, in chapter 1, several theoretical positions concerning the aetiology of disadvantage were discussed. First, the possibility that disadvantaged populations are so because of genetic difference (and inferiority) was considered; here, the work of Jensen was obviously most directly relevant. It was seen that the relationship between intelligence and race/social class is not one of crystal clarity. The issue of what intelligence itself actually *is*, the use of tests which implicitly reflect middle-class norms, and the difficulties of making accurate cross-group comparisons all suggest that this area of research is not one from which firm conclusions can be drawn. In addition, it was pointed out that, even if racial differences in intelligence *were* found to exist, it is unlikely that this would have any direct or immediate implications (especially since such differences would undoubtedly be relatively minor). Thus, the equation of disadvantage with genetic deficiency is not only unproven but also likely a non-issue in any practical sense.

Similarly rejected were views that disadvantage stems from cultural and social deprivation. Again, it was seen that studies purporting to show this are inevitably riddled with middle-class bias and assumptions about what is, and what is not, appropriate, useful or intelligent behaviour.

Thus it appears that the most reasonable hypothesis for the explanation of educational or social disadvantage is one which stresses *differences* between groups.

The attitudes, values and lifestyles of certain social groups may cause them to perform relatively poorly in situations governed by the standards and conventions of other groups. The disadvantaged thus suffer real difficulties, but these are not caused by intellectual deficiency or by cultural deprivation; rather, the problems are the result of a low-prestige group, with little social power, having to accommodate to the mainstream society. Disadvantage is therefore only possible where groups of different status interact, and where comparisons are drawn from the perspective of the higher-status group.

In chapters 2 and 3, this line of reasoning was extended to cover the language differences observed among different groups. Since languages, and language varieties, are all valid symbolic systems, distinctions among them cannot be justifiably attributed to greater or lesser logical force, accuracy etc. Examination of the speech pattern of blacks in the United States proved particularly relevant here, since it has traditionally been seen as a substandard variant of 'proper' English. The work of Labov and others, however, demonstrated quite convincingly that black English is a valid dialect which adheres to rules and thus conforms to its own internal 'logic'. That is, although we may refer to it (and other varieties) as *nonstandard*, it is clearly not *substandard*.

It was also possible to show that compensatory education, which often centres upon language and language remediation, is largely misguided. Even the term itself is inaccurate since, if disadvantaged speech is different but valid, there is nothing to compensate for. All normal children, upon entering school, possess a coherent language. If this differs from the variety which the school aims to promote then, clearly, problems may ensue. But it is important to realize that these problems do not derive from a 'poor' language for which the child must in some way be compensated.

Thus in chapters 4 and 5 I was able to consider directly the *social* nature of the problems associated with disadvantaged speech. Here the first step was to investigate the more general question of the social evaluation of speech styles *per se*. Referring to evidence drawn from North America and Britain, it was seen that disadvantaged, working-class speech is typically regarded as low in prestige and that the 'received' variety is, unsurprisingly, high in perceived status. This of course represents and reflects the association between speech styles and the social position of their speakers. Not only is disadvantaged speech viewed more unfavourably by middle-class evaluators, this social stereotype has also been internalized by speakers of nonstandard varieties themselves. Although an important sense of group identity may be fostered by these nonstandard variants, they remain inferior to the standard forms in terms of status and prestige. This was seen to have potentially harmful consequences in the job market and, indeed, in any context involving language contact.

At school, the difficulty is exacerbated by the fact that, for teachers, 'correct' language has long been of paramount importance. Thus, for the disadvantaged child, the school career may represent a long period of continuous, if subtle, downgrading of his speech style; it is not surprising that many have considered disadvantaged speech to be an impediment to school success. Although speech cues are not the only ones available to the teacher, they are of some considerable importance and are used in the categorizing processes by which some children are seen to be brighter than others, to have greater academic potential etc. Appropriate information should therefore be provided to teachers, in an attempt to lessen the likelihood of them forming expectations about children which may, quite simply, be wrong.

Chapter 6 briefly considered the special case of children of limited English-speaking ability, and of those whose dialect of English is extremely nonstandard. Since many such speakers are black they suffer, first of all, from racial prejudice. It was seen to be important not to add to this difficulty by creating disadvantage where it need not exist. Thus, many children simply have to learn a new language; others may require assistance in reducing problems due to dialect interference. In all cases, teachers should refrain from drawing conclusions about the academic potential of immigrant and ethnic group children, at least until initial language barriers have been overcome. The apparently more stable solution to the language difficulties of such children, bilingual education, was shown to represent in most cases a form of compensatory education; this may have its best potential as a vehicle for the successful integration of children of limited English-speaking ability into the school.

7.2   Conclusions

Disadvantaged speakers of nonstandard English have difficulties, most importantly at school, of a social nature. The fact that their problems are not primarily linguistic does not resolve the issue, of course. Rather, it implies that instead of 'curing' the speaker, we must direct much of our attention towards altering the social attitudes of others.

7.2.1   Teachers and teacher training

Teachers should be given the linguistic and psychological evidence which will allow them to see disadvantaged speech for what it is. Teacher training should give some attention to this work, and in addition should encourage and promote understanding of the backgrounds of disadvantaged children. This is, naturally, of greatest importance for those teachers who are likely to encounter such children in the classroom, but general information about linguistic and cultural relativism should be part of the programme for *all* trainee teachers. Throughout, the emphasis should be upon the necessity for teachers to remain flexible and open in their approach to pupils whose lifestyles may be quite unlike the teacher's own; in this way the possibility of forming premature, and perhaps erroneous, appraisals of children can be lessened.

As with all children, the teacher should approach the disadvantaged class with the knowledge that he or she will be dealing with a heterogeneous assortment of abilities, attitudes and motivations. In every case, the aim must be to assist the child in developing his fullest potential. Anything which proves an obstacle in this process should be carefully examined to ascertain whether it is a substantive difficulty, or whether it is a product of social attitude. As we have seen, a child's language, which to many teachers can appear to represent the former category is, in most instances, a manifestation of the latter.

7.2.2   Speech therapists and clinicians

On the basis of the evidence reviewed here, therapists should expect to deal with as many disadvantaged children, proportionally, as nondisadvantaged children. That is, assuming the acceptance of the *difference* position on speech, there is no reason to think that more real speech defects will be found in one population than in another. The task for therapists working with disadvantaged children is complicated, however, by the fact that in order to separate difference from defect, they must have some familiarity with the dialect concerned. The general basis for their work must be an awareness of the norms of the appropriate adult speech community; indeed, most contemporary speech therapists realize this.

Speech therapists may also find useful roles as speech teachers when specific language training is required although, as we have noted, the amount of speech teaching needed by the normal child, nonstandard speaker or not, is likely to be minimal. In this connection, therapists should not confuse the length of time a child may take to gain fluency in a second language with so-called language 'delay'.

7.2.3   Changing social attitudes

The area of social attitudes towards speech is one in which changes are at once the most likely to be of long-term benefit to the disadvantaged speaker and, at the same time, the most difficult to bring about. Evaluation of speech styles seems to be a feature of many, if not most, societies and it is simply utopian to consider that changes will occur rapidly. Indeed, although the particular speech pattern downgraded today may be held in higher esteem 20 years from now, it is probable that some other variety will then occupy its former position in the status hierarchy. In other words, it is not an unreasonable assumption that value judgements about speech will always be with us.

We can nevertheless hope that people may be more and more inclined to see their attitudes simply as matters of taste or preference, and not as judgements of the intrinsic value of speech styles. Thus, we might hope that an employer could perceive an employee as having an extremely grating voice, an unpleasant accent and a strange vocabulary and yet, at the same time, realize that the employee is intelligent, efficient and an asset to the firm. Of course, this doubtless occurs all the time even now. One simply hopes that an awareness, in general terms, of some of the recent sociolinguistic evidence, will increasingly become common knowledge and thereby decrease people's willingness to equate certain speech styles with certain personality traits.

In the educational system, especially, we might expect that the weight of evidence would have its effect more quickly than in society at large. And indeed, although there remains much room for improvement, one cannot deny that there is more educational tolerance now for nonstandard speech varieties than was previously so. Here, continuing and improving researcher-teacher communication is vital. If we wish teachers to change their attitudes, we must provide them with the evidence that they are right to do so.

7.2.4 Changing the speech of disadvantaged speakers

So far I have been discussing the views of those who work with and for disadvantaged speakers and, as mentioned at the beginning of this section, this is the most important task. Nevertheless, it is obviously unwise to ignore the fact that, while we wait and work for the millennium, disadvantage remains. Here we must realize that *practical* difficulties will continue to face nonstandard speakers, both in school and without, so long as negative evaluations of their speech persist. Hence the need for them to acquire facility in the comprehension and use of the standard variety. On the first aspect, comprehension, the evidence presented suggests that little need be done; most speakers of nonstandard English understand Standard English well enough. The second point—the *use* of SE—is more subtle. It would seem that the most appropriate action is rather indirect. Although the teacher may offer guidance as to those contexts in which SE will be most useful, the area is one in which the wishes and needs of the speakers themselves will dictate most effectively. Apart from the possibility of causing psychological stress, there is little reason to think that a policy of formal instruction in SE will bring any long-term success. Rather, it seems more appropriate that teachers, while sympathetic to the nonstandard varieties, present themselves as SE-speaking models. Over time, then, children will have the opportunity to observe and internalize the conventions applying to SE usage. And, given that reading and writing will be conducted in SE, the child can also be expected to acquire competence in these more formal language domains.

Throughout, the single most important factor is the creation by the teacher of a reasonable atmosphere in which children are not made self-conscious about their language. From this basis of acceptance, the *addition* of SE to the child's linguistic repertoire may be achieved. Any attempt at instruction which, however subtly, indicates that the nonstandard variety is less than adequate is likely to foster linguistic insecurity which is not, one would think, a good position from which to attempt the expansion of one's capabilities. Thus, to make the point once again, any policy which smacks of *replacement* of one variety with another is not only philosophically distasteful but also likely to meet with little success.

7.2.5 Future directions

It is common, at the conclusion of works such as this, to see a call made for further research in the area. Naturally, this can be repeated here; further studies of speech evaluations, of sociolinguistic attitudes in general, and of the problems faced by disadvantaged children at school are to be encouraged. At the same time, however, there is already sufficient information available in the area of language and disadvantage to allow us to give attention to the dissemination of what is known.

Therefore, it seems that this is a topic which calls for increased and sustained interdisciplinary communication. Researchers from different fields have much to say to each other (sociolinguistics itself is, of course, a hybrid), and much to say to teachers and educators. The zeal with which linguists attacked the notion of verbal deprivation can serve as a model here for further action. There is, in short, an opportunity in this line of study to apply the fruits of investigation to real-life contexts. It would be unfortunate if this opportunity were not taken. Indeed, it would be a shameful neglect.

8

Developments in disadvantage: ten years on

In terms of the aetiology of disadvantage itself, the genetic deficiency argument, while certainly still made in some quarters, has continued to receive the sort of criticism outlined in chapter 1. Apart from the difficulty in testing for some 'native' intelligence, general mental ability, or 'g' factor which would make sense in cross-population comparisons (i.e. is 'culture-free' or 'culture-fair'), it remains virtually impossible to ascertain, first, the degree of heritability of intelligence and, second, the degree to which intelligence differences across groups are due to genetic factors. The most reasonable picture, perhaps, even if somewhat less specific than we might like, is one which depicts intelligence itself as impossible to define without reference to sociocultural determinants, which can obviously vary widely. Further, the underlying, inherited capacity is probably on average much the same across human groups, differences in performance occurring because of the interaction of environmental factors. Thus, while statements like 'intelligence is 80% hereditary and 20% environmental' are silly, our knowledge of genetics would indicate that there is an interaction between the two factors. Another way of expressing things would be to say that all 'normal' people inherit basic intellectual capacities with (broadly speaking) the same range of possibility; then, non-hereditary factors operating upon this inheritance will lead to specific performance levels.

A good recent review of the nature–nurture argument about intelligence generally, and the question of racial differences specifically, is provided by Colman (1987). He outlines the rise of the intelligence-testing movement in the U.S. — a fascinating area I did not go into in chapter 1 — with its implications for eugenics, for the passage of sterilization laws in two-thirds of the country to control 'idiocy, insanity, imbecility, and criminality' (21), and for the control of immigration. It comes as no surprise to learn that mental deficiency was seen to be particularly prevalent among blacks, who, to compound the problem, were 'unusually prolific' in the view of Terman, the main force in IQ testing in the U.S., nor that many Italian, Polish and Jewish immigrants were detected as feeble-minded compared to their British and northern European counterparts. The implications of tight quotas for some categories of immigrants which followed were to have tragic results, particularly for German Jewish refugees in the 1930s.

Colman presents further details of the argument over the heritability of intelligence between Eysenck and Kamin — who have continued to be two of the main protagonists (see Eysenck and Kamin 1981) — and of the fraudulent data in twin studies presented by Sir Cyril Burt (see also Fancher 1985, Hearnshaw 1979). In fact, Colman provides impressive evidence that all studies of identical twins raised apart (see Farber 1980), of kinship correlations in general, and of adopted children are less than clearcut. Similar careful analysis exemplifies Colman's examination of black–white intelligence differences, in which many of the points made in chapter 1 are stressed — including, for example, questions of test bias and the difficulties of cross-group comparison generally. Colman finds that the case for genetically based black–white differences is not proved and, citing Bodmer (1972), not provable in societies in which environmental differences — often reflecting the prevalence of prejudice and racism —continue to be large. Colman concludes by stating that he 'was astonished to discover how little support, even of the most indirect kind, could be mustered for the hereditarian thesis' (77). Similarly, in a review of Colman, Sutherland (1988) notes that he came to the volume believing in the importance of the hereditary basis of intelligence and in innate intelligence differences across groups; after, he is unconvinced of any such difference and considers that the only evidence for any heritability of intelligence is 'that if there were none, IQ [sic] would be almost the only biological trait not influenced in this way.'

If, however, the genetic deficiency stance on disadvantage has not gained any intellectual ground in the last decade, the environmental–deficit argument continues to exert considerable force. As Harwood (1982) remarks, it has been the dominant argument since the 1930s, replacing the genetic–deficiency position (which, itself, had replaced a mid-nineteenth-century view that social reform could ameliorate the results of environmental deprivation). Consequently, the violent attacks on 'Jensenism' reflected the academic climate and, in particular, the academic involvement in environmentally-based programmes of compensatory education (see below).

An interesting commentary is that of Persell (1981). Like Colman, she reviews the arguments considering the heritability of intelligence and concludes that environmental factors are paramount. However, this is not to accept the environmental–deficit view, which the author sees as just as racist as genetic explanations, for children are seen to have a poor or deficient culture, or none at all. Even the 'difference' position on disadvantage is criticized by Persell as just a variety of the environmental–deficit view, for it too is seen to hold that disadvantaged children are deficient in 'mental capacity' or 'conceptual tools' (32; see also Smitherman-Donaldson 1988). I think this is somewhat unfair to the difference position as outlined in chapters 1 and 3, although we must always remember that the differences exhibited by disadvantaged children are commonly translated into social deficits through inaccurate or prejudiced social perceptions.

A recent Canadian study (Edwards and McKinnon 1987) demonstrates the continuing appeal of an environmental–deficit view among teachers. In northeastern Nova Scotia, 96 teachers were surveyed on their perceptions of disadvantage, using a questionnaire based upon characteristics widely cited in the literature. In part, the study was based upon the results of Edwards (1974) and a follow-up study (Archer and Edwards 1982) which demonstrated: (a) that major dimensions of importance for teachers in assessing disadvantage, as revealed by factor analysis, were a *school* factor, a *home-background* factor and an *emotional* factor; (b) that teachers' assessments made when children were five years old predicted performance on standardized achievement tests at age eight; (c) that teachers' ratings of 'at risk' children were thus of diagnostic value, and might form the basis of a screening device, simple, useful and easily administered, which has as its main feature the formalization of subjective assessments routinely made by teachers anyway (see also Lindsay 1980).

Teachers were asked to rate characteristics of disadvantage, on 5-point scales, as to their perceived importance and centrality. A number of interesting findings emerged. First, this Nova Scotia study indicated that teachers' views of disadvantage tend to have generality across a wide variety of contexts, since teachers in this study agreed, in the main, with assessments made elsewhere of the importance of certain characteristics. Second, teachers particularly stressed home-background characteristics of disadvantage, and this was seen as encouraging 'in that it shows a willingness to look behind the actual pupil characteristics which present themselves in class, and to consider underlying causal factors' (Edwards and McKinnon 1987, 343). Third, however, and less encouraging, was the evidence that most teachers seemed to endorse an environmental–deficit explanation of observed characteristics; this was revealed by comments made by teachers in addition to the rating scales themselves (see also Edwards 1986). Further notes concerning the persistence of deficit theory will be found below, when I turn specifically to language.

Ogbu (1978, 1982) has contributed to the literature his notion of the 'castelike' status possessed by some, but not all, minority or subordinate groups. This would seem to explain why not all such groups do well or poorly at school, for example, and reminds us that not all differences need become socioeducational deficits. Ogbu contrasts, for instance, the school performance of black American students with that of Chinese, Japanese and others (it is thus apparent, incidentally, that castelike status cannot simply be equated with membership of a so-called 'visible minority'). The focus of Ogbu's idea is that if a minority is socially downgraded and/or oppressed, and if social mobility is extremely difficult or impossible, regardless of efforts and achievments, then the likelihood of school failure is heightened. Ogbu was drawn to his conclusions by his perception that the difference theory of educational disadvantage and failure did not come to grips with the *success* of some immigrant children. Yet, as d'Amato (1987) observes, Ogbu's ideas are not, themselves, problem-free —principally because, like a simplified difference theory, they do not account for the behaviour and progress of all the children they purport to deal with; just as some 'different' children do not fail at school while their 'castelike' counterparts do, so some castelike children themselves succeed. Both d'Amato and Erickson (1987) suggest a useful synthesis of Ogbu's notion with the cultural difference perspective. I think this is reasonable and affords a more comprehensive understanding; indeed, at the simplest level, the notion of membership in some socially immobile caste merely reminds us that, across social and ethnic groups, some will experience a greater translation of difference into deficit — i.e. some of the disadvantaged are more disadvantaged than others.

Before turning to more specifically linguistic matters, there is one further general topic to consider. It is the status and evaluation of educational intervention efforts. As I noted in chapter 1, traditional intervention programmes of 'enrichment' or compensatory education sprang from an environmentalist background; after all, if deficits are seen to be socially caused, then there is hope for social amelioration. As well, it was pointed out that a difference perspective which rejects environmental deficit could still theoretically give rise to social programmes of assistance, even though the purely logical approach would be to remove the social judgements, comparisons and prejudices which create these *social* deficits in the first place; perhaps, while waiting and working for the millennium, we should provide practical assistance for children in current society. Nonetheless, most compensatory education interventions *have* been based upon a deficit view, and so are centrally flawed as regards their underpinning philosophy. Adherence to a difference position thus rejects the idea that there is anything to compensate for, at least in children themselves. The results of compensatory education programmes were not, in any case, very encouraging; for Head Start, for example, it can be understood that 'an educational policy whose appeal lay more in political expedience than in practical efficacy' (Harwood 1982, 51) might flounder because of insufficient groundwork.

In 1979, Zigler and Valentine edited a lengthy volume on the American Head Start programme, with great detail given of its beginnings, implementation and development. While the long-range effects of intervention are still subjects of controversy — Head Start apparently did not raise IQ scores substantially, for example — it seems clear that the programme did provide hundreds of thousands of children with positive school experiences and related services (including health care). Indeed, Zigler and Seitz (1980) note that success should be assessed in terms of improved social competence, involving physical wellbeing, motivation and achievement, as well as formal cognitive skills. Experience of an Irish programme (Kellaghan 1977) would support the view that positive effects other than IQ gains may result from intervention. Generally, it is possible that we may ask too much, in terms of future pay-offs, of educational programmes; perhaps some interventions which positively affect children's lives can be accepted as good in themselves, regardless of what they may or may not influence ten years on. We do not provide playgrounds and swings for youngsters necessarily with the view that by so doing we increase social competence, now or in the future; they are seen as pleasant in and of themselves.

Zigler and Berman (1983) provide further relevant points. First, they acknowledge that intervention efforts of the 1960s were based upon an environmental–deficit philosophy, were pre-occupied with intelligence and IQ, and were overly optimistic. Head Start, on the other hand, is described as avoiding the deficit model, emphasizing cultural relativism and difference; thus the programme is one of addition rather than replacement. As well, Zigler and

Berman state that Head Start was not, from the first, limited to IQ-raising but aimed rather for a more all-embracing social competence. Still, to the extent that it was *seen* as mainly interested in IQ gain, Head Start was open to criticism that such gain was shortlived (e.g. Jensen's views of compensatory education, chapter 1). Zigler and Berman end their overview by calling, unsurprisingly, for interventions which have a broader focus than IQ alone, and which emphasize a 'family-support' approach over more traditional, intensively scholastic programmes like, for example, the Abecedarian Project of Ramey and his associates — which would seem, as well, to reflect environmental–deficit perspectives (see Gallagher and Ramey 1987, Ramey, Collier, Sparling, Loda, Campbell, Ingram and Finkelstein 1976, Ramey and Campbell 1977, Ramey, MacPhee and Yeates 1982).

The broader-based approach to intervention is also revealed in McMichael's (1980) discussion of a British primary-school programme. Although this project was small in scale, results indicated that even 'limited and sporadic' interventions on the part of assistant head teachers were useful, and that these could prove an enjoyable episode even in the lives of children whose home situations were unsettled. The reader is also referred to the report of a Canadian pre-school intervention programme (Wright 1983) which apparently demonstrated IQ and achievement gains, as well as increased social competence. This programme, however, is clearly labelled a compensatory one and seems firmly cast in a deficit mould. Thus, the poor are characterized here as deficient in symbolic processing; children are seen as receiving insufficient cognitive stimulation from parents, whose own cognitive abilities are under-developed (Wright 1980a). Despite citing Jensen positively, the author, in another publication (1980b), apparently rejects a genetic–deficit argument, while restating the environmental–deficit view that lower-class children have an inability to think, this deriving from poor home stimulation.

Finally here, I should like to refer to a very useful article on intervention and public policy by Woodhead (1988). He discusses evaluation results of a number of American projects, acknowledging for example — with some reservations — the apparent effectiveness of Head Start programmes (which have been increasingly federally funded throughout the 1980s). But Woodhead also raises questions about the *causes* of observed effects, about the generalizability of results (e.g. *some* Head Start projects, apparently successful, can be inaccurately taken as representative of more than a thousand diverse programmes which exist under the general Head Start banner), about the duration of effects, and about the formative effects of preschool, school, family and societal interactions. Woodhead's overall message, therefore, is that interpreting the results of early intervention for public policy purposes requires a considerable amount of detail and sophistication. My final note here is that intervention policies today, as opposed to those of the past, are much more likely to be methodologically sound and, more importantly, socially aware; while the environmental–deficit philosophy has hardly been completely eradicated, there is evidence of more interventions erected on a cultural difference framework.

The difference–deficit debate continues when we turn specifically to disadvantaged language. Most readers will of course be able to confirm personally that popular prejudices still exist towards disadvantaged and nonstandard speech, and that such speech is often seen to reflect innate or learned deficiencies which go beyond speech production itself, to cognitive abilities generally. Popular writers like Reed (1981) are still able to style black 'street' speech as gibberish. These continuing reactions were predicted in chapters 4 and 7. More disturbing is the continued allegiance to a language deficit philosophy within segments of the academic community.

In 1982, Feagans and Farran edited a book devoted to the language of poor children (see also Edwards 1983a). They noted, in their preface, that the deficit model applied to language was superseded by new perspectives, and because interventions based upon it had had limited success. In this way they seem to suggest that perhaps the underlying deficit philosophy was not, in itself, inaccurate. One contributor, Blank, appears to maintain a deficit viewpoint in that she fails to make clear that while difficulties with a difference model largely have to do with understanding the range of skills possessed and valued by different social groups, those with a deficit model are linguistically overwhelming (see chapters 2 and 3). She also feels that deficit theorists were mainly interested in semantics, difference theorists with grammar; again, the implication is that the deficit stance may have some validity. Snow, another contributor, states that disadvantaged children do have deficits — they are not linguistic but are rather knowledge deficiencies which lead to reduced vocabularies. First, it is difficult to see how such deficiencies have nothing to do with language. Second, this view raises questions like 'knowledge of/for what?' which led to the formulation of the difference perspective in the first place.

Honey (1983) has recently attacked the linguistic difference viewpoint in a monograph published by the British National Council for Educational Standards. He rejects the idea that all language varieties are equally valid systems, and claims that this view undermines attempts to reintroduce school 'standards', pushing disadvantaged speakers into a language trap. That is, while what these speakers really need is help in standard English, the modern linguistic stance, out of respect for indigenous nonstandard varieties it claims are of equal status to SE, asks schools to encourage the use of NSE. A review of Honey's work (Edwards 1983b) reveals that the author falls prey to the confusion of concepts with words to describe them (thus, so-called 'primitive' tribes lack words present in more 'advanced' societies, but this says nothing about the validity of the *language* system), he misinterprets evidence bearing on the validity of one nonstandard variety in particular (BEV), he fails to see that linguistic difference can be translated into *social* deficit, and he thinks that a school policy of tolerance for nonstandard varieties must inevitably lead to an active fostering of NSE.

Teachers, too, continue to adhere to an environmental–deficit view of disadvantaged language. Gordon (1978) found, for example, that Bernstein's theory (widely, if inaccurately, connected with a deficit perspective; see chapter 2 and Edwards 1987) was attractive to a sample of British teachers, especially to those not well-versed in it, in that it acted as a confirmation of existing views. This is particularly unfortunate given that these older prejudices about language variation were to some extent giving way to difference perspectives (see Trudgill 1975 and chapter 5). Edwards and McKinnon (1987), in the survey of Nova Scotia teachers already mentioned, found support for a deficit view of disadvantaged language. Children were seen as incapable of properly articulating their thoughts and feelings, and to place little value on 'receptive and expressive' skills (see deficit theorists such as Hess, Shipman, Bereiter and Engelmann, discussed in chapter 2). Children were also seen to lack experience and language development and to require compensatory intervention; minority-group children (blacks and Acadians) were particularly singled out as having language problems. Overall, the teachers in this study demonstrated a continuing subscription to a language-deficit view which, on the basis of information presented in the first three chapters of this book, inaccurately characterizes linguistic variation. Edwards and McKinnon suggest that the persistence of this viewpoint within educational circles merely reflects its continuation outside the school gates.

In chapter 4 I noted that any form of nonstandard language may prove disadvantaging in some contexts — not because of intrinsic linguistic or aesthetic qualities, but because of social, political and economic factors. Certain dialects, therefore, are typically seen to reflect low prestige, status and speaker competence, even though they may evoke favourable evaluations of integrity and social attractiveness, may contribute to group identity and solidarity, and may possess so-called 'covert prestige'. While these latter, positive perceptions are obviously beneficial to disadvantaged, nonstandard speakers, the competence/status factor may be very damaging, particularly perhaps in the school context just discussed. One implication is that the environmental–deficit views of teachers and others find particular focus in evaluative dimensions like speaker competence; that is, there is an obvious connection among low socioeconomic status, nonstandard usage, and attributions of linguistic and cognitive deficiency. In chapter 5 the language attitudes of teachers were discussed and it was indeed demonstrated that nonstandard varieties elicited less favourable reactions towards children's personalities, backgrounds and school achievement/likely success (e.g. Edwards 1979b). Given the likely impact of teacher expectations (a very useful survey is provided by Dusek and Joseph 1983), these sorts of reactions may have harmful consequences for disadvantaged children.

Recent studies of language attitudes indicate that problems associated with speech perceptions and speech stereotyping continue (see Edwards 1982a, Edwards 1983c, Edwards and Giles 1984) and, indeed, the sentiments expressed in chapter 7 concerning the difficulties involved in changing longstanding social attitudes are just as relevant now as they were a decade ago. Edwards (1982a, 1983c) also refers to some Australian and New Zealand studies of relevance here, not cited in the first edition of this book, pointing to some anomalies concerning accent/dialect evaluation (somewhat related to those found by Crowl, MacGinitie, Nurss and Taylor, reported in chapter 5; more specifically, to the finding of Carranza and Ryan, chapter 4, that in ratings of English and Spanish the former elicited more positive evaluations on *both* status dimensions *and* solidarity traits).

Thus, a study by Berechree and Ball (1979) found that 'cultivated' Australian evoked high competence judgements compared to 'broad' and 'general' varieties, and was *also* associated with greater social attractiveness. If cultivated Australian can be understood as the standard variety — and Eltis (1980) has suggested that it is analogous to the British RP — then the result is intriguing. Perhaps this means that the relatively clear standard–nonstandard distinction found in some contexts does not apply in others. Or, as Edwards and Jacobsen (1987) have suggested, perhaps a case can be made for *regional* standards in some cases, varieties which possess both standard and regional (i.e. nonstandard) connotations.

The Edwards and Jacobsen study, of mainland Nova Scotia, Cape Breton Island (part of the province of Nova Scotia), Newfoundland and Massachusetts speakers, found that the mainland speakers evoked the higher competence ratings generally associated with standards and, because of their regional character, did not lose ground to the others along the solidarity dimensions of integrity and attractiveness. These results were seen to support the idea that, in contexts possessing regional standards, such varieties may have greater all-round favourability than do standards in settings where more clear-cut distinctions can be made between a single standard and other, nonstandard forms. Some so-called regional standards may in effect be country-wide; thus, the Berechree and Ball findings concerning 'cultivated' Australian may indicate that some other, external variety (in this case, British RP — *pace* Eltis' suggestion, above) may, because of historical and/or contemporary comparisons, have a standard status which allows solidarity responses to be made to the 'cultivated' Australian. Support for this may be found in work done by Huygens and Vaughan (1983) in New Zealand, in which RP received high status ratings. While further work clearly remains to be done in this area, the idea that some varieties may possess a broad favourability across evaluational dimensions may indicate an interesting expansion of the simple standard–nonstandard dichotomy, and of the conditions under which linguistic disadvantage (or the lack of it) is evoked.

In chapter 5 brief mention was made of the fact that studies of language attitudes in English-speaking contexts had some support in other settings too. In a German context, Ammon (1977) has investigated regional dialects at school (see Edwards and Giles 1984), and a recent work by Hagen (1987) deals with dialects and education in western Europe generally. Policies in different countries concerning standard and nonstandard language vary considerably. France, for example, has a centralist, monolithic view of standard language, whereas Italy provides an example of acceptance of regional standards. Official viewpoints naturally make their presence felt in the classroom; thus, in France, school is to reflect and promote only one standard French. But Hagen also points to some anomalies. For example, a liberal legislative view of dialects in education in the Netherlands is not always matched by actual school practice. In Flanders, on the other hand, desires that a Dutch standard be promoted in schools has not prevented the use of various Flemish dialects. Hagen notes, as well, that positive attitudes towards nonstandard dialects on the part of teachers, many of whom may be nonstandard speakers themselves, may not translate into classroom practice (of course, attitude–behaviour inconsistency is not a new topic; see Edwards 1982a). In Dutch studies, Hagen and colleagues found that three-quarters of teachers surveyed agreed that dialect use in schools was desirable, but observation revealed that virtually no dialect use occurred there. Citing Dutch and Italian work, Hagen observes that nonstandard-speaking children show dramatically declining favourable attitudes to their own varieties as they grow up, even if their maternal dialect continues to dominate in their lives. Hagen also discusses the school success of nonstandard speakers (noting several manifestations of disadvantage), questions of dialect interference, and school adaptation to the issues presented by nonstandard speakers.

Hagen adverts to differences among linguists concerning appropriate educational treatments. Trudgill (1975), for example, is seen as one with a very liberal attitude towards all aspects of nonstandard varieties at school (see chapter 5), whereas Ammon (1983), Hagen notes, sees serious difficulties for nonstandard speakers due to negative social attitudes. In fact, Ammon is presented as believing that the best 'solution' would be the disappearance of nonstandard dialects althogether. Trudgill's tolerant attitude towards dialect at school is seen to be rather unrealistic because of the negative attitudes just noted, and because of the 'functional restrictions' associated with many dialect forms (Trudgill's view that negative attitudes should be changed, not nonstandard dialects themselves, is also criticized by Davies 1985). A middle course, embracing bidilaectalism, is seen as an appropriate aim for schools and, in this, Hagen supports the thrust of this book. For, while the logical course of action, given unfavourable attitudes to certain varieties, is to alter these attitudes, this is at best a long-term strategy and, at worst, simply utopian. Besides, social needs quite reasonably dictate a common standard which, while not the maternal variety of everyone, can at least be presented to all through education, particularly in the more formal domains of reading and writing.

Before leaving the question of dialect variation, I should like briefly to say something about black English vernacular (BEV), discussed in chapter 3 as a useful test-case for nonstandard dialects in general. The evidence presented there for its linguistic validity, and for the standard English (SE) abilities of its speakers — particularly with regard to comprehension of the standard — remains strong. There have, of course, been many further studies of BEV in the last decade. Torrey (1983), for example, has reminded us that the use of BEV among black children varies. As was pointed out in chapter 3, as well, there is more than one variety of BEV, it shares much of the common English grammatical 'machinery' and it is, after all, a different dialect and not a different language (see also Edwards and Giles 1984). Torrey thus shows, in her study of New York black children, that

a teacher in a class of black children who hears BE forms frequently should not conclude that all or even most of the class members conform to the general description of BE ... some individuals use only one or two BE forms, and others completely standard forms. Furthermore, some who use many BE forms in spontaneous speech are perfectly able to handle SE in reading and other language tests. (642)

One theme noted in chapters 3 and 4 was the oral richness of the black culture.

The black speakers so profoundly misunderstood by compensatory education theorists like Bereiter and Engelmann were seen to be the possessors of a vibrant heritage by Labov and others. Bereiter and Engelmann saw black children as lacking rudimentary forms of dialogue, as unable to recognize single words, and as viewing language as something dispensable in social life. Labov saw the black child living in a community in which it was 'bathed in verbal stimulation from morning to night' (1973a, 33). A recent study by Edwards (in preparation) is relevant here. Among a rural population in Nova Scotia, three groups of 9- and 11-year-old children were studied — black children, white Acadian–French children, and white children of English-speaking background. Each child provided three types of speech sample — a set reading passage, a retold story (i.e. the experimenter tells the child a story, who then retells it), and spontaneous speech on any topic of interest to the child. Children were then evaluated by adult judges on standard personality dimensions (see chapters 4 and 5); the main intent was to see if perceived speaker favourability varied with type of speech sample evaluated. It was found, first, that black children were generally evaluated less favourably than were the other two groups; second, spontaneous speech tended, across the board, to elicit the highest ratings. Of greatest interest here, however, are the interactions found between group and speech type, and here it was found that the black children profited most, as it were, from the spontaneous speech ratings. To put it another way, differences in ratings received by black children's reading/story-retelling and spontaneous speech productions were much more marked than were those pertaining to the other two groups of children. The findings would seem to suggest that black children, whose culture is orally strong, will produce the best linguistic results ('best', that is, in the perceptions of white listeners) when the context allows them to show evidence of that strength and richness. There are rather obvious implications here, both for further study and for interpreting and reacting to language behaviour in more structured contexts (like classrooms).

The final note to be made here of BEV concerns the now-famous 'King decision'. Parents of fifteen black children from the Martin Luther King elementary school in Ann Arbor, Michigan alleged that the school had not properly educated their children. The children were doing badly at school and the parents' view was that the teachers were unaware of the important sociocultural differences between these children and their white counterparts (80% of the school's population), and that language barriers prevented school success. Indeed, the children were (inaccurately) labelled as educationally retarded and learning disabled, were relegated to speech classes for language deficiency, and were suspended, disciplined and held back. In July 1979, after a month-long trial in which several prominent linguists testified (none for the defendants), a federal court judge ruled that school authorities had failed to act to overcome language barriers, and ordered them to devise curricula to help the children acquire reading skills. Thus, the schools were to adapt. Contrary to some reports at the time, the school was *not* required to teach BEV, nor were teachers required to learn it so as to communicate with their charges — they already communicated well enough, and the problem was with the teaching of reading (see also Lucas and Borders 1987, who note that while communication *may* not have been a problem, there are few studies presenting formal linguistic evidence about communication difficulties in classrooms; their study focuses on this, and finds that dialect variation does not lead to interference; see McDermott and Gospodinoff 1981). Of great interest was the finding that BEV itself was not a barrier, but rather that negative reactions to it, coupled with inaccurate teacher expectations and, to put it bluntly, racist perceptions, constituted the barrier. Also, linguistic evidence presented enabled the judge to find that BEV was a valid and distinct English dialect. At the same time, he supported the view the SE was a necessary component of success in school and beyond; indeed, he went so far as to state that BEV was not an acceptable method of communication in many contexts.

Naturally, the case received very wide publicity, and much of the press coverage was misinformed and distorted (see Venezky 1981). As well, general opinion was divided on many aspects. Consequently, a symposium was planned, which took place in February 1980, to discuss elements and implications of the King decision; this itself became a media event with, among others, a BBC film crew and a team from the American National Public Radio organization in attendance. The symposium resulted in a book of proceedings (Smitherman 1981a; see also Zorn 1982 for a thoughtful review) which presents the fullest available account of the whole issue. Also, Smitherman (1981b) has outlined some further public policy directions she feels are indicated; they include monitoring of school effectiveness, a moratorium on standardized tests which mis-diagnose black children, promotion of public and media awareness of the legitimacy of BEV, further research of a responsive, applied nature, and comprehensive teaching of standard-language communicative competence.

Labov (1982), one of the linguists testifying at the trial, has also presented details of the case, with useful notes on the educational treatment the black children received (which led to the trial). He also observes that the judge, in invoking federal law directing educational authorities to act against language barriers impeding pupil progress, did not believe that such law applied only to foreign language (although this may have been the original thinking in the provision; see Zorn 1982, but also Bailey 1981) — the judge did *not*, then, class BEV as a separate language. Labov goes on to use the trial as an illustration of linguists' involvement in contemporary, real-life issues; to end this section, the abstract to his article is worth quoting:

> Though many linguists have shown a strong concern for social issues, there is an apparent contradiction between the principles of objectivity needed for scientific work and commitment to social action. The Black English trial in Ann Arbor showed one way in which this contradiction could be resolved. The first decade of research on Black English was marked by violent differences between creolists and dialectologists on the structure and origin of the dialect. The possibility of a joint point of view first appeared in the general reaction of linguists against the view that blacks were linguistically and genetically inferior. The entrance of black linguists into the field was a critical factor in the further development of the creole hypothesis and the recognition of the distinctive features of the tense and aspect system. At the trial, linguists were able to present effective testimony in the form of a unified view on the origins and structural

characteristics of the Black English Vernacular and argue for its validity as an alternate to standard English. (165)

As in Gordon's (1978) study — noted above — the specific influence of Bernstein has continued to arouse interest (see also Gordon 1981). Thus, Jay, Routh and Brantley (1980) and Gullo (1981), to cite but two examples, treat social class language differences from a Bernsteinian perspective, Gullo in particular apparently accepting the view that poor children's language is linked to the concrete present and is less used for abstract reasoning. Mason (1986) also deals with concrete–abstract distinctions, and notes that Bernstein's insights in this regard continue to influence teachers (see also Carrington and Williamson 1987). Overall, it would seem that this is so (Edwards 1987). However, as suggested in chapter 2, although Bernstein's influence has often been to support a deficit view of disadvantaged language, it is not at all clear that he should himself be classed as a deficit theorist. A useful new introduction to Bernstein is provided by Atkinson (1985), and this has prompted some re-examintion (e.g. A. Edwards 1987a, 1987b).

There is now the suggestion that Bernstein has indeed been badly used in support of linguistic deficit views, and that his work, properly interpreted, remains of importance in the educational setting. For example, one assertion has been that disadvantaged children do poorly because they cannot appropriately deal with the elaborated code used by the school to transmit 'universalistic orders of meaning' (Atkinson 1985, 78). Yet we know that classroom language is often quite 'restricted' to the particularistic and concrete. Both Atkinson (1985) and Edwards and Mercer (1986) thus conclude that more detailed enquiry, at the level of classroom discourse, is indicated. It is quite interesting to consider here that Bernstein's work, extending back to the late 1950s should, in some reconstructed sense at least, lead through to the modern emphasis upon discourse and conversational analysis. Nor is this the only contemporary direction of interest to students of linguistic disadvantage that can be shown to have links with Bernstein, environmental deficit, and home–school discontinuity; two others of importance are the ethnomethodological/ethnographic thrust (of particular relevance here are studies of classroom language), and the renewed call for school adaptability for disadvantaged pupils (clearly linked to Bernstein's later pronouncements; see Bernstein 1972b on compensatory education, chapter 2). Let me briefly say something about each of these.

Ethnomethodology, a term introduced by Garfinkel (1967), is the study of people's constructions of stable social worlds. It is, to say the least, a broadly-conceived notion which leans heavily upon phenomenological and holistic analysis. In concerning itself with the 'doings' constituting the social order (Sevigny 1981), its aim is to build a picture of social reality which, as it represents the perceptions and interpretations of human beings, is the only one we can know. Similarly anti-reductionist in outlook, ethnography refers to the in-depth study of social groups, leading to the comprehensive understanding of the life of a 'whole' culture; this can and should involve a wide variety of approaches, including participant observation, interviews, field studies and case studies. Of course, it is rather difficult to mount studies which investigate all aspects of a culture simultaneously; consequently, 'micro-ethnographies' result, which aim to holistically describe some fairly broad segment of social life. Of relevance here, then, are educational ethnographies (see Erickson 1981, Green and Wallat 1981, Lutz 1981) and, more particularly, ethnomethodological analyses of language use and variation. The most important feature of these is the goal of understanding language in context — and this certainly does not rule out sensitive investigations conducted under the rubrics of the sociology of language, sociolinguistics, or the social psychology of language. One thinks, for example, of the admirable work of Milroy (1980) and Cheshire (1982) on what might be called the community approach to the study of language variation, social class differences and the networks which support language patterns. Ethnographic studies *have* differed however from, say, social psychology of language ones in placing very little emphasis on experimental manipulation and quantification of findings, and are most notable for their elucidation of classroom language.

We find that discourse analysis is not an exercise restricted to investigating linguistic disadvantage. In general, it is concerned with how and what pupils learn as they become, or fail to become, successful classroom communicators and participants. But it is clearly relevant to disadvantage — if certain groups of children are generally less successful than others, and if the points made above about classroom discourse are noted, schools may effectively contribute to the maintenance of disadvantage through the use of linguistic and other practices, rules and contexts; discourse analysis may shed light on these. McDermott and Gospodinoff (1981) thus claim that schools actively maintain the continuation of group boundaries marked by code differences, reflecting in this sociopolitical forces outside the school itself, and that, in fact, current school systems are ideally constructed to sort out the disadvantaged underachievers from their achieving counterparts.

Some recent writers, particularly Potter and Wetherell (1987), feel that discourse analysis should become the central component in a reworked social psychology. If this did come to pass, it would mean an even closer intermingling of ethnomethodological perspectives, discourse/conversational analysis and social psychology/sociology. In any event, the growth of interest over the last ten years in studying classroom language would seem to be a very useful contribution to a finer understanding of school practices bearing upon the emergence and continuity of linguistic disadvantage.

Mercer and Edwards (1981), for example, have argued that an understanding of classroom communication which fully takes into account school values and practices with regard to teacher–pupil interactions will provide insights into the real-life contextual basis of linguistic disadvantage. In so doing, they demonstrate that deficit views (like those of Tough 1977 — to cite an example not referred to in the first edition of this book), with their disembodied speech analyses, do not involve the whole pattern of communication; this may include gestures, demonstrations, etc. Thus a 'disadvantaged' child's linguistic and cognitive inadequacy is supposedly evidenced by saying 'You get it like that. You squeeze it.

Go like that. And so like that', in answering a query about how a good water pistol can be made from a squeezable soap container. Mercer and Edwards note, however, that as the child was clearly demonstrating physically the operation of the container, any alleged inadequacy can only result from a misunderstanding between researcher (Tough, in this case) and child — and also, we might add, from a very restricted sense of communicative ability. This is all very reminiscent of Hawkins' study (1969), discussed in chapter 2.

Picking up on a theme mentioned above, Mercer and Edwards cite a study by Cooper which claims that *teachers* often use the 'restricted' code attributed to working-class children; thus, they may use a simple statement without accompanying explanation to silence a questioning child and remind it of their superior knowledge and status. These sorts of enquiries are of great interest, and are best conducted through a comprehensive approach to language at school. More generally, Mehan (1984) has noted that ethnographic analysis of classroom language involves such factors as: (a) the interpretation of the psychological context in which teacher–pupil interactions occur — this may include consideration of things like postural configurations, direct and indirect verbal strategies, conversational rhythms and prosody; (b) the interpretation of tacit classroom rules deriving from the teachers' need for social order — here we note such phenomena as conversational turn-taking and its indicators. Mehan observes that classroom language constitutes a cultural code which must be mastered for school success. We can then add to this the corollary that disadvantage may be understood as arising from differential mastery of this subtle and unstated style, which combines both knowledge *and* its 'appropriate' display, and from teachers' misunderstanding of why disadvantaged children's skill patterns are different (and consequent misevaluation of these patterns).

It follows from ethnographically-inspired studies of classroom discourse that a finer-grained and contextually rich analysis may lead to real and significant amelioration of disadvantage. If so, and bearing in mind the underlying difference philosophy, one would not expect that only the children would have to change. As noted in chapter 2, schools should also be ready to make adaptations; as well, throughout this book I argued for a school policy of *addition* to existing repertoires rather than *replacement* of them (with the assumption that what the child bring from home is valueless or deficient). We now see that sensitive studies of classroom dynamics can suggest practical ways in which repertoire expansion might proceed. Mehan (1984), for example, describes a study in which differences in language styles between low-status students and teachers were assessed and, following this, teachers were assisted in adapting to the children's language patterns. This lessened the passivity and 'nonverbality' of the children who now received from teachers questions phrased in their 'home style'; once their participation was thus established, children could be gradually introduced to the 'school style'. This type of educational adaptability is a long way removed from programmed intervention based upon assumptions of linguistic deprivation (see chapter 2). Argument similar to Mehan's is found in Young (1983), who observes that there may be a 'communication deficit' on the part of the school with respect to its working-class pupils. Thus, change in school practices, particularly respecting classroom language, would seem to be indicated. Young notes that this may not always be easy, however, since present practices have a longstanding tradition, based not upon questions of cognitive learning efficacy so much as on the maintenance of teacher dominance and control in the classroom.

One area of education which has already seen school adaptation to the requirements of pupils is the provision of bilingual programmes for non-English-speaking children. As noted in chapter 6, foreign-language speakers who form ethnic minorities are often also socioeconomically disadvantaged because of the common relationship between low status and ethnic group membership. It makes sense, for such children, to provide a service which may enable them to avoid failures in early education due to language barriers. However, much of recent interest derives from the perception that, in addition to purely pedagogical aims, bilingual education can be a servant to the cause of cultural pluralism, of enduring ethnolinguistic diversity. That is, given an assumed link between original language and ethnic group identity, school programmes and curricula are seen as protectors — through linguistic intervention — of identities "at risk" of assimilation to the surrounding mainstream. This is commonly held to be important not only for the specific groups concerned (see below) but also for the whole society, which would be the poorer for loss of diversity. The matter is of interest to students of disadvantage because of three factors: (a) the link between ethnic group membership and low socioeconomic status; (b) the fact that, when majority or national language competence is acquired by ethnic-group members, it is often in a nonstandard form; (c) the disadvantageous loss of identity which is presumed to attach to original–language shift and group assimilation. It is the last of these upon which I shall focus here and, since I have treated the subject in some detail elsewhere (e.g. Edwards 1981b, 1982b, 1984a, 1984b), I shall be brief; the reader is referred to the questions noted in the preface for a framework to the discussion (and to Edwards 1985 for a fuller treatment).

First, the relationship between language and identity is a complex one, but my reading of the literature and analysis of current and historical situations leads to the conclusion that continuity of the original group language need not be a necessary condition for identity continuation. The work of Barth (1969) on the maintenance of boundaries coexisting with cultural change within them is relevant here (see also Edwards 1985 for a definition of ethnic identity).

Second, the dichotomy often assumed between pluralism (good) and assimilation (bad) is unrealistic; there are types and degrees of both. Some variety of modified pluralism (e.g. Higham's notion of 'pluralistic integration', 1975), in which degrees of diversity can remain alongside minority penetration of the mainstream, would seem to appeal to (and reasonably describe) many groups and individuals if the historical record is considered (see also Glazer 1983).

Third, we should note that it is very difficult to use schools alone as agents of change, since they tend to reflect the society of which they are a part. Where education is to be used for change it is helpful, to say the least, if the direction it is asked to take is one being adopted outside the school as well; thus, given an existing social current, there is no doubt that the school's complementary role can be significant. However, the attempted revival of Irish, in a society almost totally committed to English, exemplifies the difficulty when this extra-educational current is absent. Furthermore, not only is the school's policy likely to fail, but the failure itself allows a scapegoat to be created — this resulting from an unfair burden being placed upon school in the first place.

Will education in multicultural, 'receiving' societies like the U.S., Canada and Australia be successful in promoting a permanent social, ethnolinguistic diversity? Examination of the modern centralist thrust of American bilingual education, for example, the historical attempts at bilingual education on the part of minorities themselves, and the tenor of mainstream American life should lead to a certain caution here. In all situations of language contact which appear to be leading towards linguistic assimilation and which some at least wish to transform into a stable linguistic diversity, we should remember that: (a) linguistic change rather than stasis is the historical tendency; (b) diversity tends to reduce itself over time; (c) language shift is a *symptom* of group contact. To attempt, therefore, to change aspects of language alone may well be fruitless without a much wider reworking of the social fabric which may itself be impractical, undesirable (even to those wishing language change) or impossible (short of revolutionary upheavals); (d) populations typically do not maintain two (or more) languages indefinitely, once one has come to suffice across all domains.

Situations in which identities are at risk of alteration usually result from large-scale social dynamics and group contact, yet it is in precisely these cases that schools are typically asked to intervene on behalf of pluralism and diversity; they are appealed to, in other words, at points at which existing social pressures make their task very difficult. It follows that we should not expect too much of schools alone. Supposing, however, that schools *were* to intervene on behalf of group identity, should their efforts be directed mainly at language? This has been the rationale behind some programmes of bilingual education, for example. However — in addition to the language-as-symptom caution noted above — as a marker of groupness, communicative language is very susceptible to change. This is because it is a highly visible feature which may be perceived as stigmatizing, because of pragmatic pressures to shift, or both (in the process of shift, incidentally, bilingualism is often but a stage on the road to monolingualism in the new variety). Thus, school efforts directed at identity maintenance through language preservation may indeed be battling very strong counter-trends. It may be noted here that after *communicative* language shift has occurred, the original language may still retain *symbolic* value and, in this way, continue to contribute to identity. However, this value is not particularly susceptible to educational intervention — except, perhaps, as part of a multicultural curriculum which, while not necessarily aiming to transmit given cultures in their entirety, is surely right to reflect a heterogeneous society in the classroom.

Finally here, we should recall that one of the tensions in modern education is between what Bullivant (1981) has termed 'civism' and pluralism, between a curriculum which transmits general knowledge and core elements necessary for all pupils (and perhaps especially so for minority children wishing to succeed and move in the wider society; see Stone 1981, Tomlinson 1984), and one which conveys a variety of cultural values. Of course these two elements can and should coexist to some extent, but it is certainly possible to imagine, on the one hand, schools ruthlessly insensitive to classroom heterogeneity and, on the other, schools (or programmes) seen primarily as defenders of given sociocultural policies.

* * *

With this I conclude my addendum to the first edition of this book. While not overly long, it has necessitated almost one hundred new references, and the reader who consults any of these will be led on to still more. My main purpose, as stated in the preface, has been to reinforce the original points made and, where possible, to do this through the introduction of recent information; as well, some new strands relevant to the study of disadvantage have been presented here. My perception in all of this is that, while investigations of the topic continue in various forms, there has not appeared, in the last decade, any information necessitating fundamental changes of perspective. I do not interpret this as reflecting any great skill on my part when writing the initial material; rather, it indicates that the basic and important elements in the discussion were in place ten years ago. At the conclusion of chapter 7 I noted that, while further work was indicated, existing information was sufficient to allow useful dissemination to teachers and others in contact with linguistic disadvantage. I can reiterate that here, since perhaps the most important issue in the last decade is the continuation of allegiance to a deficit philosophy of disadvantage; in my own work, this has been stressed (Edwards 1983a, 1983b, 1986; Edwards and McKinnon 1987). I hope old readers and new readers alike will agree that this remains a matter of the greatest importance in the lives of many children around the world.

References

Abbreviations:

Am. Psych.	*American Psychologist*
BJS	*British Journal of Sociology*
BJSCP	*British Journal of Social and Clinical Psychology*
Ch. Dev.	*Child Development*
Dev. Psych.	*Developmental Psychology*
Ed. Res.	*Educational Research*
Ed. Rev.	*Educational Review*
HER	*Harvard Educational Review*
J. Ed. Psych.	*Journal of Educational Psychology*
JSHD	*Journal of Speech and Hearing Disorders*
JSHR	*Journal of Speech and Hearing Research*
Lang. Sp.	*Language and Speech*
RER	*Review of Educational Research*
Soc.	*Sociology*

ABRAHAMS, R.D. 1976: *Talking Black*. Rowley, Mass.: Newbury.

ADAMS, G.R. and COHEN, A.S. 1976: Characteristics of children and teacher expectancy: An extension to the child's social and family life. *Journal of Educational Research* **70**, 87-90.

ADLAM, D.S. 1976: *Code in context*. London: Routledge & Kegan Paul.

ADLER, S. 1971: Dialectal differences: Professional and clinical implications. *JSHD* **36**, 90-100.

AGHEYISI, R. and FISHMAN, J.A. 1970: Language attitude studies: A brief survey of methodological approaches. *Anthropological Linguistics* **12**, 131-57.

AMMON, U. 1977: School problems of regional dialect speakers: Ideology and reality. *Journal of Pragmatics* **1**, 47-68.

— 1983: Soziale Bewertung des Dialektsprechers. In W. Besch et al. (eds.), *Handbuch der Dialektologie II*. Berlin: De Gruyter.

ANDERSON, E.M. 1973: *The disabled schoolchild: A study of integration in primary schools*. London: Methuen.

ANDERSON, E.N. 1969: The social factors have been ignored. *HER* **39**, 581-5.

ANDERSON, V.A. and NEWBY, H.A. 1973: *Improving the child's speech*. New York: Oxford University Press.

ANDERSSON, T. and BOYER, M. 1970: *Bilingual schooling in the United States* (2 vols.). Washington: United States Government Printing Office.

ARCHER, P. and EDWARDS, J. 1982; Predicting school achievement from data on pupils obtained from teachers: Toward a screening device for disadvantage. *J. Ed. Psych.* **74**, 761-70.

ARTHUR, B., FARRAR, D. and BRADFORD, G. 1974: Evaluation reactions of college students to dialect differences in the English of Mexican-Americans. *Lang. Sp.* **17**, 255-70.

ASHWORTH, M. 1975: *Immigrant children and Canadian schools*. Toronto: McClelland & Stewart.

ATKINSON, P. 1985: *Language, structure and reproduction*. London: Methuen.

ATKINSON, R. 1975: RP and English as a world language. *International Review of Applied Linguistics* **13**, 69-72.

BAILEY, B.L. 1966: *Jamaican Creole syntax*. London: Cambridge University Press.

BAILEY, R. 1981; Education and the law: The *King* case in Ann Arbor. In G. Smitherman (ed.), *Black English and the education of black children and youth*. Detroit: Wayne State University Press.

BARATZ, J. 1968a: Reply to Dr. Raph's article on speech and language deficits in culturally disadvantaged children. *JSHD* **33**, 299-300.

— 1968b: Language in the economically disadvantaged child: A perspective. *Asha* **10**, 143-5.

— 1969: A bi-dialectal task for determining language proficiency in economically disadvantaged Negro children. *Ch. Dev.* **40**, 889-901.

— 1970: Teaching reading in an urban Negro school system. In F. Williams (ed.), *Language and poverty*. Chicago: Markham.

— 1972: Educational considerations for teaching Standard English to Negro children. In B. Spolsky (ed.), *The language education of minority children*. Rowley, Mass.: Newbury.

BARATZ, S. and BARATZ, J. 1970: Early childhood intervention: The social science base of institutional racism. *HER* **40**, 29-50.

BARBE, W.B. 1967: Identification and diagnosis of the needs of the educationally retarded and disadvantaged. In P. Witty (ed.), *The educationally retarded and disadvantaged*. Chicago: University of Chicago Press.

BARNES, J. 1975: *Educational priority, Volume 3: Curriculum innovation in London's EPAs*. London: HMSO.

BARTH, F. 1969: *Ethnic groups and boundaries*. Boston: Little, Brown.

BERECHREE, P. and BALL. P. 1979: *A study of sex, accent-broadness and Australian sociolinguistic identity*. Paper presented at the Second Australian Conference on Language and Speech, Melbourne.

BEREITER, C. and ENGELMANN, S. 1966: *Teaching disadvantaged children in the pre-school*. Englewood Cliffs, N.J.: Prentice-Hall.

BERKO, J. 1958: The child's learning of English morphology. *Word* **14**, 150-77.

BERNSTEIN, B. 1958: Some sociological determinants of perception: An enquiry into sub-cultural differences. *BJS* **9**, 159-74.

— 1959: A public language: Some sociological implications of a linguistic form. *BJS* **10**, 311-26.

— 1960: Language and social class. *BJS* **11**, 271-6.

— 1962a: Linguistic codes, hesitation phenomena and intelligence. *Lang. Sp.* **5**, 31-46.

— 1962b: Social class, linguistic codes and grammatical elements. *Lang. Sp.* **5**, 221-40.

— 1970: A sociolinguistic approach to socialization: With some reference to educability. In F. Williams (ed.), *Language and poverty*. Chicago: Markham.

— 1971: *Class, codes and control, Volume 1: Theoretical studies towards a sociology of language*. London: Routledge & Kegan Paul.

— 1972a: Social class, language and socialization. In P. Giglioli (ed.), *Language and social context*. Harmondsworth: Penguin.

— 1972b: A critique of the concept of compensatory education. In C. Cazden, V. John and D. Hymes (eds.), *Functions of language in the classroom*. New York: Teachers College Press.

— 1973a: A brief account of the theory of codes. In V. Lee (ed.), *Social relationships and language*. Bletchley: Open University Press.

— 1973b: *Class, codes and control, Volume 2: Applied studies towards a sociology of language*. London: Routledge & Kegan Paul.

— 1975: *Class, codes and control, volume 3: Towards a theory of educational transmissions*. London: Routledge & Kegan Paul.

BERNSTEIN, B. and HENDERSON, D. 1969: Social class differences in the relevance of language to socialization. *Soc.* **3**, 1-20.

BETTS, C. 1976: *Culture in crisis: The future of the Welsh language.* Upton, Wirral: Ffynnon Press.

BEXTON, W., HERON, W. and SCOTT, T. 1954: Effects of decreased variation in the sensory environment. *Canadian Journal of Psychology* **8**, 70-6.

BIJOU, S.W. 1975: Development in the preschool years: A functional analysis. *Am. Psych.* **30**, 829-37.

BLANK, M. 1970: Some philosophical influences underlying preschool intervention for disadvantaged children. In F. Williams (ed.), *Language and poverty.* Chicago; Markham.

— 1973; *Teaching learning in the pre-school.* Columbus, Ohio: Merrill.

BLANK, M. and SOLOMON, F. 1968: A tutorial language program to develop abstract thinking in socially disadvantaged preschool children. *Ch. Dev.* **39**, 379-89.

BLOCK, N. and DWORKIN, G. 1976: *The IQ controversy.* New York: Pantheon.

BLOOM, B.S. 1969: The Jensen article. *HER* **39**, 419-21.

BLOOM, L. 1978: *Readings in language development.* New York: Wiley.

BLOOM, L. and LAHEY, M. 1978: *Language development and language disorders.* New York: Wiley.

BLOOM, R.D., WHITEMAN, M. and DEUTSCH, M. 1967: Race and social class as separate factors related to social environment. In M. Deutsch (ed.), *The disadvantaged child.* New York: Basic Books.

BODMER, W.F. 1972: Race and IQ: The genetic background. In K. Richardson, D. Spears and M. Richards (eds.), *Race, culture and intelligence.* Harmondsworth: Penguin.

BOGARDUS, E.S. 1925: Measuring social distance. *Journal of Applied Sociology* **9**, 299-308.

BOISSEVAIN, J. 1971: *The Italians of Montreal.* Ottawa: Information Canada.

BOOTH, H. 1975: Compensatory preschool: Do its effects justify its existence? *Ed. Rev.* **28**, 51-9.

BOUNTRESS, N. 1977: Approximations of selected Standard English sentences by speakers of Black English. *JSHR* **20**, 254-62.

— 1978: Comprehension of pronominal reference by speakers of Black English. *JSHR* **21**, 96-102.

BOURHIS, R., GILES, H. and TAJFEL, H. 1973: Language as a determinant of Welsh identity. *European Journal of Social Psychology* **3**, 447-60.

BOWEN, J.D. 1970: The structure of language. In A. Marckwardt (ed.), *Linguistics in school programs.* Chicago: University of Chicago Press.

BRAGG, M. and ELLIS, S. 1976: *Word of mouth.* London: BBC-TV.

BRANDIS, W. and BERNSTEIN, B. 1974: *Selection and control: Teachers' ratings of children in the infant school.* London: Routledge & Kegan Paul.

BRANDIS, W. and HENDERSON, D. 1970: *Social class, language and communication.* London: Routledge & Kegan Paul.

BREATHNACH, A. 1976: Towards the identification of educational priority areas in Dublin. *Economic & Social Review* **7**, 367-82.

BRIGHAM, J.C. 1971: Ethnic stereotypes. *Psychological Bulletin* **76**, 15-38.

BROPHY, J.E. and GOOD, T.L. 1974: *Teacher-student relationships: Causes and consequences.* New York: Holt, Rinehart & Winston.

BRUNER, J.S. 1961; The cognitive consequences of early sensory deprivation. In P. Solomon (ed.), *Sensory deprivation.* Cambridge, Mass.: Harvard University Press.

BULLIVANT, B. 1981: *The pluralist dilemma in education.* Sydney: Allen & Unwin.

BYRNE, M.C. and SHERVANIAN, C. 1977: *Introduction to communicative disorders.* New York: Harper & Row.

CARRANZA, M. and RYAN, E.B. 1975: Evaluative reactions of bilingual Anglo and Mexican American adolescents toward speakers of English and Spanish. *International Journal of the Sociology of Language* **6**, 83-104.

CARRINGTON, B. and WILLIAMSON, J. 1987: The deficit hypothesis revisited. *Educational Studies* **13**, 239-45.

CARROLL, J.B. 1972: *Language, thought and reality: Selected writings of Benjamin Lee Whorf.* Cambridge, Mass.: MIT Press.

CAZDEN, C. 1968a: Subcultural differences in child language: An inter-disciplinary review. In J. Hellmuth (ed.), *Disadvantaged child, Volume 2: Head Start and early intervention.* Seattle: Special Child Publications.

— 1968b: Some implications of research on language development for preschool education. In R. Hess and R. Bear (eds.), *Early education.* Chicago: Aldine.

— 1970: The neglected situation in child language research and education. In F. Williams (ed.), *Language and poverty.* Chicago: Markham.

— 1971; The psychology of language. In L. Travis (ed.), *Handbook of speech pathology and audiology.* New York: Appleton-Century-Crofts.

CHAZAN, M. 1973: *Compensatory education.* London: Butterworths.

CHAZAN, M., LAING, A. and JACKSON, S. 1971: *Just before school.* Oxford: Blackwell.

CHERKAOUI, M. 1977: Bernstein and Durkheim: Two theories of change in educational systems. *HER* **47**, 556-64.

CHESHIRE, J. 1982: *Variation in an English dialect.* Cambridge: Cambridge University Press.

CHEYNE, W.M. 1970: Stereotyped reactions to speakers with Scottish and English regional accents. *BJSCP* **9**, 77-9.

CHOY, S. and DODD, D. 1976: Standard-English-speaking and non-standard Hawaiian-English-speaking children: Comprehension of both dialects and teachers' evaluations. *J. Ed. Psych.* **68**, 184-93.

CLEARY, T., HUMPHREYS, L., KENDRICK, S. and WESMAN, A. 1975: Educational uses of tests with disadvantaged students. *Am. Psych.* **30**, 15-41.

COARD, B. 1971: *How the West Indian child is made educationally subnormal in the British school system.* London: New Beacon Books.

COLE, M. and BRUNER, J.S. 1972: Preliminaries to a theory of cultural differences. In I. Gordon (ed.), *Early childhood education.* Chicago: University of Chicago Press.

COLEMAN, J.S. 1966: *Equality of educational opportunity.* Washington: United States Government Printing Office.

COLES, R. 1977: The children of affluence. *Atlantic Monthly* **240(3)**, 52-66.

COLMAN, A. 1987: *Facts, fallacies and frauds in psychology.* London: Hutchinson.

COOK-GUMPERZ, J. 1973: *Social control and socialization: A study of class differences in the language of maternal control.* London: Routledge & Kegan Paul.

COOPER, H., BARON, R. and LOWE, C. 1975: The importance of race and social class information in the formation of expectations about academic performance. *J. Ed. Psych.* **67**, 312-9.

COPPLE, C. and SUCI, G. 1974: The comparative ease of processing Standard English and Black Nonstandard English by lower-class black children. *Ch. Dev.* **45**, 1048-53.

COULTHEARD, M. 1969: A discussion of restricted and elaborated codes. *Ed. Rev.* **22**, 38-50.

COVINGTON, A. 1976: Black people and Black English: Attitudes and deeducation in a biased macroculture. In D. Harrison and T. Trabasso (eds.). *Black English: A seminar.* Hillsdale, N.J.: Erlbaum.

CRONBACH, L.J. 1969: Heredity, environment, and educational policy. *HER* **39**, 338-47.

— 1975: Five decades of public controversy over mental testing. *Am. Psych.* **30**, 1-14.

CROW, J.F. 1969: Genetic theories and influences: Comments on the value of diversity. *HER* **39**, 301-9.

CROWL, T. and Mac GINITIE, W. 1974: The influence of students' speech characteristics on teachers' evaluations of oral answers. *J. Ed. Psych.* **66**, 304-8.

CROWL, T. and NURSS, J. 1976: Ethnic and regional influences on teachers' evaluations of oral answers. *Contemporary Educational Psychology* **1**, 236-40.

D'AMATO, J. 1987: The belly of the beast: On cultural differences, castelike status, and the politics of school. *Anthropology and Education Quarterly* **18**, 357-60.

d'ANGLEJAN, A. and TUCKER, G.R. 1973: Sociolinguistics correlates of speech style in

Quebec. In R. Shuy and R. Fasold (eds.), *Language attitudes: Current trends and prospects.* Washington: Georgetown University Press.

DANIELS, N. 1973: The smart white man's burden. *Harpers* **247 (1481)**, 24-6, 28, 32, 34, 40.

DAVIES, A. 1985: Standard and dialect English: The unacknowledged idealisation of sociolinguistics. *Journal of Multilingual and Multicultural Development* **6**, 183-92.

DAY, D. 1974: Language instruction for young children: What ten years of confusion has taught us. *Interchange* **5**, 59-72.

DE COSTER, W. 1974: Handicapped or different? Concepts, problems and remedies. *Council of Europe Bulletin* **1**, 57-65.

DELAHUNTY, G. 1977: Dialect and local accent. In D. ÓMuirithe (ed.), *The English language in Ireland.* Dublin: Mercier.

DENNIS, W. 1960: Causes of retardation among institutional children: Iran. *Journal of Genetic Psychology* **96**, 47-59.

DERRICK, J. 1973: The language needs of immigrant children. *London Educational Review* **2**, 25-30.

DEUTSCH, M. 1967a: Facilitating development in the preschool child: Social and psychological perspectives. In M. Deutsch (ed.), *The disadvantaged child.* New York: Basic Books.

— 1967b: The disadvantaged child and the learning process. In M. Deutsch (ed.), *The disadvantaged child.* New York: Basic Books.

— 1967c: The principal issue. In M. Deutsch (ed.), *The disadvantaged child.* New York: Basic Books.

— 1969: Happenings on the way back to the forum: Social science, IQ, and race differences revisited. *HER* **39**, 523-57.

DEUTSCH, C.P. and DEUTSCH, M. 1967: Brief reflections on the theory of early childhood enrichment programs. In M. Deutsch (ed.), *The disadvantaged child.* New York: Basic Books.

DICKSON, S. 1974: *Communication disorders.* Glenview, Illinois: Scott, Foresman & Co.

DILLARD, J.L. 1973: *Black English.* New York: Vintage.

— 1977: *American talk.* New York: Vintage.

DITTMAR, N. 1976: *Sociolinguistics: A critical survey of theory and application.* London: Edward Arnold.

DODSON, C. 1962: *The bilingual method.* Aberystwyth: Collegiate Faculty of Education.

— 1967: *Language teaching and the bilingual method.* London: Pitman.

DODSON, C., PRICE, E. and WILLIAMS, I. 1968: *Towards bilingualism.* Cardiff: University of Wales Press.

DUSEK, J. 1975: Do teachers bias children's learning? *RER* **45**, 661-84.

DUSEK, J. and JOSEPH, G. 1983: The bases of teacher expectancies: A meta-analysis. *J. Ed. Psych.* **75**, 327-46.

DUSEK, J. and O'CONNELL, E. 1973: Teacher expectancy effects on the achievement test performance of elementary school children. *J. Ed. Psych.* **65**, 371-7.

DWORKIN, G. 1974: Two views on IQs. *Am. Psych.* **29**, 465-7.

EDWARDS, A.D. 1974: Social class and linguistic inference. *Research in Education* **12**, 71-80.

— 1976: Social class and linguistic choice. *Soc.* **10**, 101-10.

— 1987a: Review of *Language, structure and reproduction* (Atkinson). *Journal of Language and Social Psychology* **6**, 67-70.

— 1987b: Language codes and classroom practice. *Oxford Review of Education* **13**, 237-47.

EDWARDS, D. and MERCER, N. 1986: Context and continuity: Classroom discourse and the development of shared knowledge. In K. Durkin (ed.), *Language development in the school years.* London: Croom Helm.

EDWARDS, J.R. 1974: Characteristics of disadvantaged children. *Irish Journal of Education* **8**, 49-61.

— 1976a: Disadvantage. *Oideas* **16**, 53-8.

— 1976b: Current issues in bilingual education. *Ethnicity* **3**, 70-81.
— 1977a: Reading, language and disadvantage. In V. Greaney (ed.), *Studies in reading.* Dublin: Educational Co.
— 1977b: The speech of disadvantaged Dublin children. *Language Problems and Language Planning* **1**, 65-72.
— 1977c: Students' reactions to Irish regional accents. *Lang. Sp.* **20**, 280-6.
— 1977d; Ethnic identity and bilingual education. In H. Giles (ed.), *Language, ethnicity and intergroup relations.* London: Academic.
— 1978: Education, psychology and eclectism. In D. Mulcahy (ed.), *Proceedings of the Second Annual Conference of the Educational Studies Association.* Cork: University College.
— 1979a: Social class differences and the identification of sex in children's speech. *Journal of Child Language,* **6**, 121-7.
— 1979b: Judgements and confidence in reactions to disadvantaged speech. In H. Giles and R. St. Clair (eds.), *Language and social psychology.* Oxford: Blackwell.
— 1981a: Disadvantage: Guilt by association. *Educational Psychology* **1**, 101-3.
— 1981b: The context of bilingual education. *Journal of Multilingual and Multicultural Development* **2**, 25-44.
— 1982a: Language attitudes and their implications among English speakers. In E. Ryan and H. Giles (eds.), *Attitudes towards language variation.* London: Edward Arnold.
— 1982b: Bilingual education revisited: A reply to Donahue. *Journal of Multilingual and Multicultural Development* **3**, 89-101.
— 1983a: Review of *The language of children reared in poverty* (Feagans and Farran). *Journal of Language and Social Psychology* **2**, 80-3.
— 1983b: Review of *The language trap* (Honey). *Journal of Language and Social Psychology* **2**, 67-76.
— 1983c: Language attitudes in multilingual settings: A general assessment. *Journal of Multilingual and Multicultural Development* **4**, 225-36.
— 1984a: The social and political context of bilingual education. In R. Samuda, J. Berry and M. Laferrière (eds.), *Multiculturalism in Canada.* Toronto: Allyn & Bacon.
— 1984b: *Linguistic minorities, policies and pluralism.* London & New York: Academic.
— 1985: *Language, society and identity.* Oxford: Blackwell.
— 1986: Language and educational disadvantage: The persistence of linguistic "deficit" theory. In K. Durkin (ed.), *Language development in the school years.* London: Croom Helm.
— 1987: Elaborated and restricted codes. In U. Ammon, N. Dittmar and K. Mattheier (eds.), *Soziolinguistik: Ein Internationales Handbuch zur Wissenschaft von Sprache und Gesellschaft.* Berlin: De Gruyter.
— (in press): Compensatory education and the characteristics of disadvantaged children.
— (in preparation): Reactions to three types of speech sample from rural black and white children in Nova Scotia.
EDWARDS, J. and GILES, H. 1984: Applications of the social psychology of language: Sociolinguistics and education. In P. Trudgill (ed.), *Applied Sociolinguistics.* London & New York: Academic.
EDWARDS, J. and JACOBSEN, M. 1987: Standard and regional standard speech: Distinctions and similarities. *Language in Society* **16**, 369-80.
EDWARDS, J. and McKINNON, M. 1987: The continuing appeal of disadvantage as deficit: A Canadian study in a rural context. *Canadian Journal of Education* **12**, 330-49.
EDWARDS, V.K. 1976a: Effects of dialect on the comprehension of West Indian children. *Ed. Res.* **18**, 83-95.
— 1976b: *West Indian language: Attitudes and the school.* London: National Association for Multiracial Education.
— 1978: Language attitudes and underperformance in West Indian children. *Ed. Rev.* **30**, 51-8.

EISENSON, J. and OGILVIE, M. 1977: *Speech correction in the schools*. New York: Macmillan.

ELASHOFF, J. and SNOW, R. 1971; *Pygmalion revisited*. Worthington, Ohio: Jones.

ELLIS, P.B. 1974: *The Cornish language and its literature*. London: Routledge & Kegan Paul.

ELTIS, K. 1980: Pupils' speech-style and teacher reaction: Implications from some Australian data. *English in Australia* **51**, 27-35.

EMERSON, S. 1978: Professor Higgins lives on. *Sunday Times*, March 5.

ENTWISLE, D.R. 1968; Developmental sociolinguistics: Inner-city children. *American Journal of Sociology* **74**, 37-49.

— 1970: Semantic systems of children: Some assessments of social class and ethnic differences. In F. Williams (ed.), *Language and poverty*. Chicago: Markham.

ERICKSON, F. 1981: Some approaches to inquiry in school-community ethnography. In H. Trueba, G. Guthrie and K. Au (eds.), *Culture and the bilingual classroom*. Rowley, Mass.: Newbury.

ERICKSON, F. 1987: Transformation and school success: The politics and culture of educational achievement. *Anthropology and Education Quarterly* **18**, 335-56.

EVANS, R 1973: The identification of children 'at risk' of educational handicap. *Urban Education* **8**, 75-96.

— 1975: Children 'at risk': Identification before school. *Aspects of Education* **20**, 10-23.

— 1976: The prediction of educational handicap. *Ed. Res.* **19**, 57-68.

EYSENCK, H.J. 1975: *The inequality of man*. London: Fontana.

EYSENCK, H.J. and KAMIN, L. 1981: *Intelligence: The battle for the mind*. London: Macmillan.

FANCHER, R. 1985: *The intelligence men: Makers of the IQ controversy*. New York: Norton.

FANTINI, M. and WEINSTEIN, G. 1968: *The disadvantaged: Challenge to education*. New York: Harper & Row.

FARBER, S. 1980: *Identical twins reared apart: A reanalysis*. New York: Basic Books.

FEAGANS, L. and FARRAN, D. 1982: *The language of children reared in poverty*. New York: Academic.

FEHR, F. 1969: Critique of hereditarian accounts of 'intelligence' and contrary findings: A reply to Jensen. *HER* **39**, 571-80.

FELDMAN, C., STONE, A., WERTSCH, J. and STRIZICH, M. 1977: Standard and nonstandard dialect competence of Hawaiian Creole English speakers. *TESOL Quarterly* **11**, 41-50.

FERGUSON, C. 1974: Language problems of variation and repertoire. In E. Haugen and M. Bloomfield (eds.), *Language as a human problem*. New York: Norton.

FERGUSON, N., DAVIES, P., EVANS, R. and WILLIAMS, P. 1971: The Plowden Report's recommendations for identifying children in need of extra help. *Ed. Res.* **13**, 210-3.

FISCHER, J.L. 1958; Social influences on the choice of a linguistic variant. *Word* **14**, 47-56.

FISHMAN, J.A. 1966: *Language loyalty in the United States*. The Hague: Mouton.

— 1970: The politics of bilingual education. *Georgetown Monographs on Languages and Linguistics* **23**, 47-58.

— 1972: *The sociology of language*. Rowley, Mass.: Newbury.

FISHMAN, J.A. and LOVAS, J. 1970: Bilingual education in a sociolinguistic perspective. *TESOL Quarterly* **4**, 215-22.

FLEMING, E. and ANTTONEN, R. 1971: Teacher expectancy or My Fair Lady. *American Educational Research Journal* **8**, 241-52.

FLORES, N. and HOPPER, R. 1975: Mexican Americans' evaluations of spoken Spanish and English. *Speech Monographs* **42**, 91-8.

FOREIT, K. and DONALDSON, P. 1971: Dialect, race and language proficiency: Another dead heat on the merry-go-round. *Ch. Dev.* **42**, 1572-4.

FRANCIS, H. 1974; Social background, speech and learning to read. *British Journal of Educational Psychology* **44**, 290-9.

FREIJO, T. and JAEGER, R. 1976: Social class and race as concomitants of composite halo in teachers' evaluative ratings of pupils. *American Educational Research Journal* **13**, 1-14.

FRENDER, R., BROWN, B. and LAMBERT, W. 1970: The role of speech characteristics in scholastic success. *Canadian Journal of Behavioural Science* **2**, 299-306.

FRENDER, R. and LAMBERT, W. 1972: Speech style and scholastic success: The tentative relationships and possible implications for lower social class children. *Georgetown Monographs on Languages and Linguistics* **25**, 237-71.

FUCHS, E. 1973: How teachers learn to help children fail. In N. Keddie (ed.), *Tinker, tailor . . . The myth of cultural deprivation*. Harmondsworth: Penguin.

GAARDER, A.B. 1970: The first seventy-six bilingual education projects. *Georgetown Monographs on Languages and Linguistics* **23**, 163-78.

GAHAGAN, D. and GAHAGAN, G. 1970: *Talk reform*. London: Routledge & Kegan Paul.

GALLAGHER, J. and BRADLEY, R. 1972: Early identification of developmental difficulties. In I. Gordon (ed.), *Early childhood education*. Chicago: University of Chicago Press.

GALLAGHER, J. and RAMEY, C. 1987: *The malleability of children*. Baltimore: Brookes.

GANS, H. 1962: *The urban villagers*. New York: Free Press.

GARDNER, R.C. and LAMBERT, W. 1972: *Attitudes and motivation in second-language learning*. Rowley, Mass.: Newbury.

GARFINKEL, H. 1967: *Studies in ethnomethodology*. Englewood Cliffs, N.J.: Prentice-Hall.

GAY, J. and TWENEY, R. 1976: Comprehension and production of standard and black English by lower-class black children. *Dev. Psych.* **12**, 262-8.

GENESEE, F. 1976: The suitability of immersion programs for all children. *Canadian Modern Language Review*, **32**, 494-515.

GILBERT, G. 1951: Stereotype persistence and change among college students. *Journal of Abnormal and Social Psychology* **46**, 245-54.

GILES, H. 1970: Evaluative reactions to accents. *Ed. Rev.* **22**, 211-27.

— 1971: Patterns of evaluation to R.P., South Welsh and Somerset accented speech. *BJSCP* **10**, 280-1.

— 1973a: Accent mobility: A model and some data. *Anthropological Linguistics* **15**, 87-105.

— 1973b: Communicative effectiveness as a function of accented speech. *Speech Monographs* **40**, 330-1.

GILES, H. and BOURHIS, R. 1973: Dialect perception revisited. *Quarterly Journal of Speech* **59**, 337-42.

— 1975: *Black speakers with white speech: A real problem?* Paper presented at Fourth International Congress of Applied Linguistics. Stuttgart.

GILES, H., BOURHIS, R. and DAVIES, A. 1975: Prestige speech styles: The imposed norm and inherent value hypotheses. In W. McCormack and S. Wurm (eds.), *Language and anthropology IV: Language in many ways*. The Hague: Mouton.

GILES, H., BOURHIS, R. and TAYLOR, D. 1977: Towards a theory of language in ethnic group relations. In H. Giles (ed.), *Language, ethnicity and intergroup relations*. London: Academic.

GILES, H., BOURHIS, R., TRUDGILL, P. and LEWIS, A. 1974: The imposed norm hypothesis: A validation. *Quarterly Journal of Speech* **60**, 405-10.

GILES, H. and POWESLAND, P. 1975: *Speech style and social evaluation*. London: Academic.

GILLIE, O. 1978: Sir Cyril Burt and the great IQ fraud. *New Statesman*, 24 November.

GINSBURG, H. 1972: *The myth of the deprived child*. Englewood Cliffs, N.J.: Prentice-Hall.

GLAZER, N. 1983: *Ethnic dilemmas, 1964-1982*. Cambridge, Mass.: Harvard University Press.

GLEITMAN, L. and GLEITMAN, H. 1970: *Phrase and paraphrase*. New York: Norton.

GOFFMAN, E. 1961: *Encounters*. New York: Bobbs-Merrill.

— 1972: The neglected situation. In P. Giglioli (ed.), *Language and social context*. Harmondsworth: Penguin.

GOLDMAN-EISLER, F. 1954: On the variability of the speed of talking and on its relation to the length of utterances in conversation. *British Journal of Psychology* **45**, 94-107.

GORDON, E.W. 1965: Characteristics of socially disadvantaged children. *RER* **35**, 377-88.

GORDON, E.W. and WILKERSON, D. 1966: *Compensatory education for the disadvantaged*. New

York: College Entrance Examination Board.

GORDON, J.C.B. 1978: The reception of Bernstein's socioloinguistic theory among primary school teachers. *University of East Anglia Papers in Linguistics* **1**.

— 1981: *Verbal deficit: A critique.* London: Croom Helm.

GORDON, J.E. 1968: The disadvantaged pupil. *Irish Journal of Education* **2**, 69-105.

GRADY, P. 1973: Language and the preschool child. *British Journal of Disorders of Communication* **8**, 42-6.

GRANGER, R., MATHEWS, M., QUAY, L. and VERNER, R. 1977: Teacher judgements of the communication effectiveness of children using different speech patterns. *J. Ed. Psych.* **69**, 793-6.

GRAY, S. and KLAUS, R. 1970: The early training project: A seventh-year report. *Ch. Dev.* **41**, 909-24.

GREAT BRITAIN: DEPARTMENT OF EDUCATION AND SCIENCE 1967: *Children and their primary schools (Plowden Report).* London: HMSO.

— 1971a: *Primary education in Wales.* London: HMSO.

— 1971b: *The education of immigrants.* London: HMSO.

— 1972: *The continuing needs of immigrants.* London: HMSO.

— 1975: *A language for life (Bullock Report).* London: HMSO.

GREEN, J. and WALLAT, C. 1981: *Ethnography and language in educational settings.* Norwood, N.J.: Ablex.

GROTBERG, E. 1965: Learning disabilities and remediation in disadvantaged children. *RER* **35**, 413-25.

— 1972: Implications of some current issues and practices for the reading teacher. In J. Figurel (ed.), *Better reading in urban schools.* Newark, Delaware: International Reading Association.

GULLO, D. 1981; Social class differences in preschool children's comprehension of Wh-questions. *Ch. Dev.* **52**, 736-40.

GUMPERZ, J. and HERNANDEZ-CHAVEZ, E. 1972; Bilingualism, bidialectalism, and classroom interaction. In C. Cazden, V. John and D. Hymes (eds.), *Functions of language in the classroom.* New York: Teachers College Press.

GUMPERZ, J. and HYMES, D. 1972: *Directions in sociolinguistics.* New York: Holt, Rinehart & Winston.

HAGEN, A. 1987: Dialect speaking and school education in western Europe. *Sociolinguistica* **1**, 61-79.

HALL, V. and TURNER, R. 1974: The validity of the 'different language explanation' for poor scholastic performance by black students. *RER* **44**, 69-81.

HALL, V., TURNER, R. and RUSSELL, W. 1973: Ability of children from four subcultures and two grade levels to imitate and comprehend crucial aspects of standard English. *J. Ed. Psych.* **64**, 147-58.

HALLIDAY, M.A.K. 1968: The users and uses of language. In J.A. Fishman (ed.), *Readings in the sociology of language.* The Hague: Mouton.

— 1969: Relevant models of language. *Ed. Rev.* **22**, 26-37.

— 1973a: *Explorations in the functions of language.* London: Edward Arnold.

— 1973b: *Foreword.* In B. Bernstein (ed.), *Class, codes and control, Volume 2: Applied studies towards a sociology of language.* London: Routledge & Kegan Paul.

— 1975: *Learning how to mean: Explorations in the development of language.* London: Edward Arnold.

— 1978: A sociosemiotic perspective on language development. In L. Bloom (ed.), *Readings in language development.* New York: Wiley.

HALSEY, A.H. 1972: *Educational priority, Volume 1: EPA problems and policies.* London: HMSO.

— 1975: The juxtaposition of social and individual approaches in compensatory education. In Director of Education and of Cultural and Scientific Affairs (ed.), *Compensatory education.* Strasbourg: Council of Europe.

HARBER, J. and BRYEN, D. 1976: Black English and the task of reading. *RER* **46**, 387-405.

HARRISON, D. 1976; Techniques for eliciting casual speech samples for the study of the Black English vernacular. In D. Harrison and T. Trabasso (eds.), *Black English: A seminar*. Hillsdale, N.J.: Erlbaum.

HARWOOD, J. 1982: American academic opinion and social change: Recent developments in the nature-nurture controversy. *Oxford Review of Education* **8**, 41-67.

HAVIGHURST, R. 1970: Deprivation and disadvantage: U.S.A. In A. Passow (ed.), *Deprivation and disadvantage: Nature and manifestations*. Hamburg: UNESCO Institute for Education.

HAWKES, N. 1966: *Immigrant children in British schools*. London: Pall Mall Press.

HAWKINS, P. 1969: Social class, the nominal group and reference. *Lang. Sp.* **12**, 125-35.

— 1977: *Social class, the nominal group and verbal strategies*. London: Routledge & Kegan Paul.

HEARNSHAW, L. 1979: *Cyril Burt: Psychologist*. London: Hodder & Stoughton.

HEBB, D.O. 1968: *A textbook of psychology*. Philadelphia: Saunders.

HEBER, M. 1974: A comparative study of the questions asked by two groups of seven year old boys differing in social class. *Soc* **8**, 245-65.

HERON, W. 1957: The pathology of boredom. *Scientific American* **196(1)**, 52-62.

— 1961: Cognitive and physiological effects of perceptual isolation. In P. Solomon (ed.), *Sensory deprivation*. Cambridge, Mass.: Harvard University Press.

HESS, R. and SHIPMAN, V. 1965: Early experience and the socialization of cognitive modes in children. *Ch. Dev.* **36**, 869-86.

— 1968a: Maternal attitudes towards the school and the role of the pupil: Some social class comparisons. In A. Passow (ed.), *Developing programs for the educationally disadvantaged*. New York: Teachers College Press.

— 1968b: Maternal influences upon early learning: The cognitive environments of urban pre-school children. In R. Hess and R. Bear (eds.), *Early education*. Chicago: Aldine.

HIGHAM, J. 1975: *Send these to me*. New York: Atheneum.

HIGHET, G. 1950: *The art of teaching*. New York: Vintage.

HOLLIDAY, F. and OLSWANG, L. 1974: *School-community program in early childhood development*. Evanston, Illinois: Evanston Public School System.

HONEY, J. 1983: *The language trap*. Kenton, Middlesex: National Council for Educational Standards.

HOPPER, R. 1977: Language attitudes in the employment interview. *Communication Monographs* **44**, 346-51.

HOPPER, R. and WILLIAMS, F. 1973: Speech characteristics and employability. *Speech Monographs* **40**, 296-302.

HOUSTON, S.H. 1970: A reexamination of some assumptions about the language of the disadvantaged child. *Ch. Dev.* **41**, 947-63.

— 1973: Syntactic complexity and informational transmission in first-graders: A cross-cultural study. *Journal of Psycholinguistic Research* **2**, 99-114.

HUDSON, L. 1973: *The cult of the fact*. New York: Harper & Row.

HUNT, B.C. 1974: Black dialect and third and fourth graders' performance on the Gray Oral Reading Test. *Reading Research Quarterly* **10**, 103-23.

HUNT, J. McV. 1961: *Intelligence and experience*. New York: Ronald Press.

— 1964: The psychological basis for using preschool enrichment as an antidote for cultural deprivation. *Merrill-Palmer Quarterly* **10**, 209-48.

— 1969: Has compensatory education failed? Has it been attempted? *HER* **39**, 278-300.

— 1972: Early childhood education and social class. *Canadian Psychologist* **13**, 305-28.

— 1975: Reflections on a decade of early education. *Journal of Abnormal Child Psychology* **3**, 275-330.

HUYGENS, I. and VAUGHAN, G. 1983: Language attitudes, social class and ethnicity in New Zealand. *Journal of Multilingual and Multicultural Development* **4**, 207-23.

HYMES, D. 1974: Speech and language: On the origins and foundations of inequality among speakers. In E. Haugen and M. Bloomfield (eds.), *Language as a human problem*. New York: Norton.

IRWIN, R. 1977: Judgments of vocal quality, speech fluency, and confidence of southern black and white speakers. *Lang. Sp.* **20**, 261-6.

JAEGER, R. and FREIJO, T. 1975; Race and sex as concomitants of composite halo in teachers' evaluative rating of pupils. *J. Ed. Psych.* **67**, 226-37.

JAY, S., ROUTH, D. and BRANTLEY, J. 1980: Social class differences in children's comprehension of adult language. *Journal of Psycholinguistic Research* **9**, 205-17.

JENSEN, A.R. 1967: The culturally disadvantaged: Psychological and educational aspects. *Ed. Res.* **10**, 4-20.

— 1968: Social class, race, and genetics: Implications for education. *American Educational Research Journal* **5**, 1-42.

— 1969a: How much can we boost IQ and scholastic achievement? *HER* **39**, 1-123.

— 1969b: Reducing the heredity-environment uncertainty: A reply. *HER* **39**, 449-83.

— 1970: Learning ability, intelligence, and educability. In V. Allen (ed.), *Psychological factors in poverty*. Chicago: Markham.

— 1973: *Educability and group differences*. New York: Harper & Row.

— 1974a: The strange case of Dr. Jensen and Mr. Hyde? *Am. Psych.* **29**, 467-8.

— 1974b: Cumulative deficit: a testable hypothesis? *Dev. Psych.* **10**, 996-1019.

— 1977: Cumulative deficit in IQ of Blacks in the rural south. *Dev. Psych.* **13**, 184-91.

JOHNSON, K. 1971: The influence of non-standard Negro dialect on reading achievement. *The English Record* **21(4)**, 148-55.

JONES, D.G. 1973: The Welsh language movement. In M. Stephens (ed.), *The Welsh language today*. Llandysul: Gomer Press.

JONES, P. and McMILLAN, W. 1973: Speech characteristics as a function of social class and situational factors. *Ch. Dev.* **44**, 117-21.

JONES, W.R. 1966: *Bilingualism in Welsh education*. Cardiff: University of Wales Press.

JOOS, M. 1967: *The five clocks*. New York: Harcourt, Brace & World.

KAGAN, J. 1969: Inadequate evidence and illogical conclusions. *HER* **39**, 274-7.

KALIN, R. and RAYKO, D. 1978: *Discrimination in evaluative judgements against foreign accented job candidates*. Paper presented at Canadian Psychological Association Conference, Ottawa.

KAMIN, L. 1974: *The science and politics of IQ*. Potomac, Maryland: Erlbaum.

— 1978: A positive interpretation of apparent 'cumulative deficit', *Dev. Psych.* **14**, 195-6.

KARLINS, M., COFFMAN, T. and WALTERS, G. 1969: On the fading of social stereotypes: Studies in three generations of college students. *Journal of Personality and Social Psychology* **13**, 1-16.

KATZ, D. and BRALY, K. 1933; Racial stereotypes in 100 college students. *Journal of Abnormal and Social Psychology* **28**, 280-90.

KATZ, I. 1970: A new approach to the study of school motivation in minority group children. In V. Allen (ed.), *Psychological factors in poverty*. Chicago: Markham.

KEDDIE, N. 1973: *Tinker, tailor... The myth of cultural deprivation*. Harmondsworth: Penguin.

KEENAN, E. 1974: Logic and language. In E. Haugen and M. Bloomfield (eds.), *Language as a human problem*. New York: Norton.

KELLAGHAN, T. 1977: *The evaluation of an intervention programme for disadvantaged children*. Windsor: NFER.

KJOLSETH, R. 1972: Bilingual education in the United States: For assimilation or pluralism? in B. Spolsky (ed.), *The language education of minority children*. Rowley, Mass.: Newbury.

KLAUS, R. and GRAY, S. 1968: The early training project for disadvantaged children: A report after five years. *Monographs of the Society for Research in Child Development* **33(4)**.

KOCHMAN, T. 1969: Social factors in the consideration of teaching Standard English. *Florida Foreign Language Reporter* **7**, 87-8.

— 1972: *Rappin' and stylin' out: Communication in urban Black America*. Chicago: University of Illinois Press.

— 1976: On the 'social reality' of American society. *Lektos* (special issue).

KOHNSTAMM, G. and WAGENAAR-HARDON, T. 1975: Evaluation of pre-school education: Research in the Netherlands. In Director of Education and of Cultural and Scientific Affairs (ed.). *Problems in the evaluation of pre-school education.* Strasbourg: Council of Europe.

KONRAD, K. and MELZACK, R. 1975; Novelty-enhancement effects associated with early sensory-social isolation. In A. Risen (ed.), *The developmental neuropsychology of sensory deprivation.* New York: Academic.

LABOV, W. 1966: *The social stratification of English in New York City.* Washington: Center for Applied Linguistics.

— 1972: Some principles of linguistic methodology. *Language in Society* **1**, 97-120.

— 1973a: The logic of nonstandard English. In N. Keddie (ed.), *Tinker, tailor... The myth of cultural deprivation.* Harmondsworth: Penguin.

— 1973b: *The transformation of experience in personal narrative.* Paper presented at McGill University, Montreal.

— 1976a: Is the black English vernacular a separate system? In W. Labov, *Language in the inner city.* Philadelphia: University of Pennsylvania Press.

— 1976b: Contraction, deletion, and inherent variability of the English copula. (Source as Labov 1976a.)

— 1976c: Negative attraction and negative concord. (Source as Labov 1976a.)

— 1976d: Some sources of reading problems for speakers of the black English vernacular. (Source as Labov 1976a.)

— 1976e: Rules for ritual insults. (Source as Labov 1976a.)

— 1976f: The linguistic consequences of being a lame. (Source as Labov 1976a.)

— 1976g: The transformation of experience in narrative syntax. (Source as Labov 1976a.)

— 1976h: The relation of reading failure to peer-group status. (Source as Labov 1976a.)

— 1977a: The social stratification of (r) in New York City department stores. In W. Labov, *Sociolinguistic patterns.* Philadelphia: University of Pennsylvania Press.

— 1977b: The study of language in its social context. (Source as Labov 1977a.)

— 1977c: The isolation of contextual styles. (Source as Labov 1977a.)

— 1977d: Hypercorrection by the lower middle class as a factor in linguistic change. (Source as Labov 1977a.)

— 1977e: The social motivation of a sound change. (Source as Labov 1977a.)

— 1982: Objectivity and commitment in linguistic science: The case of the Black English trial in Ann Arbor. *Language in Society* **11**, 165-201.

LAMBERT, W. 1967: A social psychology of bilingualism. *Journal of Social Issues.* **23**, 91-109.

LAMBERT, W., GILES, H. and PICARD, O. 1975: Evaluative reactions toward various forms of spoken French and English: The Madawaska study. *International Journal of the Sociology of Language* **4**, 127-52.

LAMBERT, W., HODGSON, R., GARDNER, R.C. and FILLENBAUM, S. 1960: Evaluational reactions to spoken languages. *Journal of Abnormal and Social Psychology* **60**, 44-51.

LAMBERT, W. and TUCKER, G.R. 1972: *Bilingual education of children: The St. Lambert experiment.* Rowley, Mass.: Newbury.

LAMBIE, D. and WEIKART, D. 1970: Ypsilanti Carnegie infant education project. In J. Hellmuth (ed.), *Disadvantaged child, Volume 3: Compensatory education: A national debate.* New York: Brunner/Mazel.

LANGACKER, R. 1972; An initial look at language. In R. Abrahams and R. Troike (eds.), *Language and cultural diversity in American education.* Englewood Cliffs, N.J.: Prentice-Hall.

LAURENT-DELCHET, M. 1975: Evaluation of pre-school education: Research in France. In Director of Education and of Cultural and Scientific Affairs (ed.), *Problems in the evaluation of pre-school education.* Strasbourg: Council of Europe.

LAWTON, D. 1969: *Social class, language and education.* London: Routledge & Kegan Paul.

LEACOCK, E. 1971: *The culture of poverty: A critique*. New York: Simon & Schuster.

LEE, R. 1971: Dialect perception: A critical review and re-evaluation. *Quarterly Journal of Speech* **57**, 410-17.

LEE, V. 1973: *Social relationships and language*. Bletchley: Open University Press.

LENNEBERG, E. 1967: *Biological foundations of language*. New York: Wiley.

LEWIS, O. 1966: The culture of poverty. *Scientific American* **215(4)**, 19-25.

LEWONTIN, R. 1976: Science and politics: An explosive mix. *Contemporary Psychology* **21**, 97-8.

LIGHT, R. and SMITH, P. 1969: Social allocation models of intelligence: A methodological inquiry. *HER* **39**, 484-510.

LINDSAY, G. 1980: The infant rating scale. *British Journal of Educational Psychology* **50**, 97-104.

LITTLE, A. 1978: *Educational policies for multi-racial areas*. London: Goldsmiths' College.

LITTLE, A. and MABEY, C. 1971: *An index for designation of Educational Priority Areas*. London: Inner London Education Authority.

LITTLE, A. and SMITH, G. 1972: *Strategies of compensation: A review of educational projects for the disadvantaged in the United States*. Paris: OECD.

LOBAN, W. 1963: *The language of elementary school children*. Champaign, Illinois: National Council of Teachers of English.

LUCAS, C. and BORDERS, D. 1987: Language diversity and classroom discourse. *American Educational Research Journal* **24**, 119-41.

LUTZ, F. 1981: Ethnography: The holistic approach to understanding schooling. In J. Green and C. Wallat (eds.), *Ethnography and language in educational settings*. Norwood, N.J.: Ablex.

MacKINNON, K. 1974: *The lion's tongue*. Inverness: Club Leabhar.

— 1977a: *Language, education and social processes in a Gaelic community*. London: Routledge & Kegan Paul.

— 1977b: Language shift and education: Conservation of ethnolinguistic culture amongst schoolchildren of a Gaelic community. *Linguistics* **198**, 31-55.

MACNAMARA, J. 1966: *Bilingualism and primary education*. Edinburgh: University of Edinburgh Press.

— 1971: Successes and failures in the movement for the restoration of Irish. In J. Rubin and B. Jernudd (eds.), *Can language be planned?* Honolulu: East-West Center Press.

MARRIOTT, L. and WELLS, J. (no date): *The University of Brixton*. London: BBC.

MARWIT, S. 1977: Black and white children's use of standard English at 7, 9, and 12 years of age. *Dev. Psych.* **13**, 81-2.

MARWIT, S. and MARWIT, K. 1973: Grammatical responses of Negro and Caucasian second graders as a function of standard and non-standard English presentation. *J. Ed. Psych.* **65**, 187-91.

— 1976: Black children's use of nonstandard grammar: Two years later. *Dev. Psych.* **12**, 33-8.

MARWIT, S., MARWIT, K. and BOSWELL, J. 1972: Negro children's use of nonstandard grammar. *J. Ed. Psych.* **63**, 218-24.

MARWIT, S. and NEUMANN, G. 1974: Black and white children's comprehension of standard and nonstandard English passages. *J. Ed. Psych.* **66**, 329-32.

MASON, M. 1986: The deficit hypothesis revisited. *Educational Studies* **12**, 279-89.

McDAVID, R. 1970: The sociology of language. In A. Marckwardt (ed.), *Linguistics in school programs*. Chicago: University of Chicago Press.

McDERMOTT, R. and GOSPODINOFF, K. 1981: Social contexts for ethnic borders and school failure. In H. Trueba, G. Guthrie and K. Au (eds.), *Culture and the bilingual classroom*. Rowley, Mass.: Newbury.

McMICHAEL, P. 1980: School intervention with disadvantaged children. *Educational Studies* **6**, 65-77.

MEDITCH, A. 1975: The development of sex-specific speech patterns in young children. *Anthropological Linguistics* **17**, 421-33.

MEHAN, H. 1984: Language and schooling. *Sociology of Education* **57**, 174-83.

MENDELS, G. and FLANDERS, J. 1973: Teachers' expectations and pupil performance. *American Education Research Journal* **10**, 203-12.

MENYUK, P. 1970: Language theories and educational practices. In F. Williams (ed.), *Language and poverty*. Chicago: Markham.

MERCER, N. and EDWARDS, D. 1981: Ground-rules for mutual understanding: A social psychological approach to classroom knowledge. In N. Mercer (ed.), *Language in school and community*. London: Edward Arnold.

MESSICK, S. and BARROWS, T. 1972: Strategies for research and evaluation in early childhood education. In I. Gordon (ed.), *Early childhood education*. Chicago: University of Chicago Press.

MIDWINTER, E. 1972: *Priority education: An account of the Liverpool project*. Harmondsworth: Penguin.

MILLER, L.B. and DYER, J.L. 1975: Four preschool programs: Their dimensions and effects. *Monographs of the Society for Research in Child Development* **40**(5/6).

MILLINS, K. 1973: The preparation of teachers to educate minority groups. *London Educational Review* **2**, 5-11.

MILROY, L. 1980: *Language and social networks*. Oxford: Blackwell.

MONSEES, E. and BERMAN, C. 1968: Speech and language screening in a summer Headstart program. *JSHD* **33**, 121-6.

MORGAN, W. 1973: *The Welsh dilemma*. Llandybie: Christopher Davies.

MORGENSTERN, J. 1956: Socio-economic factors in stuttering. *JSHD* **21**, 25-33.

MORLEY, M. 1957: *The development and disorders of speech in childhood*. Edinburgh: Livingstone.

MORRISON, A. and McINTYRE, D. 1971: *Schools and socialization*. Harmondsworth: Penguin.

MORRISON, C. 1974: *Educational priority, Volume 5: EPA: A Scottish Study*. London HMSO.

MOSS, M. 1973: *Deprivation and disadvantage*. Bletchley: Open University Press.

MOULTON, W. 1974: The nature of language. In E. Haugen and M. Bloomfield (eds.), *Language as a human problem*. New York: Norton.

MUEHL, S. and MUEHL, L. 1976: Comparison of differences in dialect speech among black college students grouped by standard English test performance. *Lang. Sp.* **19**, 28-40.

MURPHY, C. 1975: Language, idiom, accent and literacy (an interview with J.R. Edwards). *Irish Times*, November 3.

MUSGROVE, F. 1966: *The family, education and society*. London: Routledge & Kegan Paul.

NUFER, H. 1975: Evaluation of pre-school education: Research in Switzerland. In Director of Education and of Cultural and Scientific Affairs (ed.), *Problems in the evaluation of pre-school education*. Strasbourg: Council of Europe.

Ó CUÍV, B. 1969: A view of the Irish language. Dublin: Government Stationery Office.

OGBU, J. 1978: *Minority education and caste*. New York: Academic.

— 1982: Societal forces as a context of ghetto children's school failure. In L. Feagans and D. Farran (eds.), *The language of children reared in poverty*. New York: Academic.

ORWELL, G. 1964: *Inside the whale and other essays*. Harmondsworth: Penguin.

OVANDO, C. 1978: Male and female Latino college aspirations: The implications for pluralistic education. *Educational Research Quarterly* **2**, 106-22.

PASSOW, A. 1970: *Deprivation and disadvantage: Nature and manifestations*. Hamburg: UNESCO Institute for Education.

PASSOW, A. and ELLIOTT, D. 1968: The nature and needs of the educationally disadvantaged. In A. Passow (ed.), *Developing programs for the educationally disadvantaged*. New York: Teachers College Press.

PAYNE, J. 1974: *Educational priority, Volume 2: EPA surveys and statistics*. London: HMSO.

PEAR, T.H. 1971: Suggested subjects for students of speaking. *Bulletin of the British Psychological Society* **24**, 185-94.

PERNEY, L., HYDE, E. and MACHOCK, B. 1977: Black intelligence. A re-evaluation. *Journal of Negro Education* **46**, 450-5.

PERSELL, C. 1981: Genetic and cultural deficit theories: Two sides of the same racist coin. *Journal of Black Studies* **12**, 19-37.

PIAGET, J. 1952: *The language and thought of the child*. London: Routledge & Kegan Paul.

PICHÉ G., MICHLIN, M., RUBIN, D. and SULLIVAN, A. 1977: Effects of dialect-ethnicity, social class and quality of written compositions on teachers' subjective evaluations of children. *Communication Monographs* **44**, 60-72.

PLOWDEN, Lady 1970: Compensatory education and the infant school. In T. Cox and C. Waite (eds.), *Teaching disadvantaged children in the infant school*. Swansea: University College.

POTTER, J. and WETHERELL, M. 1987: *Discourse and social psychology*. London: Sage.

POWESLAND, P. and GILES, H. 1975: Persuasiveness and accent-message incompatibility. *Human Relations* **28**, 85-93.

PRICE, E. 1978: *Bilingual education in Wales 5-11*. London: Schools Council/Evans-Methuen.

PYE, M. 1976: Bad language ain't wrong (an interview with P. Trudgill). *Sunday Times*, February 29.

RAINWATER, L. 1970: Neutralizing the disinherited: Some psychological aspects of understanding the poor. In V. Allen (ed.), *Psychological factors in poverty*. Chicago: Markham.

RAMER, A. and REES, N. 1973: Selected aspects of the development of English morphology in black American children of low socioeconomic background. *JSHR* **16**, 569-77.

RAMEY, C. and CAMPBELL, F. 1977: Prevention of developmental retardation in high risk children. In P. Mittler (ed.), *Research to practice in mental retardation*. Baltimore: University Park Press.

RAMEY, C., COLLIER, A., SPARLING, J., LODA, R., CAMPBELL, F., INGRAM, D. and FINKELSTEIN, N. 1976: The Carolina Abecedarian Project: A longitudinal and multidisciplinary approach to the prevention of developmental retardation. In T. Tjossem (ed.), *Intervention strategies for high-risk infants and young children*. Baltimore: University Park Press.

RAMEY, C., MacPHEE, D. and YEATES, K. 1982: Preventing developmental retardation: A general systems mode. In L. Bond and J. Joffee (eds.), *Facilitating infant and early childhood development*. Hanover, N.H.: University Press of New England.

RAPH, J. 1965: Language development in socially disadvantaged children. *RER* **35**, 389-400.

— 1967: Language and speech deficits in culturally disadvantaged children: Implications for the speech clinician. *JSHD* **32**, 203-14.

REED, F. 1981: The color of education. *Harper's* **262** *(1569)*, 26-9.

RIESSMAN, F. 1962: *The culturally deprived child*. New York: Harper & Row.

RIST, R. 1970: Student social class and teacher expectations: The self-fulfilling prophecy in ghetto education. *HER* **40**, 411-51.

ROBINSON, P. 1976: *Education and poverty*. London: Methuen.

ROBINSON, W.P. 1965: The elaborated code in working class language. *Lang. Sp.* **8** 243-52.

— 1972: *Language and social behaviour*. Harmondsworth: Penguin.

— 1975: The dialogue of 'deficit' and 'difference' in language proficiency. *International Journal of Psycholinguistics* **3**, 27-40.

ROBINSON, W.P. and RACKSTRAW, S.J. 1972: *A question of answers* (2 vols.). London: Routledge & Kegan Paul.

RODMAN, H. 1977: Culture of poverty: The rise and fall of a concept. *The Sociological Review* **25**, 867-76.

ROSEN, H. 1972: *Language and class: A critical look at the theories of Basil Bernstein*. Bristol: Falling Wall Press.

ROSENTHAL, R. and JACOBSON, L. 1968: *Pygmalion in the classroom*. New York: Holt, Rinehart & Winston.

RUBOVITS, P. and MAEHR, M. 1971: Pygmalion analyzed: Toward an explanation of the Rosenthal-Jacobson findings. *Journal of Personality and Social Psychology* **19**, 197-203.

RUOPPILA, I. 1975: Evaluation of pre-school education: Research in Scandinavian countries. In Director of Education and of Cultural and Scientific Affairs (ed.), *Problems in the evaluation of pre-school education.* Strasbourg: Council of Europe.

RUSHTON, J. and YOUNG, G. 1975: Context and complexity in working class language. *Lang. Sp.* **18**, 366-87.

RYAN, E.B. 1979: Why do low-prestige varieties persist? In H. Giles and R. St. Clair (eds.), *Language and social psychology.* Oxford: Blackwell.

RYAN, E.B. and CARRANZA, M. 1975: Evaluative reactions of adolescents toward speakers of standard English and Mexican American accented English. *Journal of Personality and Social Psychology* **31**, 855-63.

— 1977: Ingroup and outgroup reactions to Mexican American language varieties. In H. Giles (ed.), *Language, ethnicity and intergroup relations.* London: Academic.

RYAN, E.B., CARRANZA, M. and MOFFIE, R. 1977: Reactions toward varying degrees of accentedness in the speech of Spanish-English bilinguals. *Lang. Sp.* **20**, 267-73.

SACHS, J. 1975: Cues to the identification of sex in children's speech. In B. Thorne and N. Henley (eds.), *Language and sex: Difference and dominance.* Rowley, Mass.: Newbury.

SACHS, J., LIEBERMAN, P. and ERICKSON, D. 1973: Anatomical and cultural determinants of male and female speech. In R. Shuy and R. Fasold (eds.), *Language attitudes: Current trends and prospects.* Washington: Georgetown University Press.

SAVILLE, M. and TROIKE, R. 1971: *A handbook of bilingual education.* Washington: TESOL.

SCHATZMAN, L. and STRAUSS, A. 1955: Social class and modes of communication. *American Journal of Sociology* **60**, 329-38.

SCHMALOHR, E. 1975: Evaluation of pre-school education: Research in the Federal Republic of Germany. In Director of Education and of Cultural and Scientific Affairs (ed.), *Problems in the evaluation of pre-school evaluation.* Strasbourg: Council of Europe.

SCHOOLS COUNCIL 1970: *Cross'd with adversity.* London: Evans-Methuen.

— 1972: *Research project in compensatory education: Bulletin 3.* Swansea: University College.

SEITZ, V. 1975: Integrated versus segrated school attendance and immediate recall for standard and nonstandard English. *Dev. Psych.* **11**, 217-23.

SELIGMAN, C., TUCKER, G.R. and LAMBERT, W. 1972: The effects of speech style and other attributes on teachers' attitudes toward pupils. *Language in Society* **1**, 131-42.

SEVIGNY, M. 1981: Triangulated inquiry: A methodology for the analysis of classroom interaction. In J. Green and C. Wallat (eds.), *Ethnography and language in educational settings.* Norwood, N.J.: Ablex.

SEYMOUR, H. and SEYMOUR, C. 1977: A therapeutic model for communicative disorders among children who speak black English vernacular. *JSHD* **42**, 247-56.

SHAFER, R. and SHAFER, S. 1975: Teacher attitudes towards children's language in West Germany and England. *Comparative Education* **11**, 43-61.

SHOCKLEY, W. 1970: A 'try simplest cases' approach to the heredity-poverty-crime problem. In V. Allen (ed.), *Psychological factors in poverty.* Chicago: Markham.

SHRINER, T. 1971: Economically deprived: Aspects of language skills. In L. Travis (ed.), *Handbook of speech pathology and audiology.* New York: Appleton-Century-Crofts.

SHRINER, T. and MINER, L. 1968: Morphological structures in the language of disadvantaged and advantaged children. *JSHR* **11**, 605-10.

SHUY, R. 1968: Detroit speech: Careless, awkward, and inconsistent, or systematic, graceful, and regular? *Elementary English* **45**, 565-9.

— 1970: The sociolinguists and urban language problems. In F. Williams (ed.), *Language and poverty.* Chicago: Markham.

— 1971: Sociolinguistic strategies for studying urban speech. *Bulletin of the School of*

Education (Indiana University) **47**, 1-25.

SHUY, R., WOLFRAM, W. and RILEY, W. 1967: *Linguistic correlates of social stratification in Detroit speech*. Washington: United States Government Printing Office.

SIGALL, H. and PAGE, R. 1971: Current stereotypes: A little fading, a little faking. *Journal of Personality and Social Psychology* **18**, 247-55.

SIGEL, I. and PERRY, C. 1968: Psychlinguistic diversity among 'culturally deprived' children. *American Journal of Orthopsychiatry* **38**, 122-6.

SIMONS, H. 1974: Black dialects and learning to read. In J. Johns (ed.), *Literacy for diverse learners*. Newark, Delaware: International Reading Association.

SKEELS, H. and DYE, H. 1939: A study of the effects of differential stimulation on mentally retarded children. *Proceedings of the American Association of Mental Deficiency* **44**, 114-36.

SLOBIN, D. 1974: *Psycholinguistics*. Glenview, Illinois: Scott, Foresman & Co.

SMITH, F. 1973: *Psycholinguistics and reading*. New York: Holt, Rinehart & Winston.

SMITH, G. 1975: *Educational priority, Volume 4: The West Riding project*. London: HMSO.

SMITHERMAN, G. 1981a: *Black English and the education of black children and youth*. Detroit: Center for Black Studies, Wayne State University.

— 1981b: What go round come round: *King* in perspective. *HER* **51**, 40-56.

SMITHERMAN-DONALDSON, G. 1988: Discriminatory discourse on Afro-American speech. In G. Smitherman-Donaldson and T. van Dijk (eds.), *Discourse and discrimination*. Detroit: Wayne State University Press.

SOMERVILL, M. 1974: Language of the disadvantaged: Toward resolution of conflict. *Journal of Negro Education* **43**, 284-301.

— 1975: Dialect and reading: A review of alternative solutions. *RER* **45**, 247-62.

SOMERVILL, M. and JACOBS, J. 1972; The use of dialect in reading materials for black inner-city children. *Negro Educational Review* **23**, 13-23.

SPEARMAN, C. 1927: *The abilities of man*. London: Macmillan.

SPEARMAN, C. and WYNN JONES, L. 1950: *Human ability*. London: Macmillan.

SPITZ, R. 1946: Anaclitic depression. *Psychoanalytic Study of the Child* **2**, 313-42.

SROUFE, L. 1970: A methodological and philosophical critique of intervention-oriented research. *Dev. Psych.* **2**, 140-5.

STEINER, G. 1975: *After Babel: Aspects of language and translation*. London: Oxford University Press.

STEPHENS, M. 1973: *The Welsh language today*. Llandysul: Gomer Press.

STEWART, W. 1970: Toward a history of American Negro dialect. In F. Williams (ed.), *Language and poverty*. Chicago Press.

— 1972a: Sociolinguistic factors in the history of American Negro dialects. In R. Abrahams and R. Troike (eds.), *Language and cultural diversity in American education*. Englewood Cliffs, N.J.: Prentice-Hall.

— 1972b: On the use of Negro dialect in the teaching of reading. In R. Abrahams and R. Troike (eds.), *Language and Cultural Diversity in American education*. Englewood Cliffs, N.J.: Prentice-Hall.

STINCHCOMBE, A. 1969: Environment: The cumulation of effects is yet to be understood. *HER* **39**, 511-22.

STODOLSKY, S. and LESSER, G. 1967: Learning patterns in the disadvantaged. *HER* **37**, 546-93.

STOLLER, P. 1977: The language planning activities of the U.S. Office of Bilingual Education. *Linguistics* **189**, 45-60.

STONE, M. 1981: *The education of the black child in Britain: The myth of multiracial education*. London: Fontana.

STRAUSS, A. and SCHATZMAN, L. 1960: Cross-class interviewing: An analysis of interaction and communicative styles. In R. Adams and J. Preiss (eds.), *Human organization research*. Homewood, Illinois: Dorsey.

STRONGMAN, K. and WOOSLEY, J. 1967: Stereotyped reactions to regional accents. *BJSCP* **6**, 164-7.

STUBBS, M. 1976: *Language, schools and classrooms*. London: Methuen.

SUTHERLAND, S. 1988: Review of *Facts, fallacies and frauds in psychology* (Colman). *Times Higher Education Supplement*, February 12.

SWAIN, M. 1976: Bibliography: Research on immersion education for the majority child. *Canadian Modern Language Review* **32**, 592-605.

— 1978: French immersion: Early, late, or partial? *Canadian Modern Language Review* **34**, 577-85.

SWARTZ, D. 1977: Pierre Bourdieu: The cultural transmisson of social inequality. *HER* **47**, 545-55.

SWIFT, D. 1968: Social class and educational adaptation. In H. Butcher (ed.), *Educational research in Britain*. London: University of London Press.

— 1972: What is the environment? In K. Richardson, D. Spears and M. Richards (eds.), *Race, culture and intelligence*. Harmondsworth: Penguin.

TAYLOR, L. and SKANES, G. 1977: A cross-cultural examination of some of Jensen's hypotheses. *Canadian Journal of Behavioural Science* **9**, 315-22.

TAYLOR, O. 1971: Some sociolinguistic concepts of Black language. *Today's Speech (Spring)*, 19-26.

— 1973: Teachers' attitudes toward Black and nonstandard English as measured by the Language Attitude Scale. In R. Shuy and R. Fasold (eds.), *Language attitudes: Current trends and prospects*. Washington: Georgetown University Press.

TEMPLIN, M. 1957: *Certain language skills in children*. Minneapolis: University of Minnesota Press.

THIRION, A. 1975: Evaluation of pre-compulsory education: Research in Belgium. In Director of Education and of Cultural and Scientific Affairs (ed.). *Problems in the evaluation of pre-school education*. Strasbourg: Council of Europe.

THOMAS, N. 1971: *The Welsh extremist*. London: Victor Gollancz.

THOMSON, J. 1977: Social class labelling in the application of Bernstein's theory of the codes to the identification of linguistic advantage and disadvantage in five-year-old children. *Ed. Rev.* **29**, 273-83.

THORNE, B. and HENLEY, N. 1975: *Language and sex: Difference and dominance*. Rowley, Mass.: Newbury.

THURMOND, V. 1977: The effect of Black English on the reading test performance of high school students. *Journal of Educational Research* **70**, 160-3.

TIZARD, B. 1975: *Early childhood education*. Windsor: NFER.

TOMLINSON, S. 1984: Home, school and community. In M. Craft (ed.), *Education and cultural pluralism*. London: Falmer.

TORREY, J. 1973: Illiteracy in the ghetto. In N. Keddie (ed.), *Tinker, tailor... The myth of cultural deprivation*. Harmondsworth: Penguin.

— 1983: Black children's knowledge of standard English. *American Educational Research Journal* **20**, 627-43.

TOUGH, J. 1977: *The development of meaning*. London: Allen & Unwin.

TOWNSEND, H. 1971: *Immigrant pupils in England*. Windsor: NFER.

TRAUGOTT, E.C. 1976: Pidgins, creoles, and the origins of vernacular Black English. In D. Harrison and T. Trabasso (eds.), *Black English: A seminar*. Hillsdale, N.J.: Erlbaum.

TRUDGILL, P. 1972: Sex, covert prestige and linguistic change in the urban British English of Norwich. *Language in Society* **1**, 179-95.

— 1974a: *Sociolinguistics*. Harmondsworth: Penguin.

— 1974b: *The social differentiation of English in Norwich*. London: Cambridge University Press.

— 1975: *Accent, dialect and the school*. London: Edward Arnold.

TUCKER, G.R. 1976: Summary: research conference on immersion education for the majority child. *Canadian Modern Language Review* **32**, 585-91.

TUCKER, G.R. and LAMBERT, W. 1969: White and Negro listeners' reactions to various American-English dialects. *Social Forces* **47**, 463-8.

TULKIN, S. 1972: An analysis of the concept of cultural deprivation. *Dev. Psych.* **6**, 326–39.

UNESCO, 1953: *The use of vernacular languages in education.* Paris: UNESCO.

VAN DER EYKEN, W. 1974a; Head Start onwards: Recent research in the United States. *London Educational Review* **3**, 12-18.

— 1974b: Compensatory education in Britain: A review of research. *London Educational Review* **3**, 19-24.

VAN LEER FOUNDATION, 1971: *Compensatory early childhood education: A selective working bibliography* The Hague: Bernard Van Leer Foundation.

VENEZKY, R. 1970: Nonstandard language and reading. *Elementary English* **47**, 334-45.

— 1981: Non-standard language and reading: Ten years later. In J. Edwards (ed.), *The social psychology of reading.* Silver Spring, Md.: Institute of Modern Languages.

VERDOODT, A. 1977: Educational policies on languages: The case of the children of migrant workers. In H. Giles (ed.), *Language, ethnicity and intergroup relations.* London: Academic.

WALL, M. 1969: The decline of the Irish language. In B. Ó Cuív (ed.), *A view of the Irish language.* Dublin: Government Stationery Office.

WATSON, P. 1972: Can racial discrimination affect IQ? In K. Richardson, D. Spears and M. Richards (eds.), *Race, culture and intelligence.* Harmondsworth: Penguin.

WAX, M. and WAX, R. 1971: Cultural deprivation as an educational ideology. In E. Leacock (ed.), *The culture of poverty: A critique.* New York: Simon & Schuster.

WEBER, J.L. 1968: Conspicuous deficits. *JSHD* **33**, 96.

WEDELL, K. and RAYBOULD, E. 1976: *The early identification of educationally 'at risk' children.* Birmingham: University School of Education.

WEIKART, D. and LAMBIE, D. 1968: Preschool intervention through a home teaching program. In J. Hellmuth (ed.), *Disadvantaged child, Volume 2: Head Start and early intervention.* Seattle: Special Child Publications.

WEINBERG, B. and BENNETT, S. 1971: Speaker sex recognition of 5- and 6-year-old children's voices. *Journal of the Acoustical Society of America* **50**, 1210-13.

WHITEMAN, M., BROWN, B.R. and DEUTSCH, M. 1967: Some effects of social class and race on children's language and intellectual abilities. In M. Deutsch (ed.), *The disadvantaged child.* New York: Basic Books.

WHITEMAN, M. and DEUTSCH, M. 1967: Social disadvantage as related to intellective and language development. In M. Deutsch (ed.), *The disadvantaged child.* New York: Basic Books.

WIDGREN, J. 1975: Recent trends in European migration policies. *International Review of Education* **21**, 275-85.

WIGGINS, M.E. 1976: The cognitive deficit-difference controversy: A black sociopolitical perspective. In D. Harrison and T. Trabasso (eds.), *Black English: A seminar.* Hillsdale, N.J.: Erlbaum.

WILBY, P. 1978: How racist are our schools? *Sunday Times,* February 12.

WILKINSON, A. 1965: Spoken English. *Ed. Rev.* **17** (supplement).

WILLEY, R. 1975: Teacher training for a multi-cultral society in the U.K. *International Review of Education* **21**, 335-45.

WILLIAMS, F. 1970a: Language, attitude and social change. In F. Williams (ed.), *Language and poverty.* Chicago: Markham.

— 1970b: Psychological correlates of speech characteristics: On sounding disadvantaged. *JSHR* **13**, 472-88.

— 1973: Some research notes on dialect attitudes and stereotypes. In R. Shuy and R. Fasold (eds.), *Language attitudes: Current trends and prospects.* Washington: Georgetown University Press.

— 1974: The identification of linguistic attitudes. *Linguistics* **136**, 21-32.

— 1976: *Explorations of the linguistic attitudes of teachers.* Rowley, Mass.: Newbury.

WILLIAMS, F., HOPPER, R. and NATALICIO, D. 1977: *The sounds of children.* Englewood Cliffs, N.J.: Prentice-Hall.

WILLIAMS, F., WHITEHEAD, J. and MILLER, L. 1972: Relations between language attitudes and teacher expectancy. *American Educational Research Journal* **9**, 263-77.

WILLKE, I. 1975a: About the issue. *International Review of Education* **21**, 273-4.

— 1975b: Schooling of immigrant children in West Germany-Sweden-England: The educationally disadvantaged. *International Review of Education* **21**, 357-82.

WILSON, J. and TREW, K. 1975: The educational priority school. *British Journal of Educational Psychology* **45**, 10-19.

WISEMAN, S. 1968: Educational deprivation and disadvantage. In H. Butcher (ed.), *Educational research in Britain*. London: University of London Press.

— 1973: The educational obstacle race: Factors that hinder pupil progress. *Ed. Res.* **15**, 87-93.

WOLFGANG, A. 1975: *Education of immigrant students: Issues and answers*. Toronto: Ontario Institute for Studies in Education.

WOLFRAM, W. 1969: *A sociolinguistic description of Detroit Negro speech*. Washington: Center for Applied Linguistics.

— 1973: Objective and subjective parameters of language assimilation among second generation Puerto Ricans in East Harlem. In R. Shuy and R. Fasold (eds.), *Language attitudes: Current trends and prospects.*. Washington: Georgetown University Press.

— 1976: Levels of sociolinguistic bias in testing. In D. Harrison and T. Trabasso (eds.), *Black English: A seminar*. Hillsdale, N.J.: Erlbaum.

WOODHEAD, M. 1988: When psychology informs public policy: The case of early childhood intervention. *Am. Pysch.* **43**, 443-54.

WOOTTON, A.J. 1974: Talk in the homes of young children. *Soc* **8**, 277-95.

WRIGHT, M. 1980a: Kids at college. *Alumni Gazette* (University of Western Ontario) **57(1)**, 6-8.

— 1980b: Compensatory education for preschoolers: A non-technical report on the U.W.O. preschool project. *Canadian Journal of Early Childhood Education* **1(1)**, 3-15.

— 1983: *Compensatory education in the preschool*. Ypsilanti, Michigan: High/Scope Press.

WRIGHT, P. 1960: Observational child study. In P. Mussen (ed.), *Handbook of research methods in child development*. New York: Wiley.

WYLD, H. 1934: *The best English: A claim for the superiority of Received Standard English*. Oxford: Clarendon.

YATES, R. 1970: The development and importance of language skills of disadvantaged children. In T. Cox and C. Waite (eds.), *Teaching disadvantaged children in the infants school*. Swansea: University College.

YODER, D. 1970: Some viewpoints of the speech, hearing, and language clinician. In F. Williams (ed.), *Language and poverty*. Chicago: Markham.

YOUNG, R. 1983: A school communication-deficit hypothesis of educational disadvantage. *Australian Journal of Education* **27**, 3-15.

ZIGLER, E. and BERMAN, W. 1983: Discerning the future of early childhood intervention. *Am. Psych.* **38**, 894-906.

ZIGLER, E. and SEITZ, V. 1980: Head Start as a national laboratory. Unpublished manuscript.

ZIGLER, E. and VALENTINE, J. 1979: *Project Head Start: A legacy of the war on poverty*. New York: Free Press.

ZIMBARDO, P. and RUCH, F. 1977: *Psychology and life*. Glenview, Illinois: Scott, Foresman & Co.

ZORN, J. 1982: Black English and the King decision. *College English* **44**, 314-20.

Index (names)

Index (subjects)

Cole & Whurr Journals of related interest

THE BRITISH JOURNAL OF DISORDERS OF COMMUNICATION

The British Journal of Disorders of Communication is an academically rigorous and intellectually challenging journal which presents the latest clinical and theoretical research and is a principal forum for the discussion of the entire range of communication disorders. The journal contains a representative and balanced selection of articles, with contributions from North America, Australasia and Continental Europe, as well as the UK. Among the leading articles published in recent issues are:
August 1987: Duncan & Gibbs - Acquisition of Syntax in Panjabi and English
December 1987: Gibbon and Hardcastle - Articulatory Description and Treatment of 'lateral /S/ using Electropalatography: A Case Study
April 1988: Perry - Surgical Voice Restoration following Laryngectomy: The Tracheo-oesophageal fistula technique (Singer-Blom)
August 1988: Bryan - Assessment of Language Disorders after Right Hemisphere Damage; Lebrun - Language and Epilepsy: A Review

The journal is owned by the College of Speech Therapists, and the Editor is Elspeth McCartney of Glasgow University and Jordanhill College. Issues are published three times a year and annual volumes are of up to 500 pages.

ISSN: 0007 098X

THE BRITISH JOURNAL OF EXPERIMENTAL AND CLINICAL HYPNOSIS

This is the Journal of the British Society of Experimental and Clinical Hypnosis, a learned society which brings together appropriately qualified medical professionals who have a legitimate reason for using hypnosis in their work and who share a scientific interest in the research and practical application of hypnosis. The journal provides a forum for the critical discussion of ideas, theories, findings, procedures and social policies associated with the topic of hypnosis. It also disseminates information on all aspects of theory, research and practice. A book review section is included.

ISSN:0265 1033

Please send for the Cole & Whurr catalogue.

Cole & Whurr Ltd
19b Compton Terrace, London N1 2UN
01-359 5979